PYTHON PROGRAMMING

PYTHON FOR EVERYONE

A Comprehensive Guide from eginner to Advanced Programming

Williams Asiedu

Python For Everyone

A Comprehensive Guide from Beginner to Advanced Programming

Williams Asiedu

Ouereila Publishing

Python For Everyone

A Comprehensive Guide from Beginner to Advanced Programming

ENOP0018
ISBN: 979-8-2408-0243-0

Ouereila Publishing

For permissions, inquiries or licensing requests, please contact:
Email: ouereila@gmail.com

Table of Contents

Preface

Programming is at the heart of the digital world. From education, healthcare, finance, agriculture, manufacturing, transportation, communication, entertainment, and scientific research to the applications and services used every day, software has become an essential part of modern life. Behind these technologies are programming languages that enable developers to transform ideas and problems into functional digital solutions.

The growth of artificial intelligence, machine learning, automation, data science, and other emerging technologies has made programming knowledge increasingly valuable. Understanding how software works is no longer limited to professional software developers. Students, educators, researchers, entrepreneurs, analysts, and technology enthusiasts can all benefit from the ability to understand and create computer programs.

Python is particularly well suited to this purpose. Its readable syntax provides an accessible starting point for new programmers, while its extensive capabilities and ecosystem support sophisticated applications. Python is used across a wide range of fields, including artificial intelligence, machine learning, data analysis, automation, web development, scientific computing, cybersecurity, software development, education, and more.

Python For Everyone is designed as a progressive guide for learning Python from the foundations through advanced concepts and practical applications. The book begins with the knowledge required to start programming and gradually introduces the language's syntax, rules, structures, and programming techniques. As the reader progresses, the material moves into more advanced concepts and explores how Python can be applied to practical tasks.

The emphasis throughout the book is on **understanding, practice, and application**. Concepts are explained in clear language and supported with working code examples. Readers are encouraged to study the examples, execute them, modify them, and use them as a foundation for developing their own programs.

Who Is This Book For?

Python For Everyone is written for learners at different stages of their programming journey.

It is suitable for **beginners** who have little or no programming experience and need a structured introduction to Python. It is also useful for **intermediate programmers** who want to strengthen their understanding of Python and explore additional programming concepts. More experienced Python developers may also find selected advanced topics, modules, libraries, and practical examples useful as a reference.

The book can be used for self-study, classroom instruction, academic coursework, professional development, or independent exploration. The explanations are presented in straightforward English, with technical concepts introduced progressively to make the learning process approachable.

Organization of the Book

The book follows a gradual progression from fundamental programming concepts to more advanced Python development.

The early chapters establish the foundations necessary to work effectively with Python. These include setting up the Python environment, understanding programming concepts, writing Python syntax, working with variables and data types, using operators and expressions, manipulating strings and collections, controlling program flow, and defining functions.

The book then progresses into broader and more advanced programming concepts, including object-oriented programming, regular expressions, asynchronous programming, iterators, itertools, and other important aspects of Python development.

Later topics introduce practical Python modules and libraries that demonstrate how the language can be used beyond basic programming exercises. These examples expose readers to areas such as automation, databases, natural language processing, file and document processing, media handling, image processing, and other practical applications.

The progression is intentional: readers first develop an understanding of Python's foundations and then build upon that knowledge as increasingly advanced concepts are introduced.

Learning Features

Several learning features are incorporated throughout the book to support understanding and retention.

Code Examples

Programming is best learned by writing and running code. Throughout the book, working Python examples demonstrate the syntax, methods, functions, classes, techniques, and procedures discussed in each section.

Readers are encouraged to execute the examples rather than simply read them. Changing the code and observing the results is an important part of developing programming intuition and problem-solving skills.

The examples are also intended to serve as starting points for experimentation. A simple example can often be modified into a more useful program, providing an opportunity to move from following instructions to developing independently.

Key Terms, Review Questions, and Exercises

Learning programming requires more than reading explanations. For this reason, the book includes learning activities designed to reinforce the concepts introduced throughout the chapters.

Key Terms highlight important terminology and concepts that readers should remember.

Review Questions provide multiple-choice questions that allow readers to test their understanding of the material presented in a chapter.

Review Exercises provide practical tasks that encourage readers to write code, solve problems and apply the concepts they have learned.

These activities are intended to transform passive reading into active learning and help readers identify areas that require further study or practice.

Notes and Insights

Throughout the book, **Note** and **Insight** boxes provide supplementary information.

Note boxes draw attention to important details, recommendations, distinctions or information that should not be overlooked.

Insight boxes provide additional explanations and perspectives that extend the discussion and help readers understand how a particular concept relates to broader Python programming practices.

A Note to Readers

Learning Python requires more than reading. Practice the examples, experiment with the code, learn from errors, and gradually build your own programs. Use this book as a foundation for continuous learning, problem-solving and practical development.

Learn. Practice. Experiment. Build with Python.

Happy coding, Pythonista!

Starting Python

The journey of a Python programmer begins with setting up a suitable Python environment. Fortunately, this process requires little effort because Python is relatively simple to install and configure.

Setting up Python involves preparing your computer with the Python interpreter, its required environment, and the tools needed to write and execute Python programs. Python is available for major operating systems, including Windows, macOS, and Linux.

To start using Python on your computer, follow the steps below.

Installing Python

Visit the official Python website to download the appropriate Python package for your operating system. Python provides downloads for Windows, macOS, and source distributions for Linux and other platforms.

Official Python website: https://www.python.org/

Download the latest **stable** version available for your operating system.

> **Note**
>
> Python is continuously updated with new releases and improvements. Therefore, the latest version (3.14) may change after this book is published. Unless a specific version is required for a particular example, it is recommended that you use a current stable version of Python.

Linux

Many Linux distributions include Python 3 or provide it through their official package repositories. However, the installed version depends on the Linux distribution and its release.

For Debian- or Ubuntu-based distributions, Python 3 can be installed or updated through the package manager with:

```
$ sudo apt update
$ sudo apt install python3
```

After installation, you can verify the installed version with:

```
$ python3 --version
```

Insight

The command used to install or update Python may differ between Linux distributions. The commands above apply to Debian- and Ubuntu-based systems.

Windows

After downloading the Python installer, locate the downloaded executable file and double-click it to begin the installation.
During installation, look for the option: **Add python.exe to PATH**
Select this option before proceeding with the installation. It allows Windows to locate the Python interpreter from the Command Prompt, PowerShell, and other command-line environments.
After selecting the option, continue with the installation until it is complete.

Note

If you did not select **Add python.exe to PATH** during installation, Python can be added to the PATH environment variable manually.

Manually Adding Python to PATH

If Python was not added to PATH during installation, you can configure it manually by following these steps:

1. Locate the Python installation directory.
The exact location depends on the version and installation method. For example:
C:\Users\John\AppData\Local\Programs\Python\Python314
The version number in the directory name may be different on your computer.

2. Locate the Python executable.
Inside the installation directory, look for: *python.exe*
For example:
C:\Users\John\AppData\Local\Programs\Python\Python314\python.exe
For the PATH configuration, note the **directory containing python.exe**:
C:\Users\John\AppData\Local\Programs\Python\Python314

3. Open the System Properties window.
Press: **Win + R**
The Run dialog box will appear. Type: *sysdm.cpl* and press **Enter**.
The **System Properties** window will open.

4. Open the Environment Variables window.
Select: **Advanced → Environment Variables**

5. Locate the PATH variable.
Under **User variables** or **System variables**, locate the variable named: Path
Select it and click **Edit**.

6. Add the Python directory.
Click **New** and enter the directory containing python.exe, for example:
C:\Users\John\AppData\Local\Programs\Python\Python314
Click **OK** to save the change.
Finally, close the remaining dialog boxes by clicking **OK**.

> 🧠 **Insight**
>
> When adding Python to PATH manually, add the directory containing python.exe, not the complete path ending with python.exe.

macOS

After downloading the Python installer for macOS, locate the downloaded .pkg file and double-click it to begin the installation. The macOS Installer will guide you through the installation process.
Follow the instructions displayed by the installer and accept the license agreement when prompted. For a standard installation, the default installation options are generally appropriate.

Once the installation is complete, Python will be available from the Terminal. The official Python installer also provides **IDLE**, Python's built-in development environment, in the installed Python folder under the Applications directory.
To complete the installation, the official installer may also provide an **Install Certificates command** file. Running this file installs the SSL root certificates required by Python for secure connections.

> **Note**
>
> Recent versions of macOS may already include a python3 command associated with Apple's development tools. This version should not be modified or removed. Installing Python from python.org provides a separate Python installation that can coexist with the Apple-provided tools.

Verifying the Python Installation

After installing Python, it is important to verify that the Python interpreter is correctly configured and accessible from the command line.
Open **Command Prompt** or **PowerShell** on Windows, or **Terminal** on macOS or Linux, and enter the appropriate command.

Windows

```
> python --version
```

macOS and Linux

```
$ python3 --version
```

If Python has been correctly installed and configured, the terminal will display the installed Python version. For example:
Python 3.14.6

Editors and Development Environments

Editors, or Integrated Development Environments (IDEs), are applications that enable users to write, edit, debug, and run programming code. They typically feature user-friendly interfaces with integrated tools, compilers, syntax highlighting, code completion, IntelliSense, code navigation, debugging tools, error detection, linting, refactoring, project management, integrated terminals, version-control integration, code formatting, and extensions or plugins tailored for specific languages. Some editors support multiple languages, while others are designed for a particular language.

Popular editors for Python development include:

- 📌 PyCharm
- 📌 Visual Studio Code
- 📌 Sublime Text
- 📌 Notepad++

Additionally, Python comes with its own integrated environment called IDLE. IDLE provides an interactive environment for writing and running Python code, making it particularly useful for practicing coding skills.

🧠 Insight

Python does not require a particular editor or IDE. You can write Python programs using a simple text editor and execute them using the Python interpreter. However, a capable editor or IDE can significantly improve the development experience, especially when working on larger projects.

Executing Python Code

Python is a flexible programming language that does not require a specific IDE to execute programs. Python code can be executed directly through the interpreter in an interactive session or saved in a file and executed later.

There are several ways to execute Python code. The method you choose depends on what you are trying to accomplish.

For quick experiments and small pieces of code, the **interactive interpreter** is convenient. For larger programs, it is more appropriate to write the code in a Python file and execute it using the Python interpreter or an IDE.

The following sections demonstrate three common approaches.

Running Python from the Command Line

The Python interpreter provides an interactive environment in which you can enter Python statements and immediately see their results. This is useful for learning, experimenting, testing small pieces of code and quickly prototyping ideas.

Open **Command Prompt** or **PowerShell** on Windows, or **Terminal** on macOS or Linux.

Windows

```
> python
or
> py
```

macOS and Linux

```
$ python3
```

After starting the interpreter, a prompt similar to the following will appear:

>>>

The >>> prompt indicates that the Python interpreter is ready to receive a Python statement. For example:

```
PS C:\Users\Asiedu> python
Python 3.14.0 (main, Oct 24 2025, 18:26:48) [MSC v.1933 64 bit (AMD64)] on win32
Type "help", "copyright", "credits" or "license" for more information.
>>> print("Hello World")
Hello World
>>>
```

To exit the interactive interpreter, you can use:

```
>>> exit()
```

On Windows, you can also press **Ctrl + Z** followed by **Enter**. On macOS and Linux, **Ctrl + D** can be used to exit the interpreter.

Running Python from a File

Python programs are commonly saved in files with the **.py** extension. For example: ***myfile.py***
You can create a Python file using a text editor, code editor, or IDE and write your Python code inside it.
For example

```
#myfile.py

print("Hello World")
```

Save the file as: ***myfile.py***
Open Command Prompt, PowerShell, or Terminal and navigate to the directory containing the file.
On Windows, execute the program with:

```
> python  myfile.py
```

or

```
> py myfile.py
```

On macOS and Linux:

```
$ python3 myfile.py
```

Python also allows a module to be executed using the -m option. For example:
> python -m mymodule

```
$ python -m mymodule
```

The **-m** option tells Python to locate and execute a module by its module name rather than treating the argument as a filename.

> **Note**
>
> The **.py** extension is the standard extension for Python source files. On Windows, **.pyw** can also be used for Python scripts intended to run without opening a console window. The **.pyw** extension is primarily associated with Windows.

Running Python from IDLE

IDLE stands for **Integrated Development and Learning Environment**. It is a basic development environment included with standard Python distributions. IDLE provides both an interactive Python shell and an editor for creating and editing Python programs.
The **Python Shell** allows you to enter Python statements interactively, while the **Editor** allows you to create and save complete Python programs.
To create a new Python program in IDLE, select:
File → New File
A new editor window will appear where you can write your Python code.

IDLE is included with the standard Python distribution. Its availability and launch method can vary depending on the operating system and how Python was installed.

Windows

To open IDLE on Windows, open the **Start** menu and search for: IDLE
You can then select the IDLE application associated with your installed Python version.
Depending on the installation, IDLE may also be accessible from the Python folder in the Start menu.

Linux

On Linux, IDLE can be launched from the terminal using:

```
$ python3 -m idlelib
```

Some Linux distributions also provide IDLE through their application menu or package manager.

macOS

When Python is installed from the official python.org installer, IDLE is included in the Python folder located in the **Applications** directory. Open the Python folder and select **IDLE** to launch it.
IDLE can also be launched from the Terminal with:

```
$ python3 -m idlelib
```

Python's documentation provides python -m idlelib as the command-line method for launching IDLE.

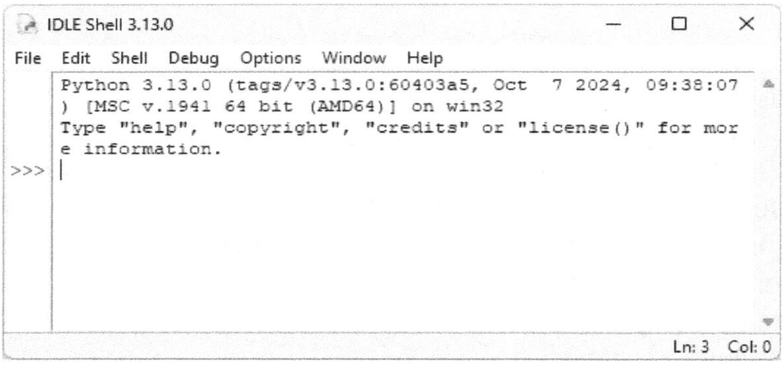

Figure: 1.0 : The Python IDLE

Key Terms

Python
IDE
IDLE
PATH / Environment Variables
Pip
PowerShell
Visual Studio Code (VS Code)
Python Interactive Shell
File Extensions
Terminal

Review Questions

1.Which command ensures you check Python 3 version on Linux or macOS?
a. python --version
b. python3 --version
c. pip --version
d. python -V
Answer: b

2.What is the primary purpose of adding Python to the PATH during installation?
a. To increase Python's execution speed
b. To allow Python to be run from any command-line interface
c. To enable automatic updates
d. To install Python packages automatically
Answer: b

3.Which file extension is used for GUI scripts on Windows that suppress the console window?
a. .py
b. .txt
c. .pyw
d. .exe
Answer: c

4.Which of the following package managers is commonly used on macOS to install Python?
a. apt
b. yum
c. Homebrew
d. pip
Answer: c

5.Which IDE comes bundled with Python and is useful for beginners to write and run code?
a. PyCharm
b. Visual Studio Code
c. Sublime Text
d. IDLE
Answer: d

Review Exercises

1.Explain the steps to install Python on Windows and how to verify the installation.

2.Describe the difference between .py and .pyw file extensions in Python.

3.Write the terminal commands to install Python 3 and pip on a Linux system.

4.Launch the Python interactive shell and demonstrate executing a simple print statement.

5.Compare the features of IDLE and Visual Studio Code for Python development.

Introduction to Programming

Python

Python is a broad and widely used programming language in the tech industry. It is well known by most individuals and developers for its simplicity, easy adaptation, and low resource requirements. Python was created by Guido van Rossum, inspired in part by ABC, Modula-3 and Lisp, a high-level programming language developed in the 1980s. It gained recognition and popularity in the early 1990s, and in 1991, the first version was officially released.
As Python became popular and gained recognition among developers, Guido van Rossum made it open source. Today, the language and its libraries are actively maintained and managed by the Python Software Foundation (PSF).

Python is largely adopted by developers because of:

1. Simple English-like syntax
Python syntax, keywords, and structure are based on the English language. For example:

- print() → displays output on the console
- sum() → totals input numbers

2. Simple rules and structure
Python syntax is much simpler compared to other programming languages. For example:

Python		*C++/ C*
print("Hello World")	=	std::cout << "Hello World" << std::endl;

3. Object-Oriented Programming (OOP)
Python is an object-oriented language that emphasizes **inheritance**, **polymorphism**, **encapsulation** and **abstraction**. For example:
object = ClassName()

4. Large community and support
Python has a vast community of developers across all domains who actively build and maintain new libraries. There are numerous Python-focused websites, online groups, and forums dedicated to tutorials and support.

5. Extensive modules (libraries) with easy installation through pip
Python, being open source, makes use of libraries or modules developed by the community. These can be easily integrated into Python programs using the syntax:

pip install module_name

6. Cross-platform compatibility

Python runs on almost all platforms and operating systems, including Windows, macOS, Linux, and mobile systems like Android.

7. Scalability and versatility

Python is used in a wide range of fields: from data analysis and machine learning to game development and automation scripts. Its flexibility allows it to scale across projects small and large.

🧠 Insight

Open Source

When the creator of a software or product allows everyone to use it freely and modify it, the program's source code is made available to the public. This concept is called open source. There are many open-source software programs, including the Python language itself.

Domains of Python

Python is one of the most popular languages spanning almost every domain in technology. It plays a key role in:

- Cybersecurity
- Artificial Intelligence (AI) and Robotics
- Graphic Design and Image Processing
- Game Development
- Mobile and Desktop Application Development
- Web Design and Development
- Data Science and Machine Learning
- Cloud Computing and Automation
- Scientific Computing

Computer Languages

When people communicate, they use natural languages (English, French, etc.), which both parties understand. Similarly, computers communicate through a language made of sequences of ones and zeros (binary). This language is called **machine language** and is difficult for humans to understand.

For example:

- Decimal 5 → Binary 101
- Decimal 3 → Binary 011

If a user wants to type 5, they would enter 0b101, and the computer interprets it as 5. But for large numbers like 1289858555, machine language quickly becomes impractical.
To make interaction easier, developers built more human-friendly programming languages. These use mnemonics (symbols) and instructions familiar to humans. Programs written in these languages are translated into machine language so that the computer can execute them.

Computer languages are broadly classified into:

1. Low-Level Language

Low-level language (machine code or assembly) is the language of circuits, written in binary (ones and zeros). It is the core language of the computer and not user-friendly.

2. High-Level Language

High-level languages contain mnemonics, structures, and instructions familiar to humans. A compiler or interpreter translates them into machine language. Modern programming languages are mostly high-level and object-oriented, with simple syntax and readability compared to older languages.
Some popular high-level languages include:

Language	Year	Origin	Developer
Fortran	1950	Assembly	IBM
Cobol	1960	FLOW-MATIC	Grace Hopper
Lisp	1958	—	John McCarthy
Pascal	1970	ALGOL	Niklaus Wirth
C	1972	BCPL, B	Dennis Ritchie
C++	1980	C	Bjarne Stroustrup
Perl	1987	C, Shell Script, AWK	Larry Wall
Python	1991	ABC, C	Guido Van Rossum
Java	1995	C, C++	James Gosling (Oracle)
JavaScript	1995	Self, Scheme	Netscape
C#	2000	C++, Java, Delphi	Anders Hejlsberg
Kotlin	2011	Java	JetBrains
Dart	2011	C, JavaScript	Google

Table 1.0

Insight

Operating System (OS)

An Operating System is software that manages and controls computer hardware and software resources. Every computer or mobile device has an operating system. Examples include:

- Windows – mostly written in C, C++, and Assembly
- Linux – written in C and Assembly
- macOS – written in C, C++, Objective-C, and Swift
- Android – based on Linux, written in Java, C, and C++
- iOS – written in Objective-C and Swift

Compiling Programs

In programming, the user writes a series of source code using an editor or an Integrated Development Environment (IDE). These editors/IDEs have built-in compilers or interpreters for specific languages and are capable of running and debugging code.
When the program runs, the IDE translates the source code into machine language.

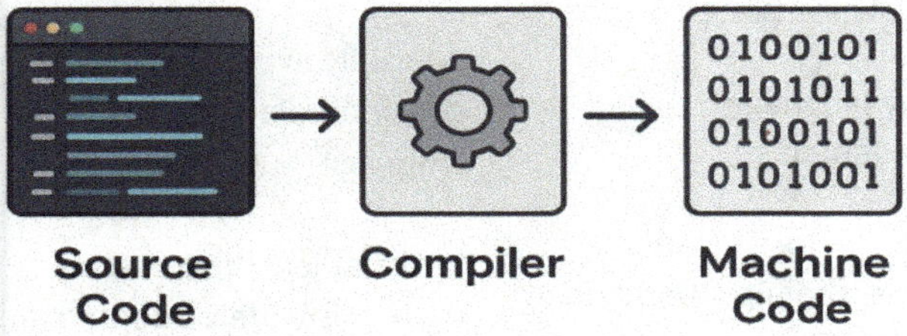

Figure 1.1 : The Compilation Process

In Python, compiling and running a program works differently compared to many other languages. Python does not translate the entire source code before execution. Instead, it interprets the code line by line (top to bottom). If a line of code contains an error, execution stops and an error message is returned.

Insight

Python is called an interpreted language because its code is executed line by line. By contrast, languages like Java, C, and C++ are compiled (the entire source code is translated before execution).

Key Terms

Lisp
Python Software Foundation (PSF)
Open Source
Python Syntax
Object-Oriented Programming
Inheritance
Polymorphism
Encapsulation
Abstraction
Libraries / Modules
Cross-Platform
Domains
Cybersecurity
Natural Language
Machine Language (Binary)
Compiler
Interpreter
Integrated Development Environment (IDE)

Review Questions

1. Who created the Python programming language?
a) Dennis Ritchie
b) James Gosling
c) Guido van Rossum
d) Bjarne Stroustrup
Answer: c

2. Python was first released in which year?
a) 1985
b) 1991
c) 1995
d) 2000
Answer: b

3. Python was inspired by which programming language?
a) Java
b) Lisp
c) Fortran
d) Pascal
Answer: b

4. Which organization currently maintains Python?
a) W3C
b) Google
c) Python Software Foundation
d) Oracle
Answer: c

5. Which of the following best describes Python?
a) Low-level compiled language
b) High-level interpreted language
c) Assembly language
d) Machine language
Answer: b

6. What does the pip command in Python stand for?
a) Python Interactive Package
b) Pip Installs Packages
c) Python Internal Program
d) Program Installation Process
Answer: b

7. Which of the following is NOT a feature of Python?
a) Object-Oriented Programming
b) Platform Independence
c) Easy syntax
d) Manual memory management
Answer: d) Manual memory management

8. Which of these is an example of a Python library?
a) NumPy
b) Windows OS
c) HTML
d) SQL
Answer: a

9. Which of these is an interpreted language like Python?
a) C
b) Java
c) C++
d) Assembly
Answer: b

Review Exercises

1. Briefly explain why Python is considered an open-source language.

2. List at least five reasons why Python is widely adopted among developers.

3. Differentiate between low-level languages and high-level languages, with examples.

4. Describe how Python executes code differently from compiled languages like C or C++.

Variables

One of the crucial roles of a computer is storing data, which can be digits, letters, or files (such as text files, media files, etc.) inside its memory. A computer can store several pieces of data in different memory addresses. When data is stored in these addresses, the computer automatically generates a memory address ID for each stored value. However, users may find it difficult to remember or work with these raw memory addresses.

To solve this, programming introduces labels that map directly to memory addresses. These labels are called variables or identifiers.
A variable is therefore an identifier that represents data stored in computer memory.

Creating Variables

In programming, creating a variable is called **defining** the variable. Variables can be made up of letters, or a combination of letters and digits. A variable is defined by assigning a value to a variable name using the equal sign (=).

Syntax

```
variableName = value
```

Example

```
Python
>>> num = 10
>>> var = "Python"
```

Multiple Assignment

In Python, a single variable is typically assigned to a single value. However, Python allows **multiple assignments**, enabling more flexible and concise code.

1. Assigning one value to multiple variables

Multiple variables can be assigned to a single value at once. In this case, all variables share the same value.

Example - one-to-one assignment,

```python
x = y = "cat"
print("x ->", x, "y ->", y)
```

```
#Output
x -> cat y -> cat
```

Explanation:
Both x and y reference the same string value "cat".

2. Assigning multiple values to multiple variables

Python also supports unpacking multiple values into multiple variables simultaneously. Each variable receives a value based on its position (order of precedence) in the assignment.

Example: many-to-one assignment,

```python
m, n, z = 10, 5, "fox"
print("m ->", m, "n ->", n, "z ->", z)
```

```
#Output
m -> 10 n -> 5 z -> fox
```

Explanation:
The variable m receives 10, n receives 5, and z receives "fox" respectively.

3. Value Swapping Using Multiple Assignment

A unique feature of Python's multiple assignment is the ability to swap variable values directly — without using a temporary variable.

Example - swap values,

```python
a, b = 5, 10
a, b = b, a
print("a ->", a, "b ->", b)
```

```
#Output
a -> 10 b -> 5
```

Explanation:
The values of a and b are swapped in a single line. This technique is widely used for data manipulation, sorting algorithms, and logic-based computations.

The None statement

Every variable must be declared with a value. However, there are situations where a variable is declared but the value is assigned later in the program. In such cases, the variable should be initialized with None to indicate that it currently has no value, but a valid value will be assigned later.

Example,

```
Python
>>> var = None
>>> var = 5
>>> print(var)
```

```
#Output
5
```

Local and Global Variables

In many programming languages, variables can have restricted access defined by keywords such as **public**, **private**, or **protected**. Python does not use these keywords in the same way. Instead, Python restricts variable access depending on where the variable is created – inside or outside a function or block.
There are two main types of variables in Python:

```
Python

var = "computer" #global variable
```

```
def function():
    num = 10      #local variable
```

1. Global Variables

A global variable is defined **outside any function or block**. It can be accessed and modified by any function or object in the program.
To view all global variables as dictionary keys, use the **globals()** function.

2. Local Variables

A local variable is defined **inside a function or block**. It can only be accessed by objects within that function or block. No code outside the block can access it. To view all local variables as dictionary keys, use the **locals()** function.

Variable Naming Conventions

1. Every variable name should start with a letter (uppercase or lowercase) or an underscore (_).
2. A variable name cannot start with a number. It may contain numbers, but they must come after a letter or underscore.
3. Variable names are case-sensitive (Name, name, and NAME are treated as different variables).
4. If two variables have the same name but different values, the latest value overrides the previous one.

Insight

Python provides a built-in function, **.isidentifier()**, to check whether a string is a valid variable name.

Example:

```
>>> "var10".isidentifier()  #True
>>> "10var".isidentifier()  #False
>>> "_5num".isidentifier()  #True
```

Creating Dynamic Variables

Normally, variables are defined explicitly by the programmer at the start or within the program flow. However, in some cases, you may want the program to create a variable name dynamically. **Dynamic variable** can be created using the **globals()** function.

Syntax:

```
globals()[variable_name] = value
```

Example:

```
••• Python
>>> var = "my_var"
>>> globals()[var] = 100
>>> print(my_var)
```

```
#Output
100
```

Explanation:
Initially, "my_var" is just a string value. With globals(), it is dynamically converted into a variable name and assigned the value 100.

Getting Variable ID

Since variables are labels that map memory addresses to stored data, the **address ID** of a variable can be retrieved using the built-in id() function.

Example,

```
••• Python
>>> num = 25
>>> print(id(num))
```

```
#Output
140711318640168
```

This prints the unique memory address where the variable's value is stored.

Comments

Sometimes, building a project or creating software is a collective effort involving a team of individuals. One person may write the code, while others review, update, or modify the source code. The common myth about programming is that programmers only understand the code they have written themselves—and even then, with time, they may find it difficult to recall what they did.

To describe what a portion of the program does, programmers can attach messages to it. This is called **commenting**. When Python is interpreting the program, it does not execute comments.
A comment can be added by using the # symbol followed by a note. The # tells the interpreter to skip that portion of the program.

For example,

Python

```python
var = "Fox" #first value(comment)
num = 2     #second value(comment)
```

Docstrings

Comments can be either a single-line note using #, or multiple-line notes with more detailed explanations. For multi-line comments, docstrings are used by enclosing the notes within either ''' ''' or """ """.

For example,

Python

```python
def myfunction():
    """
    This is a multi-line comment
    explaining the purpose of the code.
    """
```

Key Terms

Variable
Identifier
Local Variable
Global Variable
Dynamic Variable
id
Comment
Docstring
Reserved Word
globals
locals

Review Questions

Q1. Which of the following is a valid variable name in Python?
a) 2num
b) num_2
c) @value
d) class
Answer: b

Q2. Which of the following symbols is used to create a comment in Python?
a) //
b) #
c) <!-- -->
d) %%
Answer: b

Q3. What will be the output of the following code?
x = None
print(x)
a) 0
b) null
c) None
d) Error
Answer: c

Q4. Which function returns the memory address ID of a variable in Python?
a) addr()
b) getid()
c) id()
d) memory()
Answer: c

Q5. Which of the following is a global variable?
a) A variable defined inside a function.
b) A variable defined outside any function.
c) A parameter passed into a function.
d) A variable with a private keyword.
Answer: b

Q6. Which of the following is NOT allowed as a variable name in Python?
a) my_var
b) value1
c) for
d) _temp
Answer: c

Q7. In Python, docstrings are enclosed in:
a) /* */
b) ''' ''' or """ """
c) { }
d) # #
Answer: b

Q8. Which function displays all local variables in the current scope?
a) globals()
b) vars()
c) locals()
d) all()
Answer: c

Q9. What happens if you try to use a reserved keyword as a variable name in Python?
a) It will be ignored.
b) It will throw a syntax error.
c) It will store as a string.
d) It will create a hidden variable.
Answer: b

Review Exercises

1. Explain the difference between local and global variables with examples.

2. Why should programmers follow naming conventions when creating variables?

3. Differentiate between static and dynamic variables in Python.

4. What is the purpose of comments and docstrings in Python programs?

Reserved Words

Every programming language has certain keywords that cannot be used as variable names or identifiers. These are called **reserved words** or **keywords**. Each keyword performs a specific function within the language.

In Python, if you try to use a keyword as a variable, the interpreter will generate an error message.

The table below shows some keywords used in Python.

print	chr	hex	max	super	finally	yield	hash
len	else	range	raise	next	type	compile	bytearray
set	if	bin	sum	map	or	id	local
int	True	try	as	with	global	input	None
dict	False	eval	bool	while	local	elif	break
list	and	not	str	for	round	match	async
object	import	oct	ord	zip	super	filter	format
exec	del	dir	any	def	return	bytes	ascii
open	lambda	enumerate	delattr	continue	pass	help	in
assert	class	min	complex	await	pow	is	nonlocal
from	case						

Table 1.1 *Full List of Dart Reserved Keywords*

Note

Not all keywords are explained in this chapter. As you progress through the upcoming chapters, you will be introduced to the remaining keywords in detail.

Python includes a special module named **keyword**, which provides functionality for working with Python's reserved words (keywords).

This module can be used to check whether a given string is a keyword or to retrieve a list of all keywords defined in the current Python version.

Example 1 – Checking if a word is a Python keyword,

```
Python
import keyword
print(keyword.iskeyword("for"))
print(keyword.iskeyword("while"))
print(keyword.iskeyword("python"))
```

```
#Output
True
True
False
```

Example 2 – Returning a list of all the Python keywords,

```python
import keyword
print(keyword.kwlist)
```

```
#Output
['False', 'None', 'True', 'and', 'as', 'assert', 'async', 'await',
'break', 'class', 'continue', 'def', 'del', 'elif', 'else', 'except',
'finally', 'for', 'from', 'global', 'if', 'import', 'in', 'is', 'lambda',
'nonlocal', 'not', 'or', 'pass', 'raise', 'return', 'try', 'while',
'with', 'yield']
```

Built-in Functions

Python provides a wide range of built-in functions that simplify programming tasks. These functions are predefined and available for use without requiring any imports.

They help developers perform common operations efficiently, eliminating the need to write long blocks of code for basic tasks.

Built-in functions can accept arguments (input values) and may return a result after execution. Examples include commonly used functions such as **len()**, **sum()**, **max()**, **type()**, and many others.

input()

The input() function is used to receive data from the user through a prompt. By default, it takes input as a string, but the input data can be converted to any desired type and assigned to a variable.

Example 1,

```python
name = input("Enter name: ")
print("Hello", name)
```

```
#Output
Enter name: John
Hello John
```

Example 2,

```python
var1 = input("Enter first number: ")
var2 = input("Enter second number: ")
total = int(var1) + int(var2)  #Casting to integer
print("Sum of the numbers-> ", total)
```

```
#Output
Enter first number: 5
Enter second number: 10
Sum of the numbers->  15
```

Note

The **int** used above belongs to the integer data type and is used to convert or cast other types to integers. Integers and other data types will be covered in detail in the upcoming chapters

bin()

The bin returns the binary of an integer or a number.

```python
>>> bin( 8 )
... '0b1000'
```

hex()

The hex keyword returns the hexadecimal of an integer or a number.

```python
>>> hex(25)
... ' 0x19'
```

oct()

The oct() function returns the octal (base-8) representation of an integer or number.

```
Python
>>> oct(12)
... '0o14'
```

chr()

The chr function accepts an integer and returns its corresponding ASCII character.

```
Python
>>> chr( 65 )
... 'A'
>>> chr( 64 )
... '@'
```

The Following are some ASCII Characters and their corresponding Index

33	!	43	+	58	:	91	[
34	"	44	,	59	;	92	\\
35	#	45	-	60	<	93	]
36	$	46	.	61	=	94	^
37	%	47	/	62	>	97	a
38	&	48	0	63	?	98	b
39	'	49	1	64	@	165	¥
40	(	50	2	65	A	190	¾
41	)	51	3	66	B	200	È
42	*	52	4	67	C	210	Ò

Table 1.2 *Full List of Dart Reserved Keywords*

ord()

The ord function accepts an ASCII character in a string and returns its corresponding integer.

```
Python
>>> ord("m")
... 109
>>> ord("%")
... 37
```

eval()

The eval() function evaluates expressions in string format and applies mathematical operations to compute the result.

```
●●● Python
>>> result = eval("2+3*4-8/2")
>>> print(result)
... 10.0
```

id()

The id() function returns the **memory address** of a variable.

```
●●● Python
>>> var = 20.68
>>> var_id = id(var)
>>> print(var_id)
... 2993179835888
```

del

The del statement deletes a variable or object from memory. Attempting to access a deleted variable will result in an error.

```
●●● Python
>>> var = 2
>>> del var
>>> print(var)
... Traceback (most recent call last):
    File "<stdin>", line 1, in <module>
    NameError: name 'var' is not defined. Did you mean: 'vars'?
```

Key Terms

Reserved Word
Keyword
def
return
break
continue
lambda
yield
try
except
finally

Review Questions

Q1. What are reserved words in Python?
a) Words that store memory addresses.
b) Words that have predefined meanings in the language.
c) User-created variable names.
d) Function arguments.
Answer: b

Q2. Which of the following is **NOT** a reserved word in Python?
a) while
b) def
c) global
d) print
Answer: d

Q3. What will happen if you write the following in Python?
for = 20
print(for)
a) It will print 20.
b) It will store the variable for later use.
c) It will raise a SyntaxError.
d) It will return None.
Answer: c

Q4. Which keyword is used to define a function in Python?
a) func
b) def
c) function
d) lambda
Answer: b

Q5. Which keyword is used to terminate a loop in Python?
a) end
b) stop
c) break
d) exit
Answer: c

Q6. Which of these is a reserved word in Python?
a) yield
b) main
c) include
d) then
Answer: a

Q7. Reserved words in Python are:
a) Case sensitive
b) Case insensitive
c) User defined
d) Executed at runtime only
Answer: a

Q8. Which keyword is used to create an anonymous function in Python?
a) def
b) anon
c) lambda
d) func
Answer: c

Q9. Which keyword is used for exception handling?
a) try
b) except
c) finally
d) All of the above
Answer: d

Q10. How many reserved words does Python 3.11/3.13 approximately have?
a) Less than 10
b) About 20
c) Around 35+
d) Over 50
Answer: d

Review Exercises

1. What are reserved words in Python, and why can't they be used as variable names?

2. Differentiate between a **keyword** and a **built-in function** in Python with examples.

3. List at least 10 reserved words in Python and explain their uses briefly.

4. What will happen if you assign a value to a reserved word? Demonstrate with an example.

Operators

Operators play a crucial role in programming. They are special symbols used to perform mathematical operations, comparisons, assignments, validations, and evaluations in a program. Operators usually work between two values, called **operands.**
For example:

Here, the operator acts on operands to produce a result.

Operators in Python are classified into groups according to their functions.
These include:

1. Arithmetic Operators
Used for performing basic mathematical operations such as addition, subtraction, multiplication, division, etc.

2. Relational Operators
Used to compare values (e.g., greater than, less than, equal to).

3. Assignment Operators
Used to assign values to variables.

4. Logical Operators
Used to evaluate multiple conditions (e.g., and, or, not).

5. Identity Operators
Used to compare the memory locations of objects (is, is not).

6. Membership Operators
Used to check if a value is present in a sequence (in, not in).

8. Bitwise Operators
Used to perform operations at the binary level (e.g., AND &, OR |, XOR ^, shifts <<, >>).

Arithmetic Operators

Arithmetic operators are used to perform various mathematical functions on numeric data types in programming. They enable you to perform fundamental mathematical operations like addition, subtraction, multiplication, division, and more.

addition (+)

```
Python
>>> x, y = 5, 10
>>> total = x + y
>>> print(total)
```

```
#Output
15
```

subtraction (-)

```
Python
>>> m, n = 6.3, 2.5
>>> result = m - n
>>> print(result)
```

```
#Output
3.8
```

multiplication (*)

```
Python
>>> var = 4
>>> result = var * 2
>>> print(result)
```

```
#Output
8
```

division (/)

```
••• Python
>>> var = 10
>>> result = var / 2
>>> print(result)
```

```
#Output
5
```

modulo (%)

```
••• Python
>>> num, fact = 11, 3
>>> result = num % fact
>>> print(result)
```

```
#Output
2
```

floor division (//)

```
••• Python
>>> result = 9 // 2
>>> print(result)
```

```
#Output
4
```

exponential (**)

```
••• Python
>>> exp = 4 ** 2
>>> print(exp)
```

```
#Output
16
```

Relational Operators

Relational operators, also known as comparison operators, are essential components of conditional statements in Python. They are used to compare two values or operands and determine the relationship between them. Relational operators return a Boolean value, either **'True'** or **'False'**, based on the result of the comparison.

Relational operators are crucial for making decisions in programs. They help answer questions like "Is this value equal to that one?" or "Is this value greater than that one?"

equal to (==)

```
Python
>>> "computre" == "computer"
... False
>>> x = y = 3
>>> x == y
... True
```

not equal to (!=)

```
Python
>>> x, y = 3, 2
>>> x != y
... True
```

Less than (<)

```
Python
>>> result_1 = 20 < 10
>>> print(result_1)
...False
>>> result_2 = 5 < 7
>>> print(result_2)
...True
```

Less than or equal to (<=)

```
Python
>>> result = 2 <= 2
>>> print(result)
...True
```

greater than (>)

```
●●● Python
>>> x, y = 10, 5
>>> x > y
... True
```

greater than or equal to (>=)

```
●●● Python
>>> x = y = 4
>>> x >= y
... True
```

Assignment Operators

Assignment operators serve the primary function of assigning a value on the right side to a variable on the left side. This assignment results in the variable holding the assigned value, thereby making it accessible for subsequent operations or references in your code. In Python, the most commonly used assignment operator is the equals sign (=), which assigns the value on the right side to the variable on the left side. For example:

equal(=)

```
●●● Python
>>> var = 5
>>> m = n = 3
>>> x, y = 10, "cat"
```

addition assignment(+=)

The addition assignment operator adds the right operand to the left operand and assigns the result to the left operand or the variable.

```
●●● Python
>>> var = 2
>>> var += 3
>>> print(var)
... 5
```

subtraction assignment(-=)

The subtraction assignment (-=) operator subtracts the right operand from the left operand and assigns the result to the left operand or the variable.

```
••• Python
>>> num = 6
>>> num -= 3
>>> print(num)
... 3
```

multiplication assignment(*=)

The multiplication assignment (*=) operator multiplies the left operand by the right operand and assigns the result to the left operand.

```
••• Python
>>> x = 4
>>> x *= 2
>>> print(x)
... 8
```

division assignment(/=)

The division assignment (/=) operator divides the left operand by the right operand and assigns the result to the left operand or the variable. The result is always a float.

```
••• Python
>>> var = 8
>>> var /= 4
>>> print(var)
... 2.0
```

floor division assignment(//=)

The floor division assignment (//=) operator performs floor division (truncating the decimal part) and assigns the result to the left operand or the variable.

```
••• Python
>>> myvar = 10
>>> myvar //= 4
>>> print(myvar)
... 2
```

modulus assignment(%=)

The modulus assignment (%=) operator calculates the remainder when the left operand is divided by the right operand and assigns the result to the left operand or the variable.

```
Python
>>> mod = 14
>>> mod %= 3
>>> print(mod)
... 2
```

Exponential assignment(**=)

The exponentiation assignment (**=) operator raises the left operand to the power of the right operand and assigns the result to the left operand or variable.

```
Python
>>> exp = 3
>>> exp **= 2
>>> print(exp)
... 9
```

Logical Operators

Logical operators are essential elements in Python used for making logical assumptions and decisions. They operate on **Boolean** values and return either '**True**' or '**False**' based on the logical conditions they evaluate. Logical operators are or, and, not. These operators are mostly used in decision making structures.

Insight

Logical operators are mostly used in decision-making controls (**if** , **elif** clauses) for making conditional statements or decision-making. This will be studied later under Decision making statements.

or

The **or** operator returns True if at least one of the operands is True; otherwise, it returns False.

```
●●● Python
var = 5
if var == 5 or var == 2:
    print("Hello World")
```

```
#Output
Hello World
```

Key points

- In the above example, var == 5 returns True, while var == 2 returns False.
- Since one condition is True, the entire expression evaluates to True, and "Hello World" is printed.

Expression	Result
True or False	True
False or True	True
False or False	False
True or True	True

Table 1.3 *OR Logic Table*

and

The **and** operator returns True only if both operands are True; otherwise, it returns False.

```
●●● Python
var = 5
if var >= 5 and var < 10:
    print("Hello World")
```

```
#Output
Hello World
```

Key points

- In the above example, both var >= 5 and var < 10 are True.
- Since both conditions are True, the entire expression evaluates to True, and "Hello World" is printed.

Expression	Result
True and False	False
False and True	False
False and False	False
True and True	True
Table 1.4	*AND Logic Table*

not

The **not** operator returns the logical negation of the operand, meaning It reverses the result of a condition – if a condition is **True**, it becomes **False**, and vice versa.

```python
var = False
if not var:
    print("Hello World")
```

```
#Output
Hello World
```

Key points

- In the above example, var = False, and not var evaluates to **True**.
- Since the condition becomes **True**, the print() statement is executed.

Expression	Result
not False	True
not True	False
Table 1.5	*NOT Logic Table*

Identity Operators

Identity operators in Python are tools used to verify or check whether two variables or objects are stored at the same memory location. They allow you to determine if two variables or objects refer to the same entity in memory, rather than comparing their values. Identity operators are essential for understanding object identity and reference equality. The two identity operators are **is** and **is not**.

is

```
●●● Python
>>> x = y = 10
>>> z = 5
>>> var_xy = x is y
>>> print(var_xy)
... True
>>> var_zx = z is x
>>> print(var_zx)
... False
```

is not

```
●●● Python
>>> x, y = "cat", "fox"
>>> result = x is not y
>>> print(result)
... True
```

Membership Operators

Membership operators in Python are tools used to check if a specific item is present in a collection of items. These operators are invaluable for determining whether an element belongs to a set, list, tuple, string, or any other **iterable**. They provide a straightforward way to search for the presence of an item within a container.

in

```
●●● Python
>>> var = "Python"
>>> result = "P" in var
>>> print(result)
... True
>>> result = "m" in var
>>> print(result)
... False
```

not in

```python
>>> var = "Hello World"
>>> result = "Hello" not in var
>>> print(result)
... False
```

Bitwise Operators

Bitwise operators are used to perform operations on binary numbers at the **bit level**. Unlike logical operators (and, or, not) that work on Boolean values, bitwise operators work on **individual bits** of integers.

Insight

When performing bitwise operations, Python first converts the numbers into binary form, performs the operation, and then converts the result back into an integer.

1. Bitwise AND (&)

Performs a logical **AND** operation on each bit of the two numbers. The bit is set to **1** only if **both corresponding bits** are **1**.

```python
a = 10  # binary: 1010
b = 7   # binary: 0111
result = a & b
print(result)
```

```
#Output
2
```

Explanation

10	→		1010
7	→	&	0111
2	→		0010

Insight

To convert a decimal number to its binary equivalent, use the built-in **bin()** function. For example:

```
>>> bin(10)
...'0b1010'
```

2. Bitwise OR (|)

Performs a logical **OR** operation on each bit.

The bit is set to **1** if **either bit** is **1**.

```python
a = 10  # binary: 1010
b = 7   # binary: 0111
result = a | b
print(result)
```

```
#Output
15
```

Explanation

```
10  →      1010
 7  →   |  0111
           ----
15  →      1111
```

3. Bitwise XOR (^)

Performs a logical **exclusive OR** operation.

The bit is set to **1** if **only one** of the corresponding bits is **1**, but not both.

```python
a = 10  # binary: 1010
b = 7   # binary: 0111
result = a ^ b
print(result)
```

```
#Output
13
```

Explanation

10	→		1010
7	→	^	0111
13	→		1101

4. Bitwise NOT (~)

Inverts all the bits in a number.

It changes 1 to 0 and 0 to 1.

In Python, bitwise NOT of a number x gives -(x + 1) due to two's complement representation.

```
Python
a = 10
result = ~a
print(result)
```

```
#Output
-11
```

Explanation

~10 → - (10 + 1) = -11

5. Bitwise Left Shift (<<)

Shifts the bits of the number to the **left** by a specified number of positions.

Each left shift multiplies the number by 2 for each position shifted.

```
Python
a = 5
result = a << 3
print(result)
```

```
#Output
40
```

Explanation

5 → 0101 → 101000 = 40

6. Bitwise Right Shift (>>)

Shifts the bits of the number to the **right** by a specified number of positions. Each right shift divides the number by 2 for each position shifted.

```python
x = 6
result = x >> 2
print(result)
```

```
#Output
1
```

Explanation

6 → 0110 → 0001 = 1

Key Terms

Operator
Operand
is
is not
in
not in
bitwise
XOR
AND
NOT
or
and
bit

Review Questions

Q1. Which of the following is NOT an arithmetic operator in Python?
a) +
b) -
c) %
d) and
Answer: d

Q2. What is the result of 10 // 3 in Python?
a) 3.3
b) 3
c) 4
d) 3.0
Answer: b

Q3. Which operator is used for exponentiation in Python?
a) ^
b) **
c) *
d) //
Answer: b

Q4. What is the output of 5 == 5?
a) True
b) False
c) Error
d) None
Answer: a

Q5. Which of the following is a logical operator?
a) or
b) %
c) =
d) **
Answer: a

Q6. Which operator is used to assign a value to a variable?
a) ==
b) =
c) :=
d) =>
Answer: b

Q7. What is the output of x = 5; x += 3; print(x)?
a) 3
b) 5
c) 8
d) Error

Answer: c
Q8. Which operator checks if two variables refer to the same object in memory?
a) in
b) ==
c) is
d) :=

Answer: c
Q9. The operator in is used for:
a) Identity check
b) Membership check
c) Assignment
d) Bitwise shift
Answer: b

Q10. What is the result of True and False?
a) True
b) False
c) None
d) Error
Answer: b

Q11. Which of the following is a bitwise operator?
a) &
b) and
c) or
d) not
Answer: a

Review Exercises

1. Define an operator and operand with an example.

2. Differentiate between **relational operators** and **logical operators** with examples.

3. Explain the use of **assignment operators** with two code examples.

4. Describe **identity** vs **membership operators** with examples.

5. Demonstrate the difference between / and // division in Python with examples.

Data Types

The core components of programming are the program and its data. Data encompasses all raw values represented in forms such as numbers, strings of letters, special characters, and bytes. Each piece of data acts as an object of a particular Python data class.

There are approximately eight main data types in the Python language. These include:

1. Numbers (Integers and Float)
2. String
3. List
4. Tuple
5. Dictionary
6. Set
7. Boolean
8. Bytes

Insight

The **type()** function is a built-in Python function used to check the data type of a variable or object. For example

```
>>> var = 10.5
>>> t = type(var)
>>> print( t )
... <class 'float'>
```

Numbers

The **number class** consists of all positive and negative real numbers. Numbers exist in two forms:

- Numbers **without decimal points** (e.g., 25)
- Numbers **with decimal points** (e.g., 2.5)

Numbers are classified into **Integers** and **Floats**.

Integers

Integers refer to all positive and negative **whole numbers**. These numbers do not have decimal points.

Example:

... -4, -3, -2, -1, 0, 1, 2, 3, 4 ...

Insight

Type Casting

The **int()** function converts other data types into integers. Possible conversions include:

1. Float → Integer   >>> var = int(7.5) → 7
2. String → Integer   >>> var = int("26") → 26

Float

Floats include all positive and negative numbers with **decimal points**.

Example:

-2.5, -1.3, 3.2, 5.7 ...

Insight

Type Casting

The **float()** function converts other data types into floats. Possible conversions include:

1. String → Float   >>> var = float("2.1") → 2.1
2. Integer → Float   >>> var = float(6) → 6.0

Functional Operations on Numbers

Python provides several built-in functions for performing mathematical operations on numbers. These functions are part of the **core Python package** and do not require installation.
Example:

pow(x, y)

This function returns x raised to the power y (x^y).

●●● Python
```
var = 4
result = pow(var, 2)
print(result)
```

```
#Output
16
```

Note

The exponential operator ** works exactly the same as the pow() function. For example,
```
>>> result = 4 ** 2
>>> print(result)
... 16
```

round(x, y)

Rounds the number **x** to **y** decimal places. If **y** is omitted, the function rounds to the nearest whole number.

●●● Python
```
dec = 6.28564
result = round(dec, 2)
print(result)
```

```
#Output
6.29
```

abs(x)

The abs() function returns the **absolute value** of a number. It removes any negative sign and returns the number's magnitude.

```
Python
var = -3
value = abs(var)
print(value)
```

```
#Output
3
```

divmod(x, y)

The divmod() function returns both the **quotient** and **remainder** of a division as a tuple (quotient, remainder).

```
Python

result = divmod(11, 4)
print(result)
```

```
#Output
(2, 3)
```

complex(x, y)

The complex() function creates a complex number where **x** is the real part and **y** is the imaginary part.

```
Python
>>> value = complex(2, 3)
>>> print(value)
... (2+3j)
>>> result = complex(5, 2) + complex(3, 4)
>>> print(result)
... (8+6j)
```

The math Module

The math module is a powerful mathematical library used for performing numerical computations. It includes methods for working with:

- Equations
- Geometry
- Trigonometry
- Logarithms

The math module is part of the Python standard library and requires no installation.

Insight

You can explore more methods of math with the **dir()** function.
For example,

```
>>> import math
>>> for x in dir(math):
        print(x)
...
```

Function	Description
math.sqrt(x)	Returns the square root of x.
math.pow(x, y)	Returns x raised to the power of y (equivalent to x ** y).
math.exp(x)	Returns e raised to the power of x.
math.log(x)	Returns the natural logarithm (base e) of x.
math.log10(x)	Returns the logarithm of x to base 10.
math.log2(x)	Returns the logarithm of x to base 2.
math.factorial(x)	Returns the factorial of x (x!).
math.gcd(x, y)	Returns the greatest common divisor (GCD) of x and y.
math.lcm(x, y)	Returns the least common multiple (LCM) of x and y.
math.fabs(x)	Returns the absolute value of x.
math.ceil(x)	Rounds x up to the nearest integer.
math.floor(x)	Rounds x down to the nearest integer.
math.trunc(x)	Returns the truncated integer part of x.
math.modf(x)	Splits x into its fractional and integer parts as a tuple.
math.copysign(x, y)	Returns x with the sign of y.
math.fsum(iterable)	Returns the precise sum of an iterable of numbers.
math.isfinite(x)	Checks if x is a finite number.
math.isinf(x)	Checks if x is infinite (+∞ or -∞).
math.isnan(x)	Checks if x is NaN (Not a Number).

Table 1.6

pow(x, y)

```python
>>> import math
>>> result = math.pow(3, 2)
>>> print(result)
... 9.0
```

sqrt(x)

```python
>>> import math
>>> result = math.sqrt(16)
>>> print(result)
... 4.0
```

log(x)

```python
>>> import math
>>> result = math.log(4)
>>> print(result)
... 1.3862943611198906
```

floor(x)

```python
>>> import math
>>> result = math.floor(8.456)
>>> print(result)
... 8
```

ceil(x)

```python
>>> import math
>>> result = math.ceil(8.456)
>>> print(result)
... 9
```

factorial(x)

```
Python
>>> import math
>>> result = math.factorial(6)
>>> print(result)
... 720
```

gcd(integers)

```
Python
>>> import math
>>> result = math.gcd(12,16)
>>> print(result)
... 4
```

lcm(int)

```
Python
>>> import math
>>> result = math.lcm(6, 3, 4)
>>> print(result)
... 12
```

Trigonometric Functions

Function	Description
math.sin(x)	Returns the sine of x (in radians).
math.cos(x)	Returns the cosine of x (in radians).
math.tan(x)	Returns the tangent of x (in radians).
math.asin(x)	Returns the arcsine of x (inverse of sine).
math.acos(x)	Returns the arccosine of x (inverse of cosine).
math.atan(x)	Returns the arctangent of x (inverse of tangent).
math.degrees(x)	Converts x from radians to degrees.
math.radians(x)	Converts x from degrees to radians.
math.sinh(x)	Returns the hyperbolic sine of x.
math.cosh(x)	Returns the hyperbolic cosine of x.
math.tanh(x)	Returns the hyperbolic tangent of x.

math.asinh(x)	Returns the inverse hyperbolic sine of x.
math.acosh(x)	Returns the inverse hyperbolic cosine of x.
math.atanh(x)	Returns the inverse hyperbolic tangent of x.

Table 1.7

sin(x)

Python

```
>>> import math
>>> rad = math.radians(60)
>>> result = math.sin(rad)
>>> print(result)
... 0.8660254037844386
```

cos(x)

Python

```
>>> import math
>>> rad = math.radians(60)
>>> result = math.cos(rad)
>>> print(result)
... 0.5000000000000001
```

tan(x)

Python

```
>>> import math
>>> rad = math.radians(60)
>>> result = math.tan(rad)
>>> print(result)
... 1.7320508075688767
```

degrees(x)

Python

```
>>> import math
>>> rad = math.radians(60)
>>> result = math.degrees(rad)
>>> print(result)
... 59.99999999999999
```

Mathematical Constant

Function	Description
math.pi	Represents the value of π (3.14159...).
math.e	Represents Euler's number (2.71828...), the base of natural logarithms.
math.tau	Represents the constant τ (τ = 2π).
math.inf	Represents positive infinity (+∞).
math.nan	Represents "Not a Number" (NaN).

Table 1.8

pi

```
Python
>>> import math
>>> value = math.pi
>>> print(value)
... 3.141592653589793
```

e

```
Python
>>> import math
>>> value = math.e
>>> print(value)
... 2.718281828459045
```

Special Functions

Function	Description
math.erf(x)	Returns the error function of x.
math.erfc(x)	Returns the complementary error function of x.
math.gamma(x)	Returns the gamma function of x ((x-1)!).
math.lgamma(x)	Returns the natural logarithm of the absolute value of the gamma function of x.

Table 1.9

String

A string is a sequence of characters consisting of alphabets, numbers, and special characters enclosed within single quotes (' '), double quotes (" "), or triple quotes (""" """ or ''' ''').

Python

```
x = "fox"
y = 'Python is Awesome'
z = '''Programming is fun!'''
m = """consistency is the key"""
```

Insight

Type Casting

The **str()** function is used for converting other data types into strings. The possible conversions include:

1. Integer → String >>> var = str(5) → '5'
2. Float → String >>> var = str(6.28) → '6.28'
3. List → String >>> var = str([5, 2]) → '[5, 2]'
4. Tuple → String >>> var = str((4, 2)) → '(4, 2)'
5. Dictionary → String >>> var = str({'name':"John"}) → "{'name': 'John'}"
6. Set → String >>> var = str({2, 3, 5}) → '{2, 3, 5}'

String indexing

Indexing refers to the position of each character in a string. The index of a string starts from zero and goes up to the length of the string minus one (**0** to **length-1**). The first character or element of a string typically occupies index **0**, the next character takes index **1**, and so on.

For example, using "computer"

0	1	2	3	4	5	6	7
c	o	m	p	u	t	e	r
-8	-7	-6	-5	-4	-3	-2	-1

Example- Getting the index of characters,

```
Python

>>> var = "computer"
>>> index  = var[0]
>>> print("index 0-> ", index)
...index 0->  c

>>> index = var[4]
>>> print("index 4-> ", index)
...index 4->  u

>>> index = var[-2]
>>> print("index -2-> ", index)
...index -2-> e
```

String Concatenation

Two or more strings can be joined together to form a single string. This operation of adding one string to another is called **concatenation**. In Python, concatenation is performed using the plus (+) operator.

Example 1,

```
Python
var_1 = "com"
var_2 = "puter"
concat = var_1 + var_2
print(concat)
```

```
#Output
computer
```

Example 2,

```python
text1 = "Python is great."
text2 = "Consistency is the key to mastery!."
text = text1 + text2
print(text)
```

```
#Output
Python is great.Consistency is the key to mastery!.
```

Slicing Strings

A single string can be divided into individual substrings. Each character in a string has an index, which acts as the breaking or slicing point. Breaking or slicing a string can be done in two ways:

1. Using slicing syntax:

```
string[ start : end ]
```

string[start:end]	→	Returns a substring starting from the specified start index up to (but not including) the end index.
string[start:]	→	Returns a substring starting from the specified start index to the end of the string.
string[: end]	→	Returns a substring starting from the beginning (index 0) up to (but not including) the specified end index.
string[:]	→	Returns the entire string from index 0 to the last character.

```python
>>> var = "The brown fox"
>>> value  = var[4:9]          #start:4 end:9
>>> print("value-> ", value)
... value->  brown
```

```
>>> value  = var[4:]            #start:4
>>> print("value-> ", value)
... value->  brown fox

>>> value  = var[:3]            #end:3
>>> print("value-> ", value)
... value->  The

>>> value  = var[:]             # :
>>> print("value-> ", value)
... value->  The brown fox
```

2. Using string methods:

partition(sep)

Splits a string into a tuple of three substrings. The **sep** is a character (separator) that marks the breaking point.

```
Python

var = "Cats love fish and monkeys love banana."
part  = var.partition("and")
print(part)
```

```
#Output
('Cats love fish ', 'and', ' monkeys love banana.')
```

split(sep, max) and rsplit(sep, max)

The **split()** method returns a list of substrings starting from index 0 to the last index.
The **rsplit()** method splits the string starting from the last index.

- ***sep*** → defines the breaking points. By default, whitespace (" ") is used if sep is not specified.
- ***max*** → defines the number of splits. By default, the value is infinite if max is not defined.

Example 1 - *split()*

```
Python
>>> var = "apple, mango, orange, guava"
>>> sub  = var.split(",")
>>> print("sub-> ", sub)
... sub->  ['apple', ' mango', ' orange', ' guava']

>>> sub  = var.split(",", 1)    #max = 1
>>> print("sub-> ", sub)
... sub->  ['apple', ' mango, orange, guava']
```

Example 2 – *rsplit()*

```
Python

states = "Illinois@California@Florida@Texas"
sub  = states.rsplit("@", 2)
print(sub)
```

```
#Output
['Illinois@California', 'Florida', 'Texas']
```

splitlines(keepends)

Returns a list of strings split by line breaks. The separator character is **\n** (escape character for new lines). By default, substrings do not include **\n**, but if *keepends*=True, then **\n** is included in each substring.

Example 1

```
Python
cities = "New York\nLondon\nParis\nOntario"

substr  = cities.splitlines()
print("result-> ", substr)
```

```
#Output
result->  ['New York', 'London', 'Paris', 'Ontario']
```

Example 2 – keepends = True

```python
cities = "New York\nLondon\nParis\nOntario"

substr  = cities.splitlines(keepends=True)
print("result-> ", substr)
```

```
#Output
result->  ['New York\n', 'London\n', 'Paris\n', 'Ontario']
```

Methods of Strings

The string type class provides several methods for modifying, updating, editing, and checking strings. These methods are grouped according to their functionalities.

> **Note**
>
> To view the various methods available for a string, use the dir() function on a string object. For example
>
> \>>> var = "my string"
>
> \>>> methods = [x for x in dir(var)]
>
> \>>> print(methods)

Case Conversion Methods

Method	Description
upper()	Converts all characters in the string to uppercase.
lower()	Converts all characters in the string to lowercase.
capitalize()	Converts the first character of the string to uppercase and the rest to lowercase.
title()	Converts the first character of each word in the string to uppercase.
swapcase()	Swaps uppercase characters to lowercase and vice versa.

casefold()	Converts the string to lowercase, more aggressive than lower(), used for case-insensitive comparisons.

Table 2.0

Python

```
>>> #upper
>>> var = "The brown fox"
>>> result = var.upper()
>>> print(result)
...THE BROWN FOX

>>> #lower
>>> var = "The Brown Fox"
>>> result = var.lower()
>>> print(result)
... the brown fox

>>> #capitalize
>>> var = "cat hates mouse"
>>> capitalize = var.capitalize()
>>> print(capitalize)
... Cat hates mouse

>>> #title
>>> var = "cat hates mouse"
>>> title = var.title()
>>> print(title)
... Cat Hates Mouse

>>> #swapcase
>>> var = "Python is an OOP"
>>> swap = var.swapcase()
>>> print(swap)
... pYTHON IS AN oop
```

Whitespace and Padding Methods

Method	Description
strip()	Removes leading and trailing whitespace.

lstrip()	Removes leading (left-side) whitespace.
rstrip()	Removes trailing (right-side) whitespace.
zfill(width)	Pads the string with zeros (0) on the left to match the given width.
center(width, char)	Centers the string within a given width using the specified character (default is space).
ljust(width, char)	Left-aligns the string within a given width, padding with the specified character.
rjust(width, char)	Right-aligns the string within a given width, padding with the specified character.

Table 2.1

Python

```
>>> #strip
>>> var = "   programming is fun   "
>>> strip = var.strip()
>>> print(strip)
...'programming is fun'

>>> #rstrip
>>> var = "   programming is fun   "
>>> result = var.rstrip()
>>> print(result)
...'   programming is fun'

>>> #zfill
>>> var = "coding"
>>> zfill = var.zfill(10)
>>> print(zfill)
...'0000coding'

>>> #center
>>> var = "coding"
>>> center = var.center(10, '*')
>>> print(center)
...'**coding**'

>>> #rjust
>>> var = "coding"
>>> rjust = var.rjust(8, '@')
>>> print(rjust)
```

```
... '@@coding'
```

Searching and Finding Methods

Method	Description
find(substring, start, end)	Returns the index of the first occurrence of substring in the string. Returns -1 if not found.
rfind(substring, start, end)	Similar to find(), but searches from the right.
index(substring, start, end)	Similar to find(), but raises an error if the substring is not found.
rindex(substring, start, end)	Similar to rfind(), but raises an error if the substring is not found.
count(substring, start, end)	Counts the occurrences of substring in the string.

Table 2.2

```python
>>> #find
>>> pos = "roses are red".find('are')
>>> print(pos)
...6
>>> pos = "programming".find('r', 2)    #start:2
>>> print(pos)
...4

>>> #index
>>> index = "programming".index('m')
>>> print(index)
...6

>>> #count
>>> cnt = "programming".count('g')
>>> print(cnt)
...2
```

Splitting and Joining Methods

Method	Description

split(delimiter, maxsplit)	Splits the string into a list using the specified delimiter. The optional maxsplit limits the number of splits.
rsplit(delimiter, maxsplit)	Similar to split(), but splits from the right.
splitlines(keepends)	Splits the string at line breaks (\n) and returns a list. If keepends=True, line breaks are kept.
partition(separator)	Splits the string into three parts: before separator, separator, and after separator.
rpartition(separator)	Similar to partition(), but searches from the right.
join(iterable)	Joins elements of an iterable (list, tuple) into a string using the calling string as a separator.

Table 2.3

Note

The functions **split()**, **rsplit()**, **splitlines()** and **partition()** have already been discussed in the *Slicing Strings* section.
Refer to that section for a detailed explanation and practical examples.

join(iterable)

Python

```
text = "Python is awesome"
join = "-".join(text)
print(join)
```

```
#Output
P-y-t-h-o-n- -i-s- -a-w-e-s-o-m-e
```

String Modification and Replacement Methods

Method	Description
replace(old, new, count)	Replaces occurrences of old with new. The optional count limits the number of replacements.
removeprefix(char)	Removes the specified leading character or substring from a string.

removesuffix(char)	Removes the specified trailing character or substring from a string.

Table 2.4

```python
>>> #replace
>>> text = "The brown fox"
>>> new_text = text.replace("brown", "white")
>>> print(new_text)
... The white fox

>>> text = "The fat cat can jump"
>>> new_text = text.replace("a", "@", 2)
>>> print(new_text)
...The f@t c@t can jump

>>> #removeprefix
>>> text = "New York City"
>>> new_text = text.removeprefix("New")
>>> print(new_text)
... York City

>>> #removesuffix
>>> text = "kingbrown@gmail.com"
>>> new_text = text.removesuffix(".com")
>>> print(new_text)
... kingbrown@gmail
```

String Checking Methods (True or False)

Method	Description
startswith(prefix, start, end)	Returns True if the string starts with prefix.
endswith(suffix, start, end)	Returns True if the string ends with suffix.
isalpha()	Returns True if the string contains only alphabetic characters (A-Z, a-z).
isdigit()	Returns True if the string contains only digits (0-9).
isalnum()	Returns True if the string contains only alphanumeric characters (letters and numbers).
isspace()	Returns True if the string contains only whitespace characters.
islower()	Returns True if all characters in the string are lowercase.

isupper()	Returns True if all characters in the string are uppercase.
istitle()	Returns True if the string follows title case (each word starts with an uppercase letter).
isnumeric()	Returns True if the string contains only numeric characters, including Unicode numerals.
isdecimal()	Returns True if the string contains only decimal characters.
isidentifier()	Returns True if the string is a valid Python identifier (variable name).
isascii()	Returns True if the string contains only ASCII characters (0-127).

Table 2.5

Python

```
>>> #startswith
>>> test = "computer".startswith("com")
>>> print(test)
... True

>>> #endswith
>>> test = "computer".endswith("er")
>>> print(test)
... True

>>> #isalpha
>>> test = "Python".isalpha()
>>> print(test)
... True

>>> #isdigit
>>> test = "4258".isdigit()
>>> print(test)
... True

>>> #isalnum
>>> test = "Block536".isalnum()
>>> print(test)
... True

>>> #isupper
>>> test = "GEORGE".isupper()
```

```
>>> print(test)
... True

>>> #islower
>>> test = "george".islower()
>>> print(test)
... True

>>> #istitle
>>> test = "The Fat Cat".istitle()
>>> print(test)
... True

>>> #isnumeric
>>> test = "68293".isnumeric()
>>> print(test)
... True

>>> #isascii
>>> test = "roselyn_258@gmail.com".isascii()
>>> print(test)
... True
```

Formatting Strings

In programming, formatting a string means modifying it by inserting, adding or removing characters.

Python provides three core methods for formatting strings:

1. f-String

- The easiest and most flexible method.
- The string is prefixed with **f** and variables are placed within curly brackets {}.

Syntax

```
f"{ variable or expression}"
```

Example 1,

```python
name = "Marrie"
age = 25
print(f"Name: {name}, age: {age}")
```

```
#Output
Name: Marrie, age: 25
```

Example 2,

```python
book = 60
pencil = 84

stat = f"""The total average of 15 books is {book/15 }
and the average of 20 pencils is {pencil/20}
"""
print(stat)
```

```
#Output
The total average of 15 books is 4.0
and the average of 20 pencils is 4.2
```

2. .format()

- Replaces curly brackets {} with values passed inside .format().

```
" { variable } ".format( variable )
```

Example 1

```python
country = "Canada"
city = "Ontario"
```

```
result = "Country-> {}, city-> {}".format(country, city)
print(result)
```

```
#Output
Country-> Canada, city-> Ontario
```

Example 2

```
Python

cat = "meow"
dog = "woof"

animal = " The cat {1} and the dog {0}".format(dog, cat)
print(animal)
```

```
#Output
The cat meow and the dog woof
```

3. % Formatting (Old Method)

- Older versions of Python (before 3.6) used % for formatting (C-style).
- This method is mostly deprecated and has been replaced by **f-strings** and .format().

```
Python

book = 100
print( "Total book price is $%d" % book )  # %d is for integers
```

```
#Output
Total book price is $100
```

Escape Characters

Escape characters are special sequences used in strings to format text or provide commands to the compiler for display. They help create new lines, insert tab spaces, display quotes, or include special symbols.
Escape sequences always begin with a backslash (\), followed by a specific character that represents an action.

Escape Character	Description
\n	Inserts a new line (line break)
\t	Adds a horizontal tab space
\\	Inserts a backslash (\)
\'	Inserts a single quote (') inside a string enclosed in single quotes
\"	Inserts a double quote (") inside a string enclosed in double quotes
\r	Carriage return – moves the cursor to the beginning of the line
\b	Backspace – removes the previous character
\f	Form feed – moves to the next page (used in printing)
\v	Vertical tab – adds a vertical tab space
\000	Represents an octal value (e.g., \101 represents 'A')
\xhh	Represents a hexadecimal value (e.g., \x41 represents 'A')

Table 2.6

Example 1- newline (\n)

Python
```
comment = "My favorite fruits include:\napple\nmango\nstrawberry"
print(comment)
```

```
#Output
My favorite fruits include:
apple
mango
strawberry
```

Example 2- tab space (\t)

Python
```
lang = "1.Python\t\t2.JavaScript\t\t3.C++"
print(lang)
```

```
#Output
1.Python                2.JavaScript            3.C++
```

Regular Expressions

A regular expression (regex) is a way of matching or extracting substrings from a string by filtering the text against specific patterns or rules. These patterns are defined by special characters, which collectively form a matching rule.

In Python, the **re** module is used for performing regular expressions. The regex pattern is defined inside r"".

Methods of re Module

Method	Definition
compile()	Compiles a regex pattern into a regex object for repeated use.
copyreg	Provides support for object pickling (not commonly used in regex).
enum	Returns an enumeration for regex matches (not a standard regex method; likely external reference).
error	Represents regex compilation errors.
escape()	Escapes all special characters in a string.
findall()	Returns all matches of a regex pattern in a string as a list.
finditer()	Returns an iterator yielding match objects over all matches.
fullmatch()	Checks if the entire string matches the pattern.
functools	Utilities for functional programming (not part of regex).
match()	Checks if the regex matches at the beginning of the string.
purge()	Clears the cache of compiled regex patterns.
search()	Scans a string and returns the first match; returns None if not found.
split()	Splits a string at each match of the regex pattern.
sub()	Replaces matches with a replacement string.
subn()	Similar to sub(), but returns a tuple (new_string, number_of_replacements).
template()	Defines regex templates for reuse.

Table 2.7

Pattern Creation

A regex pattern defines a set of rules or guidelines to extract or match keywords in a string. Patterns are created from special characters.

Character Classes

Pattern	Meaning
.	Any character except newline

\d	Digit (0-9)
\D	Non-digit
\w	Word char (letters, digits, _)
\W	Non-word char
\s	Whitespace (space, tab, newline)
\S	Non-whitespace

Table 2.8

Dot (.)

```
Python
>>> import re
>>> text = re.findall(r"ca.", "The cat can catch the fish")
>>> print(text)
... ['cat', 'can', 'cat']
```

Digit (\d)

```
Python
>>> import re
>>> text = re.findall(r"\d","The box has 2 books and 6 pencils")
>>> print(text)
... ['2', '6']
```

Quantifiers

Pattern	Meaning
+	One or more
*	Zero or more
[ ]	Match one of the characters inside
-	Range inside [ ]
?	Zero or one
{m}	Exactly m times
{m,}	At least m times
{m,n}	Between m and n times
( )	Capture a group of characters

Table 2.9

One or more (+)

```python
>>> text=re.findall(r"\Do+\D", "The box has 2 books and 6 pencils")
>>> print(text)
... ['box', 'book']
```

Interpretation

The regex scans the text for words that:

1. Begin with a non-digit character (\D → e.g., b)
2. Contain one or more letter **'o'** (o+ → bo, boo)
3. End with a non-digit character (\D)

Hence, **'box'** and **'book'** satisfy the pattern.

Zero or more (*)

```python
>>> text = re.findall(r"ro*e*s*d*", "roses are red")
>>> print(text)
... ['ros', 're', 'red']
```

Interpretation

1. Start with **r**
2. Are optionally followed by one or more **o** (o*)
3. Optionally followed by one or more **e** (e*)
4. Optionally followed by one or more **s** (s*)
5. Optionally followed by one or more **d** (d*).

Therefore, **ros**, **re**, and **red** match.

Match one char ([ ])

```python
>>> text = re.findall(r"f[oat][txs]", "The fat fox runs fast")
>>> print(text)
... ['fat', 'fox', 'fas']
```

Interpretation

The regex matches sequences that:

1. Begin with **f**

2. Follow with **o**, **a**, or **t** ([oat])
3. End with **t**, **x**, or **s** ([txs])

Matches: **fat**, **fox**, **fas**.

Number range([1-9])

```
●●● Python
>>> text = re.findall(r"[0-9]+", "George owns 24 dogs and 650 cows")
>>> print(text)
... ['24', '650']
```

Interpretation

Matches one or more digits ranging from **0–9**.

Letter range ([A-Za-z])

```
●●● Python
>>> text = re.findall(r"[A-Za-z]e[a-z]+", "Hello, it's yellow day!")
>>> print(text)
... ['Hello', 'yellow']
```

Interpretation

1. Starts with a letter (uppercase or lowercase)
2. Followed by **e**
3. Followed by one or more lowercase letters

Result: **Hello**, **yellow**

Zero or one (?)

```
●●● Python
>>> text = re.findall(r"colou?r", "colour my world with colors")
>>> print(text)
... ['colour', 'color']
```

Interpretation

Matches **color**

Optionally followed by **u** (u?) → matches both **color** and **colour**

Exactly m times ({ m })

```
●●● Python
>>> text = re.findall(r"[1-9]{3}", "The watch cost $42587")
>>> print(text)
... ['425']
```

Interpretation
Matches a group of exactly **3 digits** between **1-9**.

Between n and m times ({ n, m })

```
●●● Python
>>> text=re.findall(r"[0-9]{2,3}", "The book is $85, $689 or $4789")
>>> print(text)
... ['85', '689', '478']
```

Interpretation
Matches a group of 2 and 3 digits between 1-9.

Anchors

Pattern	Meaning
^	Start of string
$	End of string
\b	Word boundary
\B	Non-word boundary

Table 3.0

Start of string(^)

```
●●● Python
>>> import re
>>> text = re.findall(r"^G[a-z]+", "Goodmorning, George is here")
>>> print(text)
... ['Goodmorning']
```

Interpretation
Matches strings that **begin with G** followed by **one or more lowercase letters**.

Example – Extracting emails from a text

```python
import re
message = """Contact me through my emails-> nora98@yahoo.com,
        nora10@gmail.com or norabarbie@outlook.com.
      """
text = re.findall(r"[A-Za-z0-9]+@[a-z]+\.[a-z]{3}",message )
print(text)
```

```
#Output
['nora98@yahoo.com', 'nora10@gmail.com', 'norabarbie@outlook.com']
```

Insight

The re.search(pattern, text).group() method works similarly to findall(), except that it returns **only the first match** instead of a list of all matches.

FlashText

FlashText is a text processing library used for extracting keywords from large text by scanning and identifying matches. Unlike regex, FlashText adds keywords into a **keyword list buffer** and then scans the entire text to find matches. This makes it very fast and efficient.

FlashText is not part of the Python standard library and must be installed:

```
pip install flashtext
```

Methods of Flashtext

Method	Description
add_keyword()	Adds a keyword to the keyword list.
add_keyword_from_file()	Extracts keywords from a text file.
add_keywords_from_dict()	Extracts keywords from a dictionary.
add_keywords_from_list()	Adds multiple keywords from a list.

add_non_word_boundary()	Adds exceptions for boundaries where keywords should not be matched.
case_sensitive	When set to True, differentiates uppercase and lowercase letters during matching.
extract_keywords()	Scans the text and extracts keywords.
get_all_keywords()	Returns all keywords currently stored in the buffer.
get_keyword()	Retrieves a specific keyword from the list.
keyword_trie_dict	Returns the trie dictionary storing keywords.
non_word_boundaries	Defines boundaries where keyword extraction should not apply.
remove_keyword()	Removes a specific keyword from the list.
remove_keywords_from_dict()	Removes keywords using a dictionary.
remove_keywords_from_list()	Removes keywords using a list.
replace_keywords()	Replaces matched keywords with another word or value.
set_non_word_boundaries()	Defines a custom set of non-word boundaries.

Table 3.1

Adding keywords

Python

```
from flashtext import KeywordProcessor

keyword = KeywordProcessor()
keyword.add_keyword("Python")
keyword.add_keyword("book")
keyword.add_keyword("email")
keyword.add_keyword("contact")
keyword.add_keyword("mobile")
keyword.add_keyword("location")
```

Extracting keywords

Python

```
message = """Hello Pythonista,
I'm really enjoying the Python programming book! I'd love to
learn more about FlashText and how it works.
You can reach me at email-> nobody@gmail.com.
Thank you!
"""
```

```
keys = keyword.extract_keywords(message)
print(keys)
```

```
#Output
['Python', 'book', 'email']
```

Python

```
>>> keyword.get_all_keywords()
>>> keyword.remove_keyword("book")
```

List

A list is a collection of items enclosed in square brackets [ ]. In a real-life scenario, a list can be compared to a basket of fruits containing oranges, bananas, apples, and grapes. In Python, the elements of a list are not restricted to a single type; they can include **numbers, strings, tuples, dictionaries, sets** or even other **lists**.

For example,

```python
x = [2, 4, 6.5, 8, 10.68]                        #numbers
y = ["mango", "grapes", "strawberry"]            #strings
z = [2, "id", (2,4), {'index':46}, {2,4}]        #different data types
m = [ [4, 6], [8.4, "id"] ]                      #lists
```

Insight

Type Casting
The built-in **list()** function can be used to convert other data types into a list. Possible conversions include:

1. String → List >>> var = list("sample") → ['s', 'a', 'm', 'p', 'l', 'e']
2. Tuple → List >>> var = list((2, 4)) → [2, 4]
3. Dictionary → List >>> var = list({'id' : 489}) → ['id']
4. Set → List >>> var = list({3, 5}) → [3, 5]

List Indexing

In list arrangement, every item is automatically assigned an **index number** based on its position.

- The first element always occupies **index 0**.
- The next element occupies **index 1**, followed by **index 2**, and so on.

For example:
fruits = ["orange", "banana", "apple", "grape", "strawberry"]

0	1	2	3	4
orange	**banana**	**apple**	**grape**	**strawberry**
-5	-4	-3	-2	-1

Python
```
>>> fruits = ["orange", "banana", "apple", "grape", "strawberry"]
>>> fruit = fruits[0]
>>> print(fruit)
... orange

>>> fruit = fruits[3]
>>> print(fruit)
...  grape

>>> fruit = fruits[-4]
>>> print(fruit)
...  banana
```

Note

An **IndexError** will be raised if you attempt to access an index that is **out of range**.

Joining Lists

Two or more lists can be combined to form a single list. This is done using the **addition operator** (+).

Example,

Python
```
list1 = [1, 2, 3]
list2 = [4, 5, 6]
combined = list1 + list2
print(combined)
```

```
#Output
[1, 2, 3, 4, 5, 6]
```

Splitting Lists

A list can be divided into parts or subsets using **slicing**. This is done by specifying the **start** and **end** indices:

Formulas for Slicing a List

list[start: end]	→	Returns a sub list starting from the specified start index up to (but not including) the end index.
list[start:]	→	Returns a sub list starting from the specified start index to the end of the list.
list[: end]	→	Returns a sub list starting from the beginning (index 0) up to (but not including) the specified end index.
list[:]	→	Returns the entire list from index 0 to the last character.

Note

The **end** index is exclusive, meaning the element at the end index is not included in the result.

Python

```
>>> var = ["Python", "JavaScript", "C++", "Java", "C#"]
>>> #start:1, end:4
>>> value = var[1:4]
>>> print(value)
... ['JavaScript', 'C++', 'Java']

>>> #start:2
>>> value = var[2:]
>>> print(value)
... ['C++', 'Java', 'C#']

>>> #end:3
>>> value = var[:3]
>>> print(value)
... ['Python', 'JavaScript', 'C++']
```

List Methods

Method	Description
append(item)	Adds an item to the end of the list.
extend(iterable)	Extends the list by appending elements from an iterable (e.g., another list, tuple, or set).
insert(index, item)	Inserts an item at a specified position in the list.
remove(item)	Removes the first occurrence of the specified item from the list.
pop(index=-1)	Removes and returns the item at the given index. If no index is specified, removes the last item.
clear()	Removes all elements from the list, making it empty.
index(item, start, end)	Returns the index of the first occurrence of an item. Raises an error if the item is not found.
count(item)	Returns the number of times an item appears in the list.
sort(key, reverse)	Sorts the list in ascending order by default. You can use reverse=True for descending order and key for custom sorting.
reverse()	Reverses the order of elements in the list.
copy()	Returns a shallow copy of the list.

Table 3.2

append(item)

Python

```
var = [2, 4]
var.append(6)
var.append(8)
print(var)
```

```
#Output
[2, 4, 6, 8]
```

extend(iterable)

Python

```
num = [1, 3]
num.extend([5, 7, 9])
print(num)
```

```
#Output
[1, 3, 5, 7, 9]
```

insert(index, item)

```python
cities = ["Tokyo", "Beijing", "Toronto"]
cities.insert(1, "New York")
print(cities)
```

```
#Output
['Tokyo', 'New York', 'Beijing', 'Toronto']
```

index(item, start, end)

```python
var = [2, 8, 10, 2, 15]
index = var.index(2)
print("index of 2-> ", index)

index = var.index(2, 1) #start from index 1
print("index of 2 starting from 1-> ", index)
```

```
#Output
index of 2->  0
index of 2 starting from 1->  3
```

remove(item)

```python
countries = ["Canada", "Brazil", "Japan", "Sweden"]
countries.remove("Japan")
print(countries)
```

```
#Output
['Canada', 'Brazil', 'Sweden']
```

pop()

```python
countries = ["Canada", "Brazil", "Japan", "Sweden"]
deleted = countries.pop()
print(deleted)
print(countries)
```

```
#Output
Sweden
['Canada', 'Brazil', 'Japan']
```

clear()

```python
num = [10, 12, 65]
num.clear()
print(num)
```

```
#Output
[ ]
```

copy()

```python
num = [10, 12, 65]
newlist = num.copy()
print(newlist)
```

```
#Output
[10, 12, 65]
```

count(item)

```python
var = [100, 15, 10, 20, 10]
counter = var.count(10)
print(counter)
```

```
#Output
2
```

reverse()

```python
even = [2, 4, 6, 8, 10]
even.reverse()
print(even)
```

```
#Output
[10, 8, 6, 4, 2]
```

sort(reverse= False**)**

```python
even = [4, 6, 2, 10, 8]
even.sort()
print(even)
```

```
#Output
[2, 4, 6, 8, 10]
```

Built-in Functions

Method	Description
len(list)	Returns the number of elements in the list.
max(list)	Returns the maximum value in the list (if elements are comparable).
min(list)	Returns the minimum value in the list.
sum(list)	Returns the sum of all numerical elements in the list.
list(iterable)	Converts an iterable (e.g., tuple, string, or set) into a list.
sorted(list, key, reverse)	Returns a new sorted list without modifying the original.
any(list)	Returns True if at least one element in the list is truthy, otherwise False.

all(list)	Returns True if all elements in the list are truthy, otherwise False.
enumerate(list, start)	Returns an enumerate object that contains index-value pairs.

Table 3.3

Python
```
>>> #len()
>>> cities = ["Toronto", "London", "New York", "Beijing"]
>>> len(cities)
... 4

>>> #sum()
>>> num = [6, 8, 4, 2]
>>> sum(num)
... 20

>>> #min()
>>> num = [6, 8, 4, 2]
>>> min(num)
... 2

>>> #max()
>>> num = [6, 8, 4, 2]
>>> max(num)
... 8

>>> #sorted()
>>> num = [6, 8, 4, 2]
>>> sorted = sorted(num)
... [2, 4, 6, 8]
```

Iterating Through a List

Iteration refers to accessing the members of an iterable (such as a list, tuple, dictionary, or set) **sequentially, one at a time**.
Python provides the **iter()** and **next()** functions, or their dunder equivalents __iter__() and __next__(), for manual iteration.

Example,

Python

```
num = [1, 3, 5, 7]
iterate = iter(num)

print(next(iterate))
print(next(iterate))
print(next(iterate))
```

```
#Output
1
3
5
```

Note

If you try to iterate beyond the number of elements in the list, Python will raise a **StopIteration** error.

Tuples

Tuples are collections of items that are contained within parentheses ( ). Unlike lists, tuples are **immutable** types, meaning their members cannot be changed, modified, or deleted once created. However, tuple members can still be accessed for reading and usage in programs.

Example

Python

```python
x = (4, 2, 6)                                       #numbers
y = ("Chicago", "Miami", "San Francisco")           #strings
z = ("apple", 6.58, [2, 4], {'id': 10}, {3, 6}) #different types
m = (("name", "George"), ("id", 485))               #tuples
```

Insight

Type Casting

The built-in **tuple()** function can be used to convert other data types into a tuple. Possible conversions include:

1. String → tuple >>> var = tuple("sample") → ('s', 'a', 'm', 'p', 'l', 'e')
2. List → tuple >>> var = tuple([2, 4, 6]) → (2, 4, 6)
3. Dictionary → tuple >>> var = tuple({'id' : 489}) → ('id',)
4. Set → tuple >>> var = tuple({3, 5, 7}) → (3, 5, 7)

Tuple Indexing

The arrangement of members in a tuple is much like that of a list. Each member has an **index** according to the order of arrangement in the tuple.

- The first item always occupies **index 0**.
- The second item has **index 1**.
- The next item has **index 2**, and so on.
- The last index is always (total number of items – 1).

For example,

colors = ("Red", "Blue", "Green", "Yellow", "Orange", "Purple")

0	1	2	3	4	5
Red	**Blue**	**Green**	**Yellow**	**Orange**	**Purple**
-6	-5	-4	-3	-2	-1

Getting Elements of a Tuple

Tuple items can be accessed by specifying their index inside square brackets `[]`.

Python

```
>>> colors = ("Red", "Blue", "Green", "Yellow", "Orange", "Purple")
>>> color =  colors[0]
>>> print(color)
... 'Red'

>>> color =  colors[2]
>>> print(color)
... 'Green'

>>> color =  colors[-3]
>>> print(color)
... 'Yellow'
```

Note

An **IndexError** is raised if the index is out of range.

Tuple Methods

Method	Description
index(item, start, end)	Returns the index of the first occurrence of an item. Raises an error if the item is not found.
count(item)	Returns the number of times an item appears in the tuple.

Table 3.4

index(item, start, end**)**

```python
animal = ("fox", "donkey", "cat", "dog")
index =  animal.index('donkey')
print(index)
```

```
#Output
1
```

count(item**)**

```python
num = (4, 6, 2, 4, 1)
counter =  num.count(4)
print(counter)
```

```
#Output
2
```

Built-in Functions

Method	Description
sum(iterable)	Returns the sum of all elements in a tuple (works for numeric values).
max(iterable)	Returns the maximum value in a tuple (works if elements are comparable).
min(iterable)	Returns the minimum value in a tuple.
sorted(iterable)	Returns a sorted list of tuple elements.
sum(iterable)	Returns the sum of all elements in a tuple (works for numeric values).

Table 3.5

```python
>>> #len()
>>> cities = ("Toronto", "London", "New York", "Beijing")
>>> len(cities)
```

```
... 4

>>> #sum()
>>> num = (10, 5, 1, 4)
>>> sum(num)
... 20

>>> #min()
>>> num = (2, 15, 3, 6)
>>> min(num)
... 2

>>> #max()
>>> num = (2, 15, 3, 6)
>>> max(num)
... 15

>>> #sorted()
>>> num = (2, 15, 3, 6)
>>> sorted = sorted(num)
... [2, 3, 6, 15]
```

Dictionary

A Dictionary in Python is a data structure that contains a collection of **key-value** pairs enclosed in curly braces { }. Each key is separated from its value by a colon (:), and each item (key-value pair) is separated from the next by a comma (,). In a dictionary, each key maps to its value, and every key must be unique.

Note

Keys and Values

- The **key** can be any of the following: integer, float, string, or tuple.
- The **value** can be any data type, including integer, float, string, list, dictionary, tuple, set, bytes, or even an object.

For example,

Python

```
var = {
    "name" : "George Wood",
    "id" : 4856,
    "average": 64.28,
    "hobby": ["music", "games", "reading"],
    "contact": ("+1 256 456 3578", "george@gmail.com"),
}
```

Insight

Type Casting

The **dict()** function is used for converting other data types into a dictionary. Possible conversions include:

1. String → dictionary (for example, an **encoded dictionary** or **JSON string**)
2. List → dictionary >>> var = dict([['id',20], ['avg',68]]) → {'id': 20, 'avg': 68}
3. Tuple → dictionary >>> var = dict((('id',52), ('avg',97))) → {'id': 52, 'avg': 97}

Getting Dictionary Values

In a dictionary, each value is mapped to its **unique key**. The key is used for retrieving its corresponding value. There are two primary ways to get values:

Using Square Brackets

```
value = dictionary_name[key]
```

For example,

```python
profile = {
    "name" : "John Cranston",
    "school" : "Cambridge",
    "course": "Computer Science",
    "age": 23,
    "index": 58900
}

#Getting values with keys
name = profile['name']
age = profile['age']
course = profile['course']

print(f"Name -> {name}")
print(f"Age -> {age}")
print(f"Course -> {course}")
```

```
#Output
Name -> John Cranston
Age -> 23
Course -> Computer Science
```

Note

When attempting to retrieve a value for a given key, a **KeyError** is raised if the specified key does not exist in the dictionary.

Using the get() Method

```
value = dictionary_name.get( key )
```

For example,

Python

```python
catalog = {
    "product" : "Television",
    "brand": "Samsung",
    "size" : 24,
    "price": "$1,240",
}

#Getting values with key
item = catalog.get('product')
size = catalog.get('size')
price = catalog.get('price')

print(f"Item -> {item}")
print(f"Size -> {size}")
print(f"Price -> {price}")
```

```
#Output
Item -> Television
Size -> 24
Price -> $1,240
```

Note

The get() retrieves the value associated with the key.

1. If the key does not exist, it returns **None** (or a default value if provided).
2. This prevents runtime errors that occur with square brackets.

Updating Dictionary Items

Dictionary items (key-value pairs) can be updated, modified, or expanded by adding new keys or updating existing values. Updating can be done in two ways:

Using Square Brackets

```
dictionary_name[key] = value
```

📖 **Note**

- This method updates the value of an existing key.
- If the key does not exist, a new key-value pair is added.

Example 1 – When a key exist,

```python
places = {"Brazil":"Brasília", "UK":"London", "Germany":"Hamburg"}

#updating Germany
places['Germany'] = 'Berlin'
print(places)
```

```
#Output
{'Brazil': 'Brasília', 'UK': 'London', 'Germany': 'Berlin'}
```

Example 2 – When a key does not exist,

```python
places = {"UK":"London", "Germany":"Berlin"}

#Adding Canada
places['Canada'] = 'Ottawa'
print(places)
```

```
#Output
{'UK': 'London', 'Germany': 'Berlin', 'Canada': 'Ottawa'}
```

Using the update() Method

```
dictionary_name.update( {key1 : value1,  key2 : value2, .... } )
```

Note

The **update()** updates multiple items at once by passing a dictionary of key-value pairs.

Python
```python
population = {"Europe": 458, "Africa": 238, "Asia": 805}

#update: Africa, add Australia
new_data = {"Africa": 320, "Australia" : 102 }
population.update(new_data)

print(population)
```

```
#Output
{'Europe': 458, 'Africa': 320, 'Asia': 805, 'Australia': 102}
```

Dictionary Methods

Method	Description
get(key, default)	Returns the value of the key. If the key is not found, returns the specified default value.
items()	Returns a view of all dictionary key-value pairs as tuples.
keys()	Returns a view of all dictionary keys.
values()	Returns a view of all dictionary values.
pop(key, default)	Removes and returns the value for the specified key. If the key is not found, returns the default value.
popitem()	Removes and returns the last inserted key-value pair as a tuple.
update(iterable)	Updates the dictionary with key-value pairs from another dictionary or iterable of key-value pairs.
setdefault(key, default)	Returns the value of the key if present; otherwise, inserts the key with the specified default value.
fromkeys(seq, value)	Creates a new dictionary from a sequence of keys, all having the specified value.
copy()	Returns a shallow copy of the dictionary.
clear()	Removes all key-value pairs from the dictionary.

Table 3.6

●●● Python

```
>>> #items()
>>> var = {'fruit':"apple", 'animal':"lion", 'planet':"earth"}
>>> items = var.items()
>>> print(items)
... dict_items([('fruit', 'apple'), ('animal', 'lion'), ('planet',
'earth')])

>>> #keys()
>>> var = {'fruit':"apple", 'animal':"lion", 'planet':"earth"}
>>> keys = var.keys()
>>> print(keys)
... dict_keys(['fruit', 'animal', 'planet'])

>>> #values()
>>> var = {'fruit':"apple", 'animal':"lion", 'planet':"earth"}
>>> values = var.values()
>>> print(values)
... dict_values(['apple', 'lion', 'earth'])

>>> #pop()
>>> estimate = {'pen': 4, 'pencil': 6, 'calculator': 2, "book": 9}
>>> estimate.pop("calculator")
>>> print(estimate)
... {'pen': 4, 'pencil': 6, 'book': 9}

>>> #popitem()
>>> estimate = {'pen': 4, 'pencil': 6, 'calculator': 2, "book": 9}
>>> deleted = estimate.popitem()
>>> print(deleted)
... ('book', 9)
>>> print(estimate)
... {'pen': 4, 'pencil': 6, 'calculator': 2}

>>> #copy()
>>> estimate = {'pen': 4, 'pencil': 6, 'calculator': 2, "book": 9}
>>> new_dict = estimate.copy()
```

Set

A set is an unordered collection of unique elements. Unlike lists and tuples, sets do not allow duplicate values, and the order of elements is not guaranteed. Sets enclose their members within curly braces { }.

Sets can contain members of types such as strings, integers, floats, and tuples, but not dictionaries, lists, or other sets. Sets are commonly used when there is a need to store unique items or perform mathematical operations such as **intersection**, **union**, or **symmetric difference**.

For example,

```python
x = {2, 4, 6, 8, 10 }                                  #integer
y = {4.8, 6.2, 10.53, 12.96}                           #float
z = {"lion", "elephant", "crocodile", "monkey"}        #string
m = {(2, 4), (5, 7), (6, 8)}                           #tuple
```

Insight

Type Casting

The **set()** function is used to convert other data types into a set. The Possible conversions include:

1. String → set   >>> var = set("Hello") → {'l', 'e', 'o', 'H'}
2. List → set   >>> var = set([2, 4, 6]) → {2, 4, 6}
3. Tuple → set   >>> var = set((1, 3, 5, 7)) → {1, 3, 5, 7}
4. Dictionary → set   >>> var =set({1:"USA", 2:"UK"}) → {1, 2}

Getting Elements of a Set

Since sets are unordered, items do not have an index like lists or tuples. Therefore, you cannot access set items using indices. Instead, you can:

- Use iteration (**for** loop) to access each member.
- Use the **in** keyword to check if an element exists in a set.

Example:

```python
odd = {3, 5, 7, 9, 11}
check = 7 in odd
print(check)
```

```
#Output
True
```

Set Methods

Method	Description
add(item)	Adds an element or item to the set. If the element already exists, it does nothing.
copy()	Returns a shallow copy of the set.
clear()	Removes all elements from the set, making it empty.
difference(*sets)	Returns a new set with elements that are in the original set but not in the given set(s).
difference_update(*sets)	Removes elements from the original set that are present in the given set(s). Modifies the original set.
discard(item)	Removes the specified item from the set if it exists. Does nothing if the element is not found.
remove(item)	Removes the specified item from the set. Raises a **KeyError** if the element is not found.
pop()	Removes and returns a random element from the set. Raises a **KeyError** if the set is empty.
intersection(*sets)	Returns a new set containing elements common to the original set and all given set(s).
intersection_update(*sets)	Modifies the original set to keep only elements also found in all given set(s).
isdisjoint(set)	Returns True if the set has no elements in common with other set, otherwise returns False.
issubset(set)	Returns True if all elements of the set are in other set, otherwise returns False.
issuperset(set)	Returns True if the set contains all elements of other set, otherwise returns False.
union(*set)	Returns a new set containing all unique elements from the original set and given set(s).
update(*sets)	Adds elements from given set(s) to the original set. Modifies the original set.

symmetric_difference(set)	Returns a new set with elements that are in either the set or other set, but not both.
symmetric_difference_update(set)	Modifies the original set to include only elements unique to either set.

Table 3.7

Updating a Set

Sets are mutable, meaning you can add or remove items after creation. Some common operations include:

Adding Elements

add(item)

```
Python

even = {2, 4, 6}
even.add(8)
print(even)
```

```
#Output
{8, 2, 4, 6}
```

update(iterable)

```
Python

cities = {"London", "Berlin"}
new_cities = {"New York", "Ontario"}
cities.update(new_cities)
print(cities)
```

```
#Output
{'Ontario', 'New York', 'London', 'Berlin'}
```

Removing Elements

remove(item)

```python
num = {5, 10, 15, 20}
num.remove(15)
print(num)
```

```
#Output
{10, 20, 5}
```

discard(item)

```python
fruits = {'cherry', 'grapes', 'banana', 'strawberry'}
fruits.discard('grapes')
print(fruits)
```

```
#Output
{'strawberry', 'cherry', 'banana'}
```

> **Note**
>
> Both **remove()** and **discard()** are used to delete elements from a set. The difference is that **remove()** raises a **KeyError** if the specified element is not found, while **discard()** silently ignores such cases without raising an error.

pop()

```python
var = {4, 6, 8, 10, 12}
var.pop()
print(var)
```

```
#Output
{6, 8, 10, 12}
```

Mathematical Set Operations

The set data structure provides several mathematical methods for performing operations on two or more sets. These methods are used to find common elements, differences, unions, and relationships between sets.

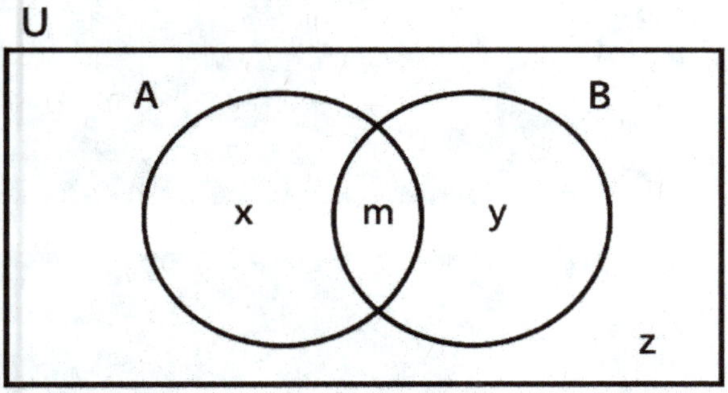

Figure 1.2: Set (Venn) Diagram

Understanding the Diagram

In the diagram:

- **A** and **B** → represent two distinct sets.
- **U** → represents the **universal set**, containing all elements of *A*, *B*, and any elements outside them.
- **x** → Members found in **A** but not in **B**
- **y** → Members found in **B** but not in **A**
- **m** → Members common to both **A** and **B**
- **z** → Members in **U** but not in **A** or **B**

union(*set)

```
Python

A = {4, 6, 8, 10, 12}
B = {3, 6, 9, 12, 15}

U = A.union(B)
print(U)
```

```
#Output
{3, 4, 6, 8, 9, 10, 12, 15}
```

difference(*set)

```
Python
A = {4, 6, 8, 10, 12}
B = {3, 6, 9, 12, 15}

x = A.difference(B)
y = B.difference(A)
print(f"region x ->", x)
print(f"region y ->", y)
```

```
#Output
region x -> {8, 10, 4}
region y -> {9, 3, 15}
```

intersection(*set)

```
Python
A = {4, 6, 8, 10, 12}
B = {3, 6, 9, 12, 15}

m = A.intersection(B)
print(f"Common members in A and B (region m)->", m)
```

```
#Output
Common members in A and B (region m)-> {12, 6}
```

symmetric_difference(*set)

```
Python
A = {4, 6, 8, 10, 12}
B = {3, 6, 9, 12, 15}

AB = A.symmetric_difference(B)
print(f"Symmetric difference ->", AB)
```

```
#Output
Symmetric difference -> {3, 4, 8, 9, 10, 15}
```

```
Python

>>> U = {1, 2, 3, 4, 5, 6, 7, 8, 9, 10}
>>> A = {2, 4, 6}
>>> B = {3, 5, 7}

>>> #issuperset(set)
>>> U.issuperset(A)
... True

>>> #issubset(set)
>>> B.issubset(U)
... True

>>> #isdisjoint(set)
>>> A.isdisjoint(B)
... True
```

Note

The symbol * has been used as a parameter in most of the examples above. The * denotes that the method must take at least one set as an argument.

Built-in Functions

Method	Description
len(iterable)	Returns the number of elements in the set.
sum(iterable)	Returns the sum of all elements in a set (works for numeric values).
max(iterable)	Returns the maximum value in a set (works if elements are comparable).
min(iterable)	Returns the minimum value in a set.
sorted(iterable)	Returns a sorted list of set elements.
in	Checks if an element exists in a set (item in set).
not in	Checks if an element is not a member of the set.

Table 3.8

●●● Python

```
>>> #len()
>>> var = {4, 2, 10, 5}
>>> length = len(var)
>>> print(length)
... 4

>>> #sum()
>>> var = {4, 2, 10, 5}
>>> total = sum(var)
>>> print(total)
... 21

>>> #min()
>>> var = {4, 2, 10, 5}
>>> minimum = min(var)
>>> print(minimum)
... 2

>>> #max()
>>> var = {4, 2, 10, 5}
>>> maximum = max(var)
>>> print(maximum)
... 10

>>> #sorted()
>>> var = {4, 2, 10, 5}
>>> sorted = sorted(var)
>>> print(sorted)
... [2, 4, 5, 10]
```

Collections Module

The **collections** module in Python provides specialized container datatypes beyond the built-in list, tuple, set, and dict.
It introduces high-performance and feature-rich alternatives that simplify tasks such as grouping, counting, and ordering data.

Collections Methods

ChainMap	UserString	UserDict	UserList
Counter	namedtuple	defaultdict	deque
OrderedDict	abc		

Table 3.9

ChainMap(*dict)

The ChainMap groups multiple dictionaries into a single, unified view.
This allows you to search for keys across several dictionaries without merging them.
Example:

Python
```
import collections
animal_A = {"domestic":"dog", "wild":"lion"}
animal_B = {"sea":"fish", "tree":"monkey"}
animal = collections.ChainMap(animal_A, animal_B)

print(animal.get('wild'))
print(animal.get('tree'))
print(animal.get('domestic'))
print(animal.get('sea'))
```

```
#Output
lion
monkey
dog
fish
```

Insight

ChainMap checks each dictionary in order until it finds the key. It's commonly used for managing multiple contexts or layered configurations.

Counter(iterable)

The **Counter** counts the occurrences of each element in an iterable and returns a dictionary-like object.

Example,

```
●●● Python
>>> import collections

>>> var = collections.Counter("programming")
>>> print(var)
... Counter({'r': 2, 'g': 2, 'm': 2, 'p': 1, 'o': 1, 'a': 1, 'i': 1, 'n':
1})

>>> var = collections.Counter((4, 2, 5, 3, 5, 2, 5))
>>> common = var.most_common()
>>> print(common)
... [(5, 3), (2, 2), (4, 1), (3, 1)]
```

deque(iterable)

A **deque** (double-ended queue) allows fast appends and pops from both ends.

Example:

```
●●● Python
>>> import collections

>>> var = collections.deque([2, 4, 6])
>>> var.appendleft(0)
>>> print(var)
... deque([0, 2, 4, 6])

>>> var = collections.deque([4, 6])
>>> var.extendleft([2, 5])
>>> print(var)
... deque([5, 2, 4, 6])

>>> var = collections.deque("Programming")
>>> print(var.count('m'))
... 2
```

Itertools Module

The **itertools** module provides efficient looping and iterator-building tools that save memory and simplify complex iteration tasks.

Insight

Iterators are objects that represent a stream of data. They produce elements one by one, saving memory compared to lists.

Itertools Methods

accumulate	compress	dropwhile	islice
chain	count	filterfalse	pairwise
combinations	cycle	groupby	permutations
product	starmap	tee	combinations_with_replacement
repeat	takewhile	zip_longest	

Table 4.0

accumulate(iterable)

Returns accumulated sums (or results of another binary function).

Example:

```python
import itertools

nums = [2, 4, 6]
result = list( itertools.accumulate(nums) )
print(result)
```

```
#Output
[2, 6, 12]
```

chain(iterables)

Combines multiple iterables into a single sequence.

Example:

```python
import itertools

var_A = (2, 4)
var_B = (6, 8)
result = tuple( itertools.chain(var_A, var_B) )
print(result)
```

```
#Output
(2, 4, 6, 8)
```

combinations(iterables, max)

Generates all possible combinations (without replacement).

Example:

```python
from itertools import combinations

var= "ABC"
result = tuple( combinations(var, 2) )
print(result)
```

```
#Output
(('A', 'B'), ('A', 'C'), ('B', 'C'))
```

combinations_with_replacement(iterables, max)

Allows elements to repeat in combinations.

Example,

```python
from itertools import combinations_with_replacement

var= "ABC"
result = tuple( combinations_with_replacement(var, 2) )
print(result)
```

```
#Output
(('A', 'A'), ('A', 'B'), ('A', 'C'), ('B', 'B'), ('B', 'C'), ('C', 'C'))
```

permutations(iterable, max)
Perms all members of the iterable.
Example:

```
Python
from itertools import permutations

var= ("cow", "dog", "fish")
result = tuple( permutations(var, 3) )
print(result)
```

```
#Output
(('cow', 'dog', 'fish'), ('cow', 'fish', 'dog'), ('dog', 'cow', 'fish'), ('dog',
'fish', 'cow'), ('fish', 'cow', 'dog'), ('fish', 'dog', 'cow'))
```

compress(iterable, selector)
Filters data according to a selector list.
Example:

```
Python
from itertools import compress

var= {"UK","Germany","Japan","Brazil"}
selector = [0, 1, 1, 0]
result = list( compress(var, selector) )
print(result)
```

```
#Output
['Brazil', 'Japan']
```

count(start, step)
Creates an infinite iterator that counts from a start number by a step.
Example,

```
Python
from itertools import count

for i in count(0, 5):
    if i > 15:
        break
    print(i)
```

```
#Output
0
5
10
15
```

cycle(iterable)

Repeats an iterable indefinitely.

Example,

```python
from itertools import cycle

cnt = 0
var = ["design", "code"]
for i in cycle(var):
    print(i)
    cnt += 1
    if cnt == 6:
        break
```

```
#Output
design
code
design
code
design
code
```

dropwhile(function, iterable)

Skips items while a condition is true, then returns the rest.

Example,

```python
from itertools import dropwhile

var = ["fruit","orange","apple","animal","fox","cat"]
result = list(dropwhile(lambda x : x != 'animal', var))
print(result)
```

```
#Output
['animal', 'fox', 'cat']
```

takewhile(function, iterable)

Takes items from an iterable as long as the condition is true.

```
••• Python
from itertools import takewhile

var = ["fruit","orange","apple","animal","fox","cat"]
result = list( takewhile(lambda x : x != 'animal', var) )
print(result)
```

```
#Output
['fruit', 'orange', 'apple']
```

groupby(iterable)

Groups consecutive elements with the same key.

```
••• Python
from itertools import groupby

var = [2, 2, 4, 6, 6, 6]
for key, group in groupby(var):
    print(key, list(group))
```

```
#Output
2 [2, 2]
4 [4]
6 [6, 6, 6]
```

repeat(object, count)

Repeats an object a specified number of times.

```
••• Python
from itertools import repeat

for i in repeat("Hello World!",3):
    print(i)
```

```
#Output
Hello World!
Hello World!
Hello World!
```

Key Terms

Numbers
Integers
Floats
Slicing
Concatenation
Complex Numbers
Indexing
Formatting
Mutable
Shallow Copy
Iteration
Immutable
Casting
Unordered

Review Questions

1. Which of the following is a valid type casting in Python?
a) int("12.5")
b) int("12")
c) float("abc")
d) complex("hello")
Answer: b

2. What is the output of the following code?
import math
print(math.divmod(15, 4))
a) (3, 3)
b) (3, 4)
c) (3, 3.75)
d) (3, 3)
Answer: a

3. Which of the following statements about Python numbers is TRUE?
a) Floats can only be positive.
b) Integers cannot be negative.
c) Complex numbers have a real and imaginary part.
d) int() can convert any string to an integer.
Answer: c

4. What will be the output of the following code?
text = "Python is fun"
print(text[7:])
a) Python
b) is fun
c) Python is
d) fun
Answer: b

5. Which method would you use to remove leading and trailing whitespace from a string?
a) strip()
b) rstrip()
c) ljust()
d) center()
Answer: a

6. What will be the output of the following code?
numbers = [2, 4, 6, 8]
numbers.append([10, 12])
print(numbers)
A. [2, 4, 6, 8, 10, 12]
B. [2, 4, 6, 8, [10, 12]]
C. [10, 12, 2, 4, 6, 8]
D. [2, 4, 6, 8]
Answer: b

7. Which method returns a new sorted list without modifying the original list?
A. list.sort()
B. sorted(list)
C. list.reverse()
D. list.copy()
Answer: b

8. What does my_list[-1] return?
A. The first element
B. The last element
C. An IndexError
D. A sublist
Answer: b

9. Which of the following statements is true about tuples?
A. Tuples are mutable
B. Tuples allow duplicate items
C. Tuple elements must be of the same type
D. Tuples cannot contain lists
Answer: b

10. What will the following code return?
x = ('a', 'b', 'c', 'a')
print(x.count('a'))
A. 1
B. 2
C. 3
D. Error
Answer: b

11. Which method returns the index of the first occurrence of an item in a tuple?
A. count()
B. index()

C. find()
D. search()
Answer: b

12. Which of the following is true about sets?
A. Sets allow duplicate elements
B. Sets are ordered
C. Sets do not allow duplicate elements
D. Sets can contain lists as elements
Answer: C

13. What is the difference between discard() and remove() in a set?
A. Both do the same thing
B. discard() raises KeyError if element not found
C. remove() raises KeyError if element not found
D. discard() can only remove numeric values
Answer: C

14. What will the following code print?
A = {1, 2, 3}
B = {3, 4, 5}
print(A.union(B))
A. {1, 2, 3}
B. {3, 4, 5}
C. {1, 2, 3, 4, 5}
D. {1, 2, 4, 5}
Answer: C

15. Which method would you use to check if all elements of set A exist in set B?
A. isdisjoint()
B. issubset()
C. issuperset()
D. union()
Answer: b

Review Exercises

1. Write a Python program that converts a float string "7.5" into a float, then into an integer, and prints both values.

2. Using the math module, calculate the square root, factorial, and greatest common divisor (GCD) for the numbers 16, 5, and 12.
3. Create two sets, A = {1, 2, 3, 4} and B = {3, 4, 5, 6}.
4. Find the union, intersection, difference (A-B), and symmetric difference of the sets.
5. Check if A is a subset of B.
6. Add a new element 7 to set B.
7. Remove element 1 from set A using discard().

Decision Making Statements

Decision making is crucial in programming, especially when you want your program to execute only when a certain condition is true or false. These statements, known as conditional statements, are based on a Boolean value (True or False).
The structure of a conditional statement is a block that may contain one or more programs or instructions. In Python, there are **three** different kinds of conditional statements:

The if Statement

The if **statement** is the simplest decision-making statement. In this structure, a program or statement is placed within the if **block**, which has a condition.

- If the condition is satisfied (evaluates to True), then the program executes.
- Otherwise, the program skips the block and continues executing the rest of the program.

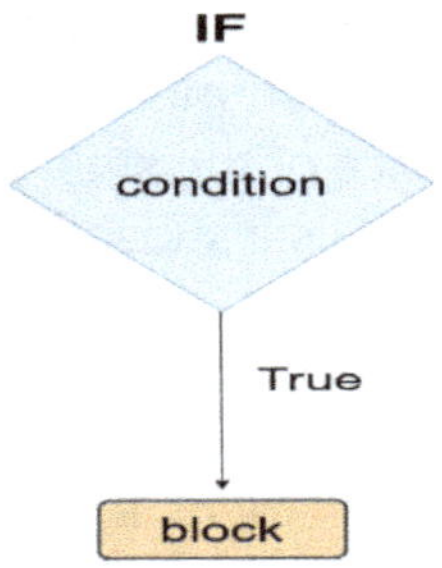

Figure 1.3 : The IF flowchart

True statement

Example – A program to print a message when a condition is true,

```
Python
isMessage = True
if isMessage:
    print("Hello World!")

print("Python is a great programming language")
```

```
#Output
Hello World!
Python is a great programming language
```

Key Point

- When the condition inside the **if** statement evaluates to True, the indented block of code under it is executed.
- After executing the block, the program continues with the next statement outside the **if** block.

False statement

Example 2 – A program to return a rainy message when condition is true,

```
●●● Python
weather = "sunny"
message = "It's sunny today ☀"

if weather == "rainy":
    message = "It's rainy today ☔"

print(message)
```

```
#Output
It's sunny today ☀
```

Key Point

- When the condition inside the **if** statement evaluates to False, the block under the **if** statement is skipped, and the program continues executing the next line of code.
- The value of message remains unchanged because the condition weather == "rainy" was not satisfied.

Example 3 – A program to accept a number and identify as an odd or even,

```
●●● Python
num = int(input("What is your favorite number-> "))

if num % 2 ==0:
    print(f"{num} is an even number")

if num % 2 != 0:
    print(f"{num} is an odd number")

print("let's try again!")
```

```
#Output
What is your favorite number-> 8
8 is an even number
let's try again!
```

The if-else Statement

The **if-else statement** provides two blocks: an **if block** and an **else block**. Each block contains different programs or statements.

- The **if block** has a condition. When this condition is satisfied (True), the program within the block executes.
- If the condition is not satisfied (False), the program within the else block executes instead.

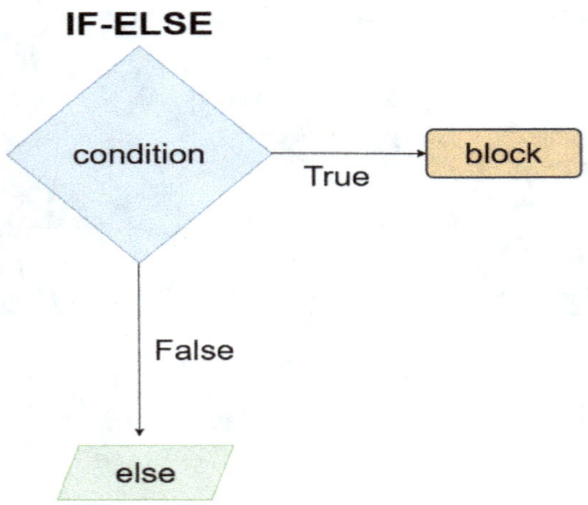

Figure 1.4 : The IF-ELSE flowchart

Example 1 – A program to determine if a person qualifies to be at the cinema,

```
Python
age = 15

if age < 18:
    print("Sorry!, you're underage.\nYou can't be at the cinema")
else:
    print("Congratulations!\nYou can be at the cinema")
```

```
#Output
Sorry!, you're underage.
You can't be at the cinema
```

Key Point

- The ***if*** statement checks the condition age < 18.
- If the condition evaluates to True, the indented block under if is executed.
- If the condition evaluates to False, the block under the ***else*** statement is executed

instead.

- The else statement provides an alternative path when the initial condition is not met.

Example 2 – A program to accept a number and decide a win or a lose,

```python
guess = int(input("Guess a number -> "))

if guess in [10, 15, 20, 40]:
    print("You have won!")
else:
    print("Wrong guess")
```

```
#Output
Guess a number -> 4
Wrong guess
```

Key Point

- The program checks if the entered number (guess) exists within the given list [10, 15, 20, 40].
- If the value is found in the list, the **if** block runs and prints "You have won!".
- If not found, the condition is False, so the **else** block executes and displays "Wrong guess".
- The **else** clause ensures that the program responds appropriately when the condition fails.

The if-elif-else Statement

The **if-elif-else statement** is used for more complex decision making involving multiple conditions. It consists of:

- An **if block** (with a condition)
- One or more **elif blocks** (each with its own condition)
- An **else block** (without condition)

Execution flow:

1. If the condition in the **if block** is satisfied, its statement executes. Otherwise, control passes to the first **elif block**.

2. The first **elif** condition is checked. If satisfied, its statement executes. If not, control moves to the next **elif block**.
3. If none of the conditions in **if** or any **elif blocks** are satisfied, the else block executes.

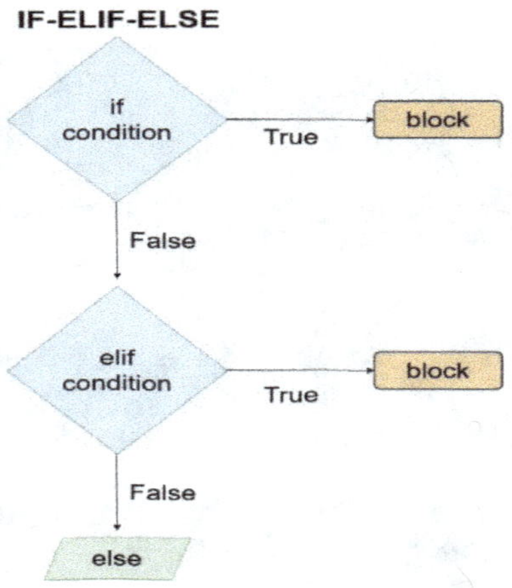

Figure 1.5 : The ELIF flowchart

Example 1 – A program to categorize scores into "Pass", "Very Good" and "Excellent"

```
Python
score = 53

if score < 40:                      #below 40
    print("Pass")

elif score >= 40 and  score < 60:   #between 39 and 60
    print("Very Good")

else:
    print("Excellent")              #above 59
```

```
#Output
Very Good
```

Key Point

- The **elif** statement allows multiple conditional checks in a sequence.
- The program first checks the **if** condition (score < 40). If True, it executes that block and skips the rest.
- If the **if** condition is False, Python evaluates the next condition under **elif**.
- The **else** block runs only if all previous conditions (**if** and **elif**) are False.
- This structure makes it possible to handle three or more logical outcomes in a single decision flow.

Example 2 – A Simple calculator program,

```python
x , y = 4, 2
operation = "*"

if operation == "-":
    result = x - y
    print(result)

elif operation == "*":
    result = x * y
    print(result)

elif operation == "/":
    result = x / y
    print(result)

else:
    result = x + y
    print(result)
```

```
#Output
8
```

Key Point

- Multiple **elif** blocks allow the program to match different operations and execute the correct arithmetic expression.
- Only one block is executed — the first condition that evaluates to True.
- The **else** clause acts as a fallback or default case when none of the prior conditions are met.
- This structure improves code readability and prevents the need for multiple nested **if** statements.

Nested Conditional Statements

There are situations where, if the condition of a block is satisfied, another condition within that block is checked before executing a statement.

Nested conditional statements are simply conditional statements that contain further conditional statements, creating a network of logic.

The nested condition is suitable for complex logic where a statement needs to be validated by multiple conditions before execution.

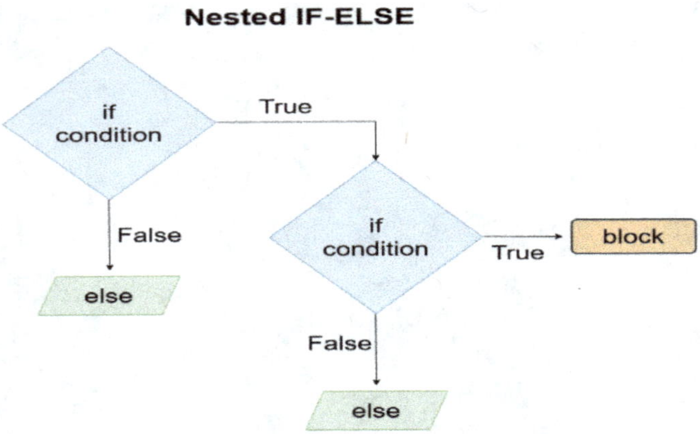

Figure 1.6 : A simple nested IF-ELSE flowchart

Example – A program to determine if a person qualifies for bonuses. All women and men less than 18 years old are qualified,

```python
gender = "male"
age = 16

if gender == "male":
    if age < 18:
        print("Young boy.\nQualified for bonuses.")
    else:
        print("Adult man.\nNot qualified for bonuses")

else:
    print("Woman.\nQualified for bonuses.")
```

```
#Output
Young boy.
Qualified for bonuses.
```

Key Point

- A **nested if** means placing one **if statement** inside another, allowing the program to make decisions based on multiple related conditions.
- The outer **if** checks the first condition (gender == "male").
- If that condition is True, the inner **if** then checks the next condition (age < 18).
- Each nested block executes only when all enclosing conditions are True.
- This technique is useful when conditions are hierarchical or depend on one another — for example, checking gender first, then age.

Key Terms

Conditional statement
Boolean value
Nested if
True/False evaluation
Hierarchical condition

Review Questions

1 .Which statement executes only when a specified condition is True?
A. else
B. if
C. elif
D. nested if
Answer: b

2. What will the following code print?

```
x = 10
if x > 15:
    print("Greater")
else:
    print("Smaller or equal")
```

A. Greater
B. Smaller or equal
C. Nothing
D. Error
Answer: b

3. Which statement allows multiple conditional checks in sequence?
A. if
B. elif
C. else
D. nested if
Answer: b

4. In a nested if, when does the inner block execute?
A. Always
B. When the outer condition is False
C. When the outer condition is True
D. Only if all conditions are False
Answer: c

5. What is the output of the code below?

```
num = 7
if num % 2 == 0:
    print("Even")
elif num % 2 != 0:
    print("Odd")
else:
    print("Unknown")
```

A. Even
B. Odd
C. Unknown
D. Error
Answer: b

Review Exercises

1. Write a Python program to accept a number and print whether it is positive, negative, or zero using if-elif-else.

2. Write a program to accept a grade (A, B, C, D, F) and print “Excellent”, “Good”, “Average”, “Poor”, or “Fail” using if-elif-else.

3. Using nested if statements, write a program to check if a person is eligible to vote:
   Age must be ≥ 18
   Must be a citizen (True/False)

4. Modify the odd/even program to use a single if-else statement instead of two separate if statements.

Loop

Programs can be made to run a task repeatedly for a number of times or until a condition becomes false. Running a program this way requires the use of **loops**.
A ***loop*** is a control structure that repeatedly executes a block of statements or tasks. Loops are automated and are controlled by conditions or a range of values. They use the block statement structure where the statements of the task are placed within the block.

In Python, there are **two** types of loops:

1. for loop
2. while loop

Importance of Loops in a Program

1. Loops handle repetitive execution of a program.
2. Loops help in iterating through collections such as lists, tuples, sets, and dictionaries.
3. Loops reduce code redundancy by eliminating the need for repetitive code blocks.
4. Loops enable automation of data generation and repetitive computations.
5. Loops are essential for tasks like searching, sorting, and applying operations to multiple data values.
6. Loops provide control flow for programs that require repeated execution.
7. Loops are useful for implementing simulations, animations, and time-based processes.

The for Loop

The **for loop** is a control statement that controls the recursive execution of tasks or statements for a given number of times. Unlike the while loop, the **for** loop does not depend on conditions but rather on a **range of values** or an **iterable** sequence.

Example 1,

```
Python
animal = ["lion", "cow", "rhinoceros", "donkey"]

for i in animal:
    print(i)
```

```
#Output
lion
cow
```

```
rhinoceros
donkey
```

Example 2,

```python
students = {
        'George':"Harvard",
        'Marrie':"Cambridge",
        'Kelvin':"MIT",
        'Gloria':"Oxford"
}

for name, school in students.items():
    print(f"{name} -> {school}")
```

```
#Output
George -> Harvard
Marrie -> Cambridge
Kelvin -> MIT
Gloria -> Oxford
```

The range() Function

The **range()** function is commonly used in **for** loops to define the number of repetitions. It controls where to begin, where to end, and the step size used for the loop.

range(start, end, step)

- **start (int):** Optional. Specifies where the loop should begin. Default is 0.
- **end (int):** Required. Specifies where the loop should end (not inclusive).
- **step (int):** Optional. Specifies the increment (or decrement) between numbers. Default is 1.

Example 1,

```python
for var in range(3):
    print(f"{var} Hello World!")
```

```
#Output
0 Hello World!
1 Hello World!
2 Hello World!
```

Example 2,

```
Python

total = 0
for var in range(1, 5):
    total = total + var
    print(f"{var} total -> {total}")
```

```
#Output
1 total -> 1
2 total -> 3
3 total -> 6
4 total -> 10
```

Example 3,

```
Python

for var in range(0, 10, 2):
    print(var)
```

```
#Output
0
2
4
6
8
```

The while Loop

The **while loop** is a control statement that recursively executes statements as long as a condition evaluates to True.

- The **while** loop checks the condition before execution.
- If the condition is True, the statements within the block execute.
- Once execution finishes, the condition is checked again.
- The process continues until the condition evaluates to False, at which point the loop stops.

Example 1,

```
Python
i = 0
while i < 3:
    i = i + 1
    print(f"{i} Hello World!")
```

```
#Output
1 Hello World!
2 Hello World!
3 Hello World!
```

Key Point

- Every **while** loop has a **condition** that is evaluated **before each iteration**.
- The condition **i < 3** is initially True, so the loop begins executing.
- The statement **i = i + 1** increments the value of **i** by 1 in each iteration.
- When **i** is no longer less than 3, the condition becomes False, and the loop **terminates** automatically.

Example 2,

```
Python
count = 2
while count <= 10:
    print(f"{count} {count * '*'}")
    count = count + 2
```

```
#Output
2 **
4 ****
6 ******
8 ********
10 **********
```

Infinite Loop

Some applications require infinite execution of a certain program or task. These programs may include:

- Daemons (background services)
- Animations
- Date and time trackers
- Logging services
- Continuous monitoring systems
- Buffer cleaning and releasing

Such programs do not end as long as the application continues to run.
The while loop is particularly suitable for infinite execution. This is achieved by setting the condition to always evaluate to True.

Example 1- A program that continuously accepts numeric inputs and returns the sum of all entries when the user enters "=",

```python
entries = []

while True:
    num = input("Enter a number or = : ")
    if num == "=":
        total = sum(entries)
        print(f"sum -> {total}")
        break

    else:
        entries.append(float(num))
```

```
#Output
Enter a number or = : 4
Enter a number or = : 6
Enter a number or = : 20
Enter a number or = : =
sum -> 30.0
```

Example 2 – A program designed to repeatedly display the message "Happy coding, Pythonista!" at 2-second intervals,

```
Python
```

```python
import time

count = 0
while True:
    count += 1
    print(count, " Happy coding Pythonista \U0001F602 \U0001F389")
    time.sleep(2)
```

```
#Output
1  Happy coding Pythonista 😂  🎉
2  Happy coding Pythonista 😂  🎉
3  Happy coding Pythonista 😂  🎉
4  Happy coding Pythonista 😂  🎉
```

🧠 **Insight**

In debugging or testing, pressing **Ctrl + C** interrupts execution and stops an infinite loop.

The break Statement

The break statement is a Python keyword mostly used in loop structures to **halt or terminate execution prematurely** once a given condition is met.

For example,

●●● Python

```python
for i in range(1, 10):
    if i == 5:
        break

    print(f"{i} Hello World!")
```

```
#Output
1 Hello World!
2 Hello World!
3 Hello World!
4 Hello World!
```

The continue Statement

The continue statement is another Python keyword used in loops. Instead of stopping the loop entirely, it **skips the current iteration** and moves to the next iteration when a certain condition is true.

For example,

```
Python
for i in range(1, 10):
    if i in [4, 6, 8]:
        continue

    print(f"{i} Hello World!")
```

```
#Output
1 Hello World!
2 Hello World!
3 Hello World!
5 Hello World!
7 Hello World!
9 Hello World!
```

Nested Loop

A **nested loop** refers to a loop placed inside another loop. In other words, it is a loop within a loop.

Nested loops are necessary when working with multi-dimensional data, pattern generation, matrix operations, or when performing repeated iterations over multiple sets of data.

They allow you to repeat one sequence of operations for every iteration of another loop.

How Nested Loops Work

1. The **outer loop** contains one or more **inner loops**.
2. When the program runs, the outer loop starts its first iteration and then pauses.
3. The inner loop begins to execute:
    - It iterates **all its steps** if it doesn't contain another loop.

- It iterates **only the first step** and pauses if it contains another inner loop, following the same pattern.

4. Once the inner loop finishes executing, the outer loop resumes its next iteration.
5. This cycle continues until the outer loop completes all its iterations.

Example 1,

Python

```
for i in range(1, 5):     #outer loop
    print(f"step {i}-> ", end="")  #inner loop
    for m in range(5):
        print(m, end=" ")
    print()
```

```
#Output
step 1-> 0 1 2 3 4
step 2-> 0 1 2 3 4
step 3-> 0 1 2 3 4
step 4-> 0 1 2 3 4
```

Key Point

- The **outer loop** controls the number of steps (or iterations) – in this case, it runs from 1 to 4.
- For **each iteration** of the outer loop, the **inner loop** executes completely, printing numbers from 0 to 4.
- After the inner loop finishes, the print() statement without arguments moves the cursor to a new line before the next outer iteration begins.

Insight

The parameter **end**="" in the print() function specifies what should be printed at the end of each output. By default, **end**="\n", which inserts a newline character after every **print()** call. Setting **end**="" prevents the automatic line break.

Example 2 – Printing triangle of numbers,

```python
Python
for i in range(1, 6):
    for m in range(1, i):
        print(m, end=" ")
    print()
```

```
#Output
1
1 2
1 2 3
1 2 3 4
```

Example 3 – Printing pattern of stars,

```python
Python
end = 6
for i in range(1, end):
    for m in range(end-i):
        print('*', end=" ")
    print()
```

```
#Output
* * * * *
* * * *
* * *
* *
*
```

Data Generation Using Loops

Data and programs are the core components of any application or software, making them essential resources in programming.

- Programs process data to perform tasks.
- Data can either be provided by users or generated automatically by the system.

Manually generating large datasets is tedious, but loops make this process efficient by **automating data generation** in both structured and unstructured patterns.

In Python, **for loops** are particularly suitable for generating data efficiently, such as creating number sequences, synthetic datasets, or repetitive structures.

List Comprehension

Example 1 - Generating a list of squared numbers from 1 to 10,

```
••• Python

square  = [x**2 for x in range(1, 11)]
print(square)
```

```
#Output
[1, 4, 9, 16, 25, 36, 49, 64, 81, 100]
```

Example 2 - Generating a list of odd numbers from 0 to 15

```
••• Python

odd = [ item  for item  in range(15)  if item%2 != 0]
print(odd)
```

```
#Output
[1, 3, 5, 7, 9, 11, 13]
```

Example 3 - Generating a matrix (list of lists) filled with random numbers,

```
••• Python
import random

data = [[random.randrange(9) for _ in range(3)] for _ in range(3)]
print(data)
```

```
#Output
[ [4, 0, 1], [7, 3, 5], [5, 3, 2] ]
```

Set Comprehension

Example 1 - Generating a set of even numbers between 0 and 10

```
●●● Python

var = { x for x in range(0,10) if x % 2 == 0}
print(var)
```

```
#Output
{0, 2, 4, 6, 8}
```

Example 2 - Generating a set of random numbers,

```
●●● Python
from random import randrange

var = { randrange(100) for x in range(10)}
print(var)
```

```
#Output
{73, 80, 19, 84, 24, 89, 58, 29, 30, 57}
```

Dictionary Comprehension

Example - Generating a dictionary of numbers and their cubes (1 to 5)

```
●●● Python

data = { x: x**3  for x  in range(1, 6) }
print(data)
```

```
#Output
{1: 1, 2: 8, 3: 27, 4: 64, 5: 125}
```

Key Terms

for
while
iterables
comprehension
continue
break
infinite

Review Questions

1. Which loop executes a block of code while a condition is True?
A. for loop
B. while loop
C. nested loop
D. break
Answers: b

2. What is the output of the following code?

```
for i in range(1, 5):
    if i == 3:
        break
    print(i)
```

A. 1 2 3
B. 1 2
C. 1 2 3 4
D. 3 4
Answers: b

3. Which statement skips the current iteration and continues with the next?
A. break
B. continue
C. pass
D. exit
Answers: b

4. What does the following list comprehension produce?
[x**2 for x in range(1, 4)]
A. [1, 2, 3]
B. [1, 4, 9]
C. [1, 8, 27]
D. [2, 4, 6]
Answers: b

5. Which of the following is **not** a valid use of loops?
A. Iterating through a list
B. Performing repeated calculations
C. Automatically stopping without a condition in a while loop
D. Generating sequences of numbers
Answers: c

Review Exercises

1. Write a Python program using a **for loop** to print all numbers divisible by 3 between 1 and 30.

2. Write a program using a **while loop** that continuously asks the user to enter a number until they enter 0. The program should print the sum of all entered numbers.

3. Write a program to print the following pattern using a **nested for loop**:
   1
   1 2
   1 2 3
   1 2 3 4

4. Use **list comprehension** to generate a list of all multiples of 5 between 1 and 50, and **dictionary comprehension** to generate a dictionary of numbers from 1 to 5 and their factorials.

Function

A **function** is a block of organized and related statements designed to perform a specific task. It can contain variables, loops, decision-making statements, other functions, and objects that can be reused across different parts of a program. Functions are also referred to as *methods*, *procedures*, *subprograms*, *routines*, or *subroutines*.

Importance of Functions

1. Enhanced Readability and Comprehensibility
Functions improve the readability of a program by breaking it into smaller logical units. Since each function performs a distinct task, it becomes easier for a programmer (or another reader) to understand and maintain the code.

2. Efficiency through Minimization of Repetitions
Functions encapsulate repetitive tasks into reusable blocks. This minimizes code duplication, reduces redundancy, and makes programs more efficient to manage.

3. Breaking Complex Programs into Smaller Segments
By using functions, large or complex programs can be decomposed into smaller, manageable units. Each function is responsible for one aspect of the program's logic, simplifying development, debugging, and maintenance.

4. Improved Time Efficiency
Organizing code into reusable functions saves development time. Once a function is written, it can be reused multiple times in the same program or even in other programs, eliminating the need to rewrite the same logic.

Types of Functions

Python supports two kinds of functions:

1. **Built-in functions**
2. **User-defined functions**

Built-in Functions

Built-in functions are an integral part of the **Python Standard Library**. These functions come pre-installed with Python and are readily available for use without any additional setup. They perform a wide range of tasks, including mathematical computations, data type conversions, string manipulations, file handling, and more.

Examples of built-in functions include:

Function	Definition
sum()	Returns the total of all numbers in an iterable.
eval()	Evaluates and executes a string expression as Python code.
bin()	Converts an integer to its binary string representation.
oct()	Converts an integer to its octal string representation.
chr()	Returns the character represented by the specified Unicode code point.
ord()	Returns the Unicode code point (integer) of a character.
dir()	Returns a list of methods and properties of an object.
del	Keyword used to delete objects, variables, or elements from data structures.
max()	Returns the maximum (highest) value in an iterable.
min()	Returns the minimum (lowest) value in an iterable.
len()	Returns the length (number of items) of an iterable.

Table 4.1

Note

Many of these built-in functions have been well explored in earlier chapters of this book.

User-defined Functions

User-defined functions are custom functions created by the programmer using the **def** keyword. They enable developers to group related statements that perform a specific task into a single, reusable block of code. This approach promotes **modularity**, **readability**, and **reusability**, allowing you to call the same function multiple times throughout your program without rewriting the same logic.

Syntax

```
def sample(args):
    #statement

    return value
```

- **def** → Keyword used to define or declare a function.
- **sample** → A label that identifies the function. It must follow Python's naming rules.

- **args** → Optional values passed to a function to provide input data. Declared inside parentheses.
- colon (:) → Indicates the start of the function body.
- statement(s) → The block of logic that performs the intended task.
- **return** → Optional keyword to return a value from the function. If omitted, the function returns None.

Example 1 – A function to print "Hello World!",

Python

```python
def greet():
    message = "Hello World!"
    print(message)
```

Example 2 – A function to return an addition of two numbers.

Python

```python
def add():
    x, y = 10, 6
    result = x + y
    return result
```

Rules for Naming Functions

Naming functions follows the same rules as naming variables:

1. A function name can begin with a letter.
2. Function names cannot start with a digit. Example: **12myfunction**
3. A function name can start with an underscore. Example: **_myfunction**
4. Functions can be a mix of letters, digits, and underscores, but the first character must be a letter or underscore. Example: **myfunction23**
5. Function names are case-sensitive. Example: **myfunction** ≠ **Myfunction**.

Calling a Function

A function call occurs when a defined function is executed to perform its intended task. Functions are called by writing their name followed by parentheses (), which may include **arguments** if required.

During program execution, Python locates the function definition by name, processes the statements within its block, and returns control to the calling point once execution is complete. Function calls can be made directly within the program or invoked from within another function, allowing for flexible and structured program flow.

Example 1 - Calling a function in a program directly,

```python
def greet():
    message = "Hello World!"
    print(message)

#Calling the function
greet()
```

```
#Output
Hello World!
```

Example 2 - Calling a function in a program directly,

```python
def add():
    x, y = 10, 6
    result = x + y
    return result

#Calling the function
result  = add()
print(result)
```

```
#Output
16
```

Example 3 - Calling a function within another function,

```python
def add():
    x, y = 10, 6
    result = x + y
    return result

def square():
    #Calling the function
    result = add()
    return result ** 2
```

Argument Functions

Functions can be designed to receive input data before performing a task. These inputs—called **arguments**—are passed into the function and used by variables or objects within its block to execute specific operations.

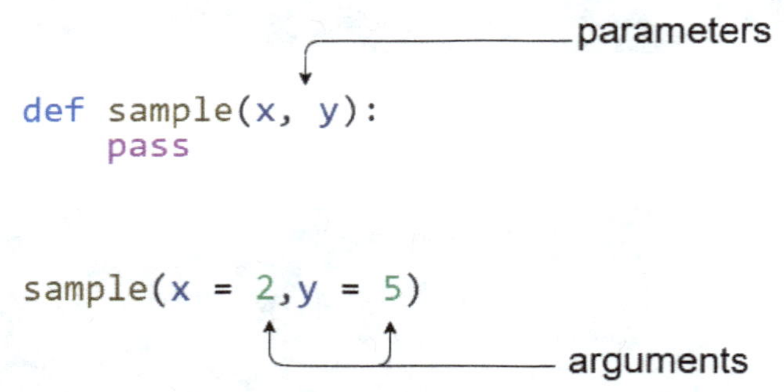

Arguments can be any data type or object, including:

- Numbers
- Strings
- Lists
- Tuples, dictionaries, sets
- Bytes, files, or even other functions
- Object

Functions that require data before execution are called **argumentative functions**, while those that don't need input are called **argumentless functions**.

In Python, function **parameters** (the variable names inside the parentheses of a function definition) represent the data expected by the function. When a function takes **multiple arguments**, their order is crucial because Python assigns each argument value according to its position.

Unlike some languages, Python does not require you to explicitly declare the type of each parameter—the interpreter determines the type dynamically at runtime.

Example 1 – A function to get a name and returns a greeting message,

```python
def greet(name):
    message = f"Hello {name} \nWishing you a happy coding"
    return message

#Calling the function
result  = greet(name = "Charles")
print(result)
```

```
#Output
Hello Charles
Wishing you a happy coding
```

Example 2 – A function to accept two numbers and return their sum ,

```python
def add(x, y):
    result = x + y
    return result

#Calling the function
result  = add(4, 6)
print(result)
```

```
#Output
10
```

Order of Arguments

When supplying arguments to a function, the order in which the arguments are provided is extremely important. Typically, the **first parameter** corresponds to the **first argument**, the **second parameter** to the **second argument**, and so on.

Example,

```
sample(x, y, z)  →  sample(1, 2, 3)
```

In the example above:

- Parameter **x** = 1
- Parameter **y** = 2
- Parameter **z** = 3

> 📖 **Note**
>
> If the order of the arguments is changed accidentally, the function's logic and output will also change — which may lead to unexpected results.

To avoid depending on strict order, arguments can be passed by specifying parameter names or keywords explicitly. This method allows you to arrange arguments in any order while maintaining accuracy.

```
sample(x, y, z)  →  sample(z=2, x=3, y=1)
```

In this case, Python assigns each value to the correct parameter regardless of order, improving flexibility and readability.

Example,

```python
def subtract(x, y):
    answer = x - y
    print(f"{x} - {y} =  {answer}")

#Positional arguments
subtract(10, 6)

#Keyword arguments
subtract(y=6, x=10)
```

```
#Output
10 - 6 =  4
10 - 6 =  4
```

Optional and Required Arguments

In Python, some functions can run even if no argument is supplied because they have **default** values. These are known as **optional arguments**.
Other functions require that arguments be passed every time they are called. If not, Python raises a **TypeError**. These are known as **required arguments**.

Optional Arguments

Have default values. If not supplied, the function uses the default.

Example,

```python
def multiplier(num, factor = 10):
    value = num * factor
    return value


#Calling without a factor arg
value1 = multiplier(num = 5)
print(f"Default factor -> {value1}")


#Calling with a factor arg
value2 = multiplier(num=5, factor=3)
print(f"Factor of 3-> {value2}")
```

```
#Output
Default factor -> 50
Factor of 3-> 15
```

Required Arguments

Must be provided when calling a function, or a TypeError will occur.

Example,

Python

```
def average(num1, num2, num3):
    total = num1 + num2 + num3
    avg = total / 3
    return avg

#supplying all arguments
result1 = average(5, 3, 6)
print(f"Average -> {result1}")

#missing one argument
result2 = average(8, 4)
print(f"Average -> {result2}")
```

```
#Output
Average -> 4.666666666666667
TypeError: average() missing 1 required positional argument: 'num3'
```

Note

Optional and required arguments can be combined within the same function definition. However, all required arguments must come before optional ones, which include their default values.

Example,

```
def sample( x = value, y):    → Wrong
    pass

def sample( y,  x = value):   → Correct
    pass
```

Unlimited Positional Arguments(*args)

Positional arguments are the most common type of arguments in Python. They are assigned to parameters based on their position in the function call. However, when designing applications that may need to handle **many or unknown numbers of arguments**, defining a fixed number of parameters becomes impractical.

To handle such scenarios, Python allows you to use a positional variable argument, represented by an asterisk * before the parameter name – commonly written as *args. *args collects multiple positional arguments into a **tuple**, allowing iteration through each item.

Example,

```
Python

def add(*args):
    total = sum(args)
    print(f"Sum of all entries-> {total}")


#Entering unlimited data
add(6, 3, 2, 4)
add(10, 30, 40)
```

```
#Output
Sum of all entries-> 15
Sum of all entries-> 80
```

Key Point:

- *args allows your function to accept any number of arguments.
- The arguments are stored as a tuple, which can be iterated using a loop.
- The use of *args makes your function flexible and scalable.

Keyword Arguments (**kwargs)

In some cases, you may want your function to accept an **unknown number of keyword** arguments (key–value pairs). This is achieved using **kwargs.

- *args → collects multiple **positional arguments** into a tuple.
- **kwargs → collects multiple **keyword arguments** into a dictionary.

This makes functions flexible and adaptable for different scenarios.

Example,

```python
def student(**kwargs):
    name = kwargs.get('name')
    score = kwargs.get('score')
    credit = kwargs.get('credit')
    GPA = score/credit

    print(f"Name:{name}\nScores:{score}\nCredits:{credit}\nGPA:{GPA}")

student(credit= 120, score= 450, name="Marrie")
```

```
#Output
Name: Marrie
Scores: 450
Credits: 120
GPA: 3.75
```

Here, the function can accept any number of key–value pairs without prior declaration.

Insight

The names *args and **kwargs are only conventions. You can use any valid identifiers, such as *myentries or **myentries. What matters is the presence of the single asterisk (*) or double asterisk (**), which determines how arguments are passed to the function.

Using both *args and **kwargs

Use *args and **kwargs together when you want your function to handle both unlimited positional and keyword arguments.

Example – A function that returns sales report from previous and current date,

```python
def sales(*today, **previous):
    today_sales = sum(today)
    today_units = len(today)

    item = previous.get("item")
    previous_sales = previous.get("sale")
```

```
    previous_units = previous.get("units")

    total_units = today_units + previous_units
    total_sales = today_sales + previous_sales

    stats = f"Item->{item}\nSales->{total_sales}\nUnits-> {total_units}"
    return stats


#Supplying both *args and **kwargs
report= sales(100, 240, 160,  item="Meat Pizza", sale=300, units=2)
print(report)
```

```
#Output
Item-> Meat Pizza
Sales-> 800
Units-> 5
```

Anonymous Functions (lambda)

In Python, functions are usually defined using the **def** keyword. However, there are situations where you need small, one-line functions for quick tasks. For such cases, Python provides **anonymous functions**, also called **lambda** functions.

A **lambda** function does not require a name (though it can be assigned one). It is defined using the **lambda** keyword followed by parameters and an expression.

Syntax:

```
lambda argument : expression
```

argument: These are the input values provided to the lambda function.
expression: This is the logic that defines the function. The expression is automatically returned.

Example 1 - Lambda function to add two numbers,

```
Python
var = lambda x,y : x+y
print(var(4, 6))
```

```
#Output
10
```

Example 2 - Lambda function to return the square of a number,

```python
square = lambda x : x**2
print(square(3))
```

```
#Output
9
```

Example 3 - Lambda function to check if a number is even,

```python
even = lambda x  : x % 2 == 0
print(even(8))
print(even(5))
```

```
#Output
True
False
```

Using map() and filter() with Lambda

Lambda functions can be used to create new iterables by transforming or filtering elements from an existing iterable. This is achieved using the **map()** and **filter()** functions.

map()

The map() function applies a given function to each element of an iterable and returns a new iterable with the modified values.

```
type(map(lambda argument: expression, iterable))
```

Example 1 - Lambda function to return a list of squared numbers,

```python
numbers = [1, 2, 3, 4]
squared = list(map(lambda x: x**2, numbers))
print(squared)
```

```
#Output
[1, 4, 9, 16]
```

Example 2 - Lambda function to return the square root of numbers.

```python
from math import sqrt

var = [9, 16, 25, 64, 81, 100]
square_root = list(map(lambda x: sqrt(x), var))
print(square_root)
```

```
#Output
[3.0, 4.0, 5.0, 8.0, 9.0, 10.0]
```

filter()

The filter() function is used to select elements from an iterable based on a given condition. It returns a new iterable containing only elements that satisfy the condition.

Syntax

```
type(filter(lambda argument:condition, iterable))
```

Example 1 - Lambda function to return a list of even numbers,

```python

numbers = [1, 2, 3, 4, 5, 6]
evens = list(filter(lambda x: x % 2 == 0, numbers))
print(evens)
```

```
#Output
[2, 4, 6]
```

Example 2 - Lambda function to return multiples of three,

```python
numbers = [2, 3, 4, 5, 6, 7, 8, 9]
multiple_three = tuple(filter(lambda x: x % 3==0, numbers))
print(multiple_three)
```

```
#Output
(3, 6, 9)
```

Recursion in Functions

Recursion is a programming technique where a function calls itself directly or indirectly in order to solve a problem. It is a powerful concept because many complex problems can be broken down into smaller, similar sub-problems that are easier to solve.

When a recursive function is defined, it must contain two essential parts:

1. **Base Case:**
   The condition that stops the recursion. Without a base case, the function will call itself endlessly, leading to an infinite recursion error.

2. **Recursive Case:**
   The part of the function where it calls itself with a smaller or reduced version of the problem.

Example 1: Factorial using Recursion,

```python
def factorial(n):
    if n == 0 or n == 1:    # Base case
        return 1
    else:                   # Recursive case
        return n * factorial(n - 1)

print(factorial(5))
```

```
#Output
120
```

Explanation:

- When n =5, the function keeps calling itself:
  5 * factorial(4) → 5 * 4 * factorial(3) → 5 * 4 * 3 * factorial(2) → 5 * 4 * 3 * 2 * factorial(1) → 5 * 4 * 3 * 2 * 1.
- Finally, the base case factorial(1) returns 1, ending the recursion.

Example 2: Fibonacci Sequence using Recursion

The Fibonacci sequence is defined as:

- F(0) = 0, F(1) = 1
- F(n) = F(n-1) + F(n-2)

```python
def fibonacci(n):
    if n == 0:          # Base case
        return 0
    elif n == 1:        # Base case
        return 1
    else:               # Recursive case
        return fibonacci(n - 1) + fibonacci(n - 2)

for i in range(6):
    print(fibonacci(i), end=" ")
```

```
#Output
0 1 1 2 3 5
```

Advantages of Recursion

1. Provides a **natural and clean solution** for problems that can be broken into subproblems (divide-and-conquer).
2. Makes code shorter and easier to understand in cases such as tree traversal, factorial, Fibonacci, and backtracking algorithms.
3. Eliminates the need for explicit loops in some cases.

Disadvantages of Recursion

1. **Performance overhead:** Recursive calls consume more memory due to the function call stack.
2. **Risk of infinite recursion:** Without a proper base case, recursion may run indefinitely and crash the program.
3. In some problems, iterative solutions are **more efficient** than recursion.

Insight

Recursion vs Iteration

- **Recursion** solves problems by breaking them down and calling the same function again.
- **Iteration** solves problems by repeating steps using loops (for, while).
- Many recursive problems can also be solved using iteration, but recursion often provides a more elegant approach.

The pass Keyword

The pass keyword, as used in the function block above, is not limited to functions alone—it can also be used in other code structures such as loops and conditional statements.

It serves as a **placeholder** when a function, loop, or block of code is defined but does not yet contain any statements. This is useful when writing code that will be implemented later, preventing syntax errors that would occur if the block were left empty.

A function or block cannot be left empty without using pass, as Python requires at least one statement inside it.

Example,

Python

```python
def sample():
    pass
```

Concurrent Execution

Concurrent execution refers to the execution of multiple functions or processes simultaneously. In programming, functions are typically executed sequentially in a linear manner, following a first-come, first-served basis. This means that the function called first is executed before any subsequent functions. Execution progresses from the top of the program to the bottom, and any function waiting to execute must remain idle until the currently running function completes. This happens because execution occurs within the system's single thread by default.

Example,

```python
def english():
    print("English -> Good morning and happy Coding")

def french():
    print("French -> Bonjour et bon codage")

def german():
    print("Germany -> Guten Morgen und viel Spaß beim Programmieren!")

english()
french()
german()
```

```
#Output
English -> Good morning and happy Coding
French -> Bonjour et bon codage
Germany -> Guten Morgen und viel Spaß beim Programmieren!
```

In the program above, the functions are executed **sequentially**—that is, one after another in the order they are called.

- english() executes first.
- french() waits until english() finishes execution before it begins.
- german() then executes only after french() completes.

This behavior occurs because, by default, Python runs code on a **single thread**—meaning only one task can be processed at a time.

Drawbacks of Sequential Execution

1. **Execution Delays** – Each function must wait for the previous one to complete before starting, which can slow down overall performance.
2. **Inefficient for Multi-Core Systems** – Even though modern processors have multiple cores, sequential execution uses only **one core**, leaving the others idle.
3. **Poor Performance with Heavy Tasks** – Programs that involve CPU-intensive operations (e.g., data processing, file compression, or image rendering) become slow because tasks are not distributed across multiple cores.
4. **Limited Responsiveness** – Applications that rely on real-time operations or background processing may freeze or lag since only one operation runs at a time.

Multiprocessing or **threading** solves these problems by allowing multiple functions or tasks to run simultaneously on different CPU cores using **threads**. Each function runs as a separate process, with its own memory space and resources, enabling true parallel execution.

This approach significantly improves performance for CPU-bound tasks and ensures full utilization of multi-core processors.

Threading

Threading allows multiple functions or processes to execute simultaneously without waiting for the completion of another process before starting. This improves performance by enabling parallel execution. In Python, the **threading** module provides various methods for managing and working with threads.

Threading Methods

Method	Description
Thread()	Creates a thread
active_count()	Returns the currently executing thread object.
current_thread()	Returns a list of all active Thread objects.
enumerate()	Returns a list of all active Thread objects.
excepthook()	Used to handle uncaught exceptions in threads.
get_ident()	Returns the thread identifier (a unique integer for each thread).
get_native_id()	Returns the native (OS-level) thread identifier.
getprofile()	Retrieves the profiling function for the current thread.
gettrace()	Returns the trace function for the current thread.
local()	Creates thread-local data storage. Each thread maintains its own separate copy.
main_thread()	Returns the main thread object.
setprofile()	Used to set a profiling function for threads.
settrace()	Sets a trace function for debugging threads.
stack_size()	Returns the stack size used when creating new threads.

Table 4.2

Thread(target, name, args, kwargs, daemon, group **)**

target → Specifies the function that the thread will execute when started. If None, no function runs, and the thread does nothing.

name → A string representing the thread's name. If **None**, a default name like "Thread-1", "Thread-2", etc., is assigned.

args → A tuple containing arguments to pass to the target function.
If the function requires multiple arguments, they must be passed as a tuple.

kwargs → A dictionary containing keyword arguments (key=value pairs) for the target function.

daemon → Determines whether the thread is a **daemon thread** (runs in the background and stops when the main program exits). If **None,** it inherits the main thread's daemon status.

group → Reserved for future implementation. Always set to **None**.

Example 1

```
Python
import threading
import time

def english():
    time.sleep(2)   #delay execution for 2 seconds
    print("English -> Good morning and happy Coding")

def french():
    time.sleep(1)  #delay execution for 1 seconds
    print("French -> Bonjour et bon codage")


def german():
    print("Germany -> Guten Morgen und viel Spaß beim Programmieren!")


#Creating Threads
threading.Thread(target= english).start()
threading.Thread(target= french).start()
threading.Thread(target= german).start()
```

```
#Output
Germany -> Guten Morgen und viel Spaß beim Programmieren!
French -> Bonjour et bon codage
English -> Good morning and happy Coding
```

Explanation

In the example above, the threading module is used to execute multiple functions concurrently, meaning they run *independently* of each other.

Each function is executed on a **separate thread**, allowing them to start and complete at different times.

Each function runs in its own thread

The threading.Thread(target=function_name) creates a separate thread for each function and starts it immediately using .start().

time.sleep() introduces a delay

The time.sleep() function pauses the execution of that particular thread for a specified duration (in seconds).

- english() waits 2 seconds before executing.
- french() waits 1 second.
- german() executes immediately.

Threads run concurrently

Unlike sequential execution, threads do not wait for each other to finish. All threads are active simultaneously, allowing the program to perform multiple tasks at the same time.

Execution order is non-deterministic

The order of outputs may vary depending on thread scheduling and execution timing controlled by the Python interpreter and operating system.

Example 2

```
Python
import threading

def add(*data):
    result = sum(data)
    print(result)

#Creating Threads
threading.Thread(target= add, args = (10, 20)).start()
threading.Thread(target= add, args = (4, 6, 5)).start()
```

```
#Output
30
15
```

Thread Object Methods

Method	Description
start()	Starts the execution of the thread.
daemon	A boolean attribute that determines whether a thread is a daemon thread. Daemon threads run in the background and automatically terminate when the main program exits.
name	Retrieves or sets the thread's name.
ident	Returns the thread's unique identifier (assigned by Python).
is_alive()	Returns True if the thread is still running, False otherwise.
join()	Waits for the thread to finish execution before continuing.

native_id()	Returns the OS-assigned native thread ID.
run()	Defines the code that runs when the thread starts. Typically, you override this method when creating a custom thread class.

Table 4.3

Example,

```
Python
from threading import Thread

def subtraction(x, y):
    result = x - y
    print(result)

def average(total, n):
    result = total / n
    print(result)

#Creating Threads
thread1 = Thread(target= average, args = (100, 25), daemon= True)
thread2 =Thread(target= subtraction, args=(15, 10), name="second_thread")

#Starting threads
thread2.start()

#the next thread has to wait
thread2.join()
thread1.start()

#daemon
print(f"Is thread1 daemon-> {thread1.daemon}")

#name
print(f"Name of thread1-> {thread1.name}")
print(f"Name of thread2-> {thread2.name}")

#is_alive
print(f"Is thread1 alive-> {thread1.is_alive()}")

#native_id
print(f"Native id of thread2-> {thread2.native_id}")
```

```
#Output
5
4.0
Is thread1 daemon-> True
Name of thread1-> Thread-1 (average)
Name of thread2-> second_thread
Is thread1 alive-> False
Native id of thread2-> 35912
```

Multiprocessing

The **multiprocessing** module is an alternative approach in Python for running concurrent and memory-intensive processes. Unlike threading, which shares the same memory space, multiprocessing creates separate processes, each with its own Python interpreter and memory resources.

This allows true parallel execution on multiple CPU cores, making it ideal for **CPU-bound** tasks such as computations, data processing, or simulations.

When a multiprocessing program is executed, each process runs **independently**, meaning that the **Global Interpreter Lock (GIL)** does not restrict execution as it does in threading. This makes multiprocessing more efficient for parallel computation, even though it requires more system resources than threading.

For example,

Python
```
import multiprocessing

def square(x):
    result = x * x
    print(f"Square of {x} -> {result}")


if __name__ == "__main__":
    # Creating processes
    p1 = multiprocessing.Process(target=square, args=(4,))
    p2 = multiprocessing.Process(target=square, args=(3,))

    p1.start()
    p2.start()

    # Waiting for both processes to finish
    p1.join()
    p2.join()
    print("All processes completed.")
```

```
#Output
Square of 3 -> 9
Square of 4 -> 16
All processes completed.
```

Asynchronous Programming

The limitation or disadvantage of running programs on a single thread is that all tasks are queued in memory, and each task must wait for the previous one to finish executing. This causes delays in performance, reduces speed, and prevents efficient use of system resources such as multi-core processors. Tasks that rely on network access, file I/O, or other slow operations can especially slow down overall execution.

Aside from using **multithreading** (as discussed in the previous section) to address these limitations, Python provides another powerful mechanism called **asynchronous** programming, which allows programs to manage execution timing and concurrency efficiently.

Asynchronous programming enables Python to perform multiple operations without blocking the main thread. Instead of waiting for one task to finish, the program can *pause* one operation while waiting (such as for input/output) and *continue* executing another.

This is made possible through the **asyncio** module, which is part of Python's standard library and does not require additional installation. It is primarily used for writing concurrent code using the **async** and **await** keywords.

Example 1 – A simple asynchronous program,

Python
```python
import asyncio

async def add(x, y):
    value = x + y
    await asyncio.sleep(2)
    return f"The sum of {x} and {y} -> {value}"


result =  asyncio.run(add(5, 6))
print(result)
```

```
#Output
The sum of 5 and 6 -> 11
```

Explanation:

- async marks a function as asynchronous (called a coroutine).
- await pauses the function until the awaited task completes.
- asyncio.run() executes the event loop.

Example 2 – Running multiple asynchronous programs,

```
Python
import asyncio

async def add(x, y):
    value = x + y
    await asyncio.sleep(2)
    print(f"The sum of {x} and {y} -> {value}")

async def square(x):
    value = x * x
    await asyncio.sleep(1)
    print(f"The square of {x} -> {value}")


async def main():
    await asyncio.gather(add(5, 2), square(4))


asyncio.run(main())
```

```
#Output
The square of 4 -> 16
The sum of 5 and 2 -> 7
```

Explanation:

- asyncio.gather() allows multiple coroutines to run concurrently.

Methods of asyncio

all_tasks	format_helpers	proactor_events	streams
as_completed	futures	protocols	subprocess
base_events	gather	queues	sys
base_futures	get_child_watcher	run	taskgroups
base_subprocess	get_event_loop	run_coroutine_threadsafe	tasks
base_tasks	get_event_loop_policy	runners	threads
constants	get_running_loop	selector_events	timeout
coroutines	iscoroutine	set_child_watcher	timeout_at
shield	iscoroutinefunction	set_event_loop	timeouts
sleep	isfuture	set_event_loop_policy	to_thread
create_task	locks	create_subprocess_exec	transports
current_task	log	create_subprocess_shell	wait
ensure_future	mixins	sslproto	wait_for
events	new_event_loop	staggered	windows_events

exceptions	open_connection	start_server	windows_utils

Table 4.4

create_tasks()

Schedules the execution of a coroutine concurrently as a Task.

```python
import asyncio
async def sample():
    await asyncio.sleep(2)
    print("Hello World!")

async def main():
    task = asyncio.create_task(sample())
    await task

asyncio.run(main())
```

all_tasks()

Returns a set of all tasks that are currently running in the event loop.

```python
import asyncio
async def sample():
    await asyncio.sleep(2)
    print("Hello World!")

async def main():
    t1 = asyncio.create_task(sample())
    print(asyncio.all_tasks())

asyncio.run(main())
```

```
#Output
{<Task pending name='Task-1' coro=<main() running at d:\python.py:22>
cb=[_run_until_complete_cb() at C:\python\Lib\asyncio\base_events.py:180]>,
<Task pending name='Task-2' coro=<sample() running at d:\python.py:15>>}
```

wait_for()

Runs a coroutine with a timeout period.

```python
import asyncio
async def sample():
    await asyncio.sleep(2)
    print("Hello World!")

async def main():
    try:
        result = await asyncio.wait_for(sample(), timeout=3)
        print(result)
    except asyncio.TimeoutError:
        print("Task took too long!")

asyncio.run(main())
```

as_completed()

Runs multiple coroutines concurrently and yields results as they are completed.

```python
import asyncio

async def delay(x):
    await asyncio.sleep(x)
    return f"Completed after {x} seconds"

async def main():
    tasks = [delay(2), delay(1), delay(3)]
    for result in asyncio.as_completed(tasks):
        print(await result)

asyncio.run(main())
```

```
#Output
Completed after 1 seconds
Completed after 2 seconds
Completed after 3 seconds
```

Key Terms

Procedure
Built-in Function
User-defined Function
Arguments
Parameters
Anonymous
Lambda
Recursion
Recursive
Sequential Execution
Threading
Multiprocessing
Asynchronous
pass Keyword
Daemon
Global Interpreter Lock (GIL)

Review Questions

1. Which of the following is a correct way to define a user-defined function in Python?
A) function greet(): print("Hello")
B) def greet(): print("Hello")
C) func greet() { print("Hello") }
D) greet function(): print("Hello")
Answer: B

2. What will len([1, 2, 3, 4]) return?
A) 3
B) 4
C) 5
D) Error
Answer: B

3. *Which of the following is true about args?*
A) Stores keyword arguments in a dictionary
B) Stores positional arguments in a tuple
C) Allows only one argument
D) Must be the last parameter
Answer: B

4. Which statement about recursion is FALSE?
A) Recursion requires a base case
B) Recursive functions can call themselves
C) Recursion always uses less memory than iteration
D) Fibonacci can be implemented recursively
Answer: C

5. What is the output of this lambda function?
square = lambda x: x**2
print(square(5))
A) 5
B) 10
C) 25
D) None
Answer: C

6. Which threading method waits for a thread to finish before continuing execution?
A) start()
B) join()
C) is_alive()
D) daemon()
Answer: B

7. Which of the following correctly uses a keyword argument?
A) add(3, 4)
B) add(x=3, y=4)
C) add(4=y, 3=x)
D) add((3,4))
Answer: B

8. What is the purpose of the async keyword in Python?
A) To create a new thread
B) To mark a function as asynchronous
C) To execute a function immediately
D) To pause the program
Answer: B

9. Which of these is a built-in Python function?
A) factorial()
B) greet()
C) square()
D) my_function()
Answer: A

Review Exercises

1. Create a user-defined function called greet_user() that asks for a user's name and prints a greeting message.

2. Write a function multiply_numbers(*args) that accepts any number of numbers and returns their product.

3. Implement a recursive function factorial(n) to calculate the factorial of a given number.

4. Use a lambda function and map() to create a list of the cubes of numbers from 1 to 5.

5. Threading Exercise: Create three functions (task1, task2, task3) that print messages, then execute them concurrently using the threading module.

Class and Object

Python is a multi-paradigm language, but it is primarily **object-oriented (OOP)**, meaning everything in Python is treated as an object. Even fundamental data types such as integers, floats, strings, lists, dictionaries, functions, and modules are all objects.
Object-Oriented Programming (OOP) is based on five major principles:

1. **Class and Object**
2. **Inheritance**
3. **Polymorphism**
4. **Encapsulation**
5. **Abstraction**

Class

A class is a blueprint or template for creating objects. It is a user-defined data type, similar to built-in types like list, dict, str, float, and int. A class may contain functions (methods) and variables (attributes).
When a class is defined, no memory is allocated until an object is created.

Object

An object is a specific instance of a class. Objects store data and behavior defined by their class.

Attributes and Methods

Classes are composed of two main components:

1. **Methods**
   A *method* is a function defined inside a class. It implements the logic **or** behavior that characterizes the class. In simple terms, a function inside a class is called a method.

2. **Attributes**
   An *attribute* is a variable declared within a class to hold data. Thus, a variable inside a class is called an attribute.

Example – *Car Class Analogy*
A Car can serve as an example of a class, containing both attributes and methods.

Methods(functions)

brake	Stops the car
steer	Controls direction
gear	Changes speed or reverses

Attributes (Variables)

color	Color of the car.
speed	Represents the current speed of the car
fuel	Fuel level of the car.
brand	Manufacturer name.
model	Specific model name.

Creating a Class

A class is defined using the **class** keyword followed by the class name.

```
class Sample:
    pass
```

Or

```
class Sample():
    pass
```

Note

Both forms are valid. The second form (class Sample():) is often used when the class inherits from another class, for example:
class Sample(AnotherClass):
However, it can still be used independently.

Naming Conventions for Classes

1. Class names can start with either uppercase or lowercase letters, but UpperCamelCase (PascalCase) is preferred. eg MyClass
2. Class names cannot start with a digit (e.g., 12Sample is invalid).
3. Class names are case-sensitive (MyClass ≠ Myclass).
4. A class name can begin with an underscore, but this is uncommon.
5. Class names can combine letters and digits (e.g., MyClass23).

Example – The Car Class

```python
class Car:
    speed = 10
    fuel = 64.23

    def brake(self):
        return "Stop me when traffic light is red"

    def gear(self):
        status = "reversing"
        return status
```

Key Points

1. The class **Car** is defined using the **class** statement.
2. speed and fuel are **attributes** of the class.
3. brake() and gear() are **methods** of the class.
4. The keyword **self** represents the instance of the class.

Creating an Object

To instantiate a class, assign it to an object name:

```python
class Sample:
   pass

var = Sample()
```

The object (var) behaves like a variable that can access the class's methods and attributes.

Insight

Understanding Class as Module

In earlier chapters, we imported modules such as math. These modules are Python files (.py) that may contain classes, functions and variables defined in Python's library.

For example

›› import math

›› square_root = math.sqrt(16)

Here:

- math → class (module)
- sqrt → method (function)
- square_root → object (variable holding result)

Accessing Methods and Attributes

One of the core features of object-oriented programming (OOP) in Python is the ability to define classes and create objects (instances) from them.

Each object can access the attributes (data) and methods (functions) defined within its class.

When a class is defined—whether in the same program or imported from another module—its attributes and methods can be accessed and manipulated through its objects using dot notation.

Steps

1. Defining the class

```
class Sample:

    var = "sample"

    def sample_method(self):
        pass
```

2. Creating an object

```
sample = Sample()
```

3. Accessing methods and attributes

```
method = sample.sample_method()
attribute = sample.var
```

Example 1 – A simple class,

```python
class MyClass:

    num = 5.0

    def square(self, x):
        return x * x
```

```python
myclass = MyClass()
square = myclass.square(4)
var = myclass.num

print('Square of the number ->', square)
print('Attribute ->', var)
```

```
#Output
Square of the number -> 16
Attribute -> 5.0
```

Example 2 - Creating a Simple Math Class,

```python
class SimpleMath:

    pi = 3.1415
    def add(self, x, y):
        return x + y

    def sub(self, x, y):
        return x - y


simplemath = SimpleMath()

result1 = simplemath.add(3, 5)
result2 = simplemath.sub(10, 6)
pi_value = simplemath.pi

print("Using add() -> ", result1)
print("Using sub() -> ", result2)
print("Value of pi -> ", pi_value)
```

```
#Output
Using add() ->  8
Using sub() ->  4
Value of pi ->  3.1415
```

Creating Module

In Python, classes and their members (methods and attributes) can be defined in one program and used in another. This is made possible through the use of **modules**. A module is simply a Python file (**.py**) that contains definitions of classes, functions, and variables which can be imported and reused in other programs.
By organizing classes into separate modules, you can make your code more structured, reusable, and easier to maintain. This concept forms the foundation of **modular programming** in Python.

This promotes:

1. Code reusability
2. Modularity
3. Simplified maintenance
4. Reduced redundancy

Steps to Create and Use a Custom Module

1. Navigate to your working directory and create a new Python file named **smallmath.py**.
2. Write the following code inside **smallmath.py**:

```
#smallmath.py

class Math:

    def rectangle(self, width, height):
        area = width * height
        return f"Area is {area} cm²"
```

3. In the same directory, create another file named **geometry.py**.
4. Import the module in geometry.py:

```
#geometry.py

import smallmath                # Importing all classes
from smallmath import Math      # Importing a specific class
```

5. Access the class and method:

```
#geometry.py

from smallmath import Math

smallmath = Math()
print(smallmath.rectangle(4, 6))
```

```
#Output
Area is 24 cm²
```

Static Methods

In the examples above, the first parameter in every method is **self**. **self** represents the **instance** of the class and allows access to attributes and methods within it. Without **self**, the method cannot reference the instance or be accessed externally.

If you want a method to be used without the **self** parameter, you can declare it as a **static method** using the **@staticmethod** decorator.

Example – Static Method

```
Python

class Math:

    @staticmethod
    def add(x, y):
        return x + y


#Accessing method without instantiating the class:
result = Math.add(4, 6)
print(result)
```

```
#Output
10
```

Inheritance

Inheritance is a key feature of Object-Oriented Programming (OOP) that allows one class to inherit the attributes and methods of another class. It promotes code reusability, hierarchical organization, and extension of existing logic without rewriting code.

When a class **B** inherits from another class **A**, all the methods and attributes of class **A** become available to class **B**, unless they are declared **private** or explicitly restricted.
To inherit from a class, the parent class is placed inside parentheses after the child class definition.

Example 1 – Creating an Animal Class and Inheriting It

Python

```
class Animal:
    def cat(self):
        return "milk"

    def monkey(self):
        return "banana"


# Inheriting the Animal class
class Feed(Animal):

    def favorites(self):
        cat = self.cat()
        monkey = self.monkey()
        return f"Cats love {cat}\nMonkeys love {monkey}"


feed = Feed()
fav = feed.favorites()
print(fav)
```

```
#Output
Cats love milk
Monkeys love banana
```

Key Points

1. cat() and monkey() methods are defined in the **Animal** class.
2. The **Feed** class inherits **Animal** by placing (Animal) in its definition.

3. The **self** keyword allows access to inherited methods as though they were defined in the current class (Feed).

Example 2 – Inheriting a class from a different file

script1.py

```python
class Data:

    def add(self,data):
        size = len(data)
        total = sum(data)
        return {'size':size, 'total':total}
```

script2.py

```python
from script1 import Data

class Main(Data):

    def average(self, *args):
        result = self.add(args)
        size = result.get('size')
        total = result.get('total')

        avg = total/size
        return f"Average is -> {avg}"


main = Main()
print(main.average(4, 5, 10, 3))
```

```
#Output
Average is -> 5.5
```

Polymorphism

Polymorphism (meaning *many forms*) is another major principle of OOP. It allows different classes to define methods with the same name but possibly different implementations.
This provides flexibility, as a single method name can behave differently across various objects.

Example – Multiple Classes with a Common Method,

```python
class English:
    def greet(self):
        return "Hello"

class French:
    def greet(self):
        return "Bonjour"

class Italian:
    def greet(self):
        return "Ciao"

languages = [English(), French(), Italian()]

for obj in languages:
    print(obj.greet())
```

```
#Output
Hello
Bonjour
Ciao
```

Key Points

1. Three classes (English, French, Italian) define the same method greet().
2. The **for** loop iterates through a list of class instances and calls greet() for each.
3. Despite using the same method name, the output differs depending on the class.

Polymorphism simplifies code by treating different objects with a shared interface uniformly.

The __init__() Method (Constructor)

The __init__() method is a constructor in Python classes.
It is automatically called when a class object (instance) is created. Its main purpose is to initialize attributes and prepare the class for use.

Key Roles of __init__()

1. Initializes class attributes and methods.
2. Automatically executes when an object is instantiated.
3. Receives arguments passed during object creation.
4. Declares **global instance attributes** using the self keyword.

> **Note**
>
> Attributes that are not prefixed with **self** are **local** and cannot be accessed by other methods within the class. The **self** keyword makes attributes instance-wide and accessible throughout the class.

Example – Creating a Circle Class,

Python

```
class Circle:
    def __init__(self):
        self.pi = 3.1415

    def area(self, radius):
        result = self.pi * pow(radius, 2)
        return result


circle = Circle()
result = circle.area(25)
print(result)
```

```
#Output
1963.4375
```

Encapsulation

Encapsulation is the concept of **restricting access** to certain parts of an object to protect data integrity. It hides internal details of a class from the outside world, allowing only specific interfaces (methods) to modify or access data.
In Python:

- **Protected attributes** start with a single underscore (_attribute) – these are intended for internal use but can still be accessed if needed.
- **Private attributes** start with a double underscore (__attribute) – these are name-mangled and cannot be accessed directly outside the class.

Example – Creating a Car Class with Private Attributes,

Python

```python
class Car:
    def __init__(self):
        self.__speed = 10.26

    def get_acceleration(self):
        return self.__speed


class Automobile:
    def __init__(self):
        self.car = Car()
        # Trying to access private attribute
        self.speed = self.car.__speed


auto = Automobile()
```

```
#Output
AttributeError: 'Car' object has no attribute '_Automobile__speed'
```

Key Points

1. The attribute __speed is private in the Car class.
2. Automobile creates an instance of Car but cannot directly access __speed.
3. Attempting to do so raises an AttributeError.

Insight

To properly access a private attribute, you should provide a **getter** or **setter** method within the class.

Example – Accessing Private Attributes Safely,

```
Python
class Car:
    def __init__(self):
        self.__speed = 10.26

    def get_speed(self):
        return self.__speed


car = Car()
print(car.get_speed())
```

```
#Output
10.26
```

- This maintains data protection while still allowing controlled access.

Argument Class (Parameterized)

Just like functions, classes can receive arguments. Arguments are passed to the class through the __init__() constructor and become accessible to all methods via **self**.
Arguments can be of any data type — numbers, strings, lists, tuples, dictionaries, files, or even other objects.

Example 1 – Math Class with Parameterized Constructor,

```
Python
import math

class Math:
    def __init__(self, x):
        self.x = x
        sqr = self.square()
        fact = self.factorial()

        print(f"The square of {x} is {sqr}")
        print(f"The factorial of {x} is {fact}")

    def square(self):
        return self.x ** 2
```

```
    def factorial(self):
        return math.factorial(self.x)


Math(4)
```

```
#Output
The square of 4 is 16
The factorial of 4 is 24
```

Example 2 – Rectangle Class,

```
Python

class Rectangle:
    def __init__(self, length, width):
        self.length = length
        self.width = width

    def area(self):
        return self.length * self.width

    def perimeter(self):
        return 2 * (self.length + self.width)

rect = Rectangle(20, 10)

print("Area of a rectangle -> ", rect.area())
print("Perimeter of a rectangle -> ", rect.perimeter())
```

```
#Output
Area of a rectangle ->  200
Perimeter of a rectangle ->  60
```

The __str__() or __repr__() Method

The **__str__()** method is a **special (magic) method** that defines how an object should be represented as a string. It is automatically called when the object is passed to **print()** or converted to a string using **str()**.
This allows a class to behave like a built-in function by returning a human-readable string instead of a memory reference.

Example – Average Class,

Python

```python
class Average:
    def __init__(self, *args):
        self.entries = args

    def __str__(self):
        return f"{self.avg()}"

    def avg(self):
        total = sum(self.entries)
        length = len(self.entries)
        return total / length


result = Average(10, 20, 30)
print(result)
```

```
#Output
20.0
```

Insight

The *args syntax allows the class to receive an unknown number of arguments, making it flexible and dynamic.

Abstraction

Abstraction is the process of hiding complex implementation details and exposing only essential features to the user. It helps reduce complexity and increases program clarity by separating *what* an object does from *how* it does it.

In Python, abstraction is achieved through **abstract classes** and **abstract methods** defined in the abc (Abstract Base Class) module.

Example – Using Abstraction in Python,

```python
from abc import ABC, abstractmethod

class Shape(ABC):
    @abstractmethod
    def area(self):
        pass

class Rectangle(Shape):
    def __init__(self, width, height):
        self.width = width
        self.height = height

    def area(self):
        return self.width * self.height


class Circle(Shape):
    def __init__(self, radius):
        self.radius = radius

    def area(self):
        return 3.1415 * (self.radius ** 2)


shapes = [Rectangle(5, 10), Circle(7)]

for shape in shapes:
    print(shape.area())
```

```
#Output
50
153.9335
```

Key Points

1. Shape is an abstract class — it cannot be instantiated directly.
2. The method area() is an abstract method that must be implemented in all subclasses.

Key Terms

Polymorphism
Constructor (__init__)
Instance Attributes
Encapsulation
Private Attributes
Getter/Setter Methods
Parameterized Constructor
Magic Methods (__str__, __repr__)
Abstract Class
Abstraction

Review Questions

1. Which of the following is true about polymorphism in Python?
a) Methods must have different names in each class
b) Objects of different classes can use the same method name
c) Only inheritance enables polymorphism
d) Python does not support polymorphism
Answer: b

2. What does the __init__() method do in Python classes?
a) Declares class methods
b) Initializes instance attributes when an object is created
c) Destroys an object
d) Converts a class to a string
Answer: b

3. Which of the following indicates a private attribute in Python?
a) __speed
b) _speed
c) speed
d) speed__
Answer: a

4. What is the purpose of the @abstractmethod **decorator?**
a) To create a static method
b) To hide a method
c) To initialize a class attribute
d) To enforce implementation in subclasses
Answer: d

5. What does the __str__() method in a class do?
a) Returns a developer-readable representation of an object
b) Returns a human-readable string of an object
c) Initializes the object
d) Defines private attributes
Answer: b

Review Exercises

1. Explain the difference between class attributes and instance attributes.
2. How does Python achieve polymorphism without requiring inheritance?
3. Why are getter and setter methods important for encapsulation?
4. What is the difference between __str__() and __repr__() methods in Python?
5. Describe how abstract classes enforce abstraction in Python.

Random, Calendar and Datetime

Random Module

The random module is one of Python's most widely used libraries, particularly in areas such as game development, simulations, cryptography, and statistical modeling. It allows for the generation of random numbers and the selection of elements in a non-linear or unsequential manner.

Random Methods

Function	Definition
random.random()	Returns a random floating-point number between 0.0 and 1.0.
random.choice(iterable)	Randomly selects a single element from a sequence (list, tuple, string, etc.).
random.choices(iterable)	Returns a list of k randomly selected elements from a sequence, with optional weights for probability control.
random.randint(a, b)	Returns a random integer between a and b (both inclusive).
random.randrange(start, end)	Returns a random integer within a range, similar to range().
random.shuffle(iterable)	Randomly rearranges the elements of a mutable sequence.
random.uniform(a, b)	Returns a random float in the range [a, b].
random.triangular(low,high, mode)	Returns a random float from a Triangular distribution.
random.sample(population, k)	Returns a unique list of k elements randomly selected from the population.
random.seed()	Initializes the random number generator with a seed to produce repeatable results.
random.randbytes(n)	Returns a bytes object with n random bytes.
random.getstate()	Returns the current internal state of the random number generator.
random.setstate(state)	Restores the random number generator state to a previously saved state.
random.betavariate(alpha,beta)	Returns a random float from a Beta distribution with parameters alpha and beta.
random.binomialvariate(n, p)	Returns a random number based on a Binomial distribution, where n is the number of trials and p is the probability of success in each trial.
random.expovariate(lambda)	Returns a random number from an Exponential distribution with a given lambda (λ), which determines the rate of decay.
random.gammavariate(alpha,beta)	Returns a random number based on a Gamma distribution with shape alpha and scale beta.
random.gauss(mu, sigma)	Generates a random number from a Gaussian (Normal) distribution with mean mu and standard deviation sigma.
random.getrandbits(k)	Returns a random integer represented by k random bits.
random.lognormvariate(mu,sigma)	Generates a number from a Log-normal distribution, where mu and sigma determine the shape.
random.normalvariate(mu,sigma)	Returns a random number based on a Normal (Gaussian) distribution.

random.paretovariate(alpha)	Generates a random number following a Pareto distribution with a shape parameter alpha.
random.vonmisesvariate(mu,kappa)	Generates a random number from a Von Mises distribution (used in circular data analysis).
random.weibullvariate(alpha,beta)	Returns a random number based on a Weibull distribution, which is commonly used in reliability engineering.

Table 4.5

random()

Python

```
from random import random

value1 = random()
value2 = random()
print(value1)
print(value2)
```

```
#Output
0.4418865459215676
0.38348600994947124
```

randint(a, b)

Python

```
from random import randint

value1 = randint(1, 10)
value2 = randint(15, 20)
print(f"Values between 1-10 -> {value1}")
print(f"Values between 15-20 -> {value2}")
```

```
#Output
Values between 1-10 -> 4
Values between 15-20 -> 19
```

randrange(start, end, step)

Python

```
from random import randrange

value1 = randrange(10)          #start=0, end=10, step=1
value2 = randrange(100, 150)    #start=100, end=150, step=1
```

```
value3 = randrange(10, 30, 5)    #start=10, end=30, step=5

print(f"Values range from 0-10 -> {value1}")
print(f"Values range from 100-150 -> {value2}")
print(f"Values range from 10-30 -> {value3}")
```

```
#Output
Values range from 0-10 -> 4
Values range from 100-150 -> 130
Values range from 10-30 -> 15
```

choice(iterable)

```
Python
from random import choice

value1 = choice(["Python", "C++", "Java", "JavaScript"])
value2 = choice((4, 10, 20, 5))
print(value1)
print(value2)
```

```
#Output
JavaScript
10
```

choices(iterable)

```
Python
from random import choices

var1 = choices(["lion", "tiger", "crocodile"])
var2 = choices((100, 150, 200, 250, 300))
print(var1)
print(var2)
```

```
#Output
['tiger']
[200]
```

gauss(a, b)

```
Python
from random import gauss

value = gauss(1, 10)
print(value)
```

```
#Output
-14.414841715143382
```

sample(iterable, size, count)

```
Python
from random import sample

var1 = sample(["berry", "grapes", "orange", "apple"], 3)
var2 = sample(["berry", "grapes", "orange", "apple"], 1)
var3 = sample(["berry","grapes","orange","apple"],2,counts=[1,0,0,1])
print(var1)
print(var2)
print(var3)
```

```
#Output
['apple', 'berry', 'grapes']
['grapes']
['berry', 'apple']
```

uniform(a, b)

```
Python
from random import uniform

result = uniform(10, 100)
print(result)
```

```
#Output
29.433741695382583
```

Insight

The Guess Game

The Guess Game is an interactive game where the user inputs a number within a specified range. If the entered number matches the randomly generated number by the program, the user wins. Otherwise, they must continue guessing until they find the correct number. However, the game can be terminated at any time by entering a non-digit character.

```
from random import randint

def guess():

    while True:
        guessed = randint(1, 10)
        entry = input("Enter a number between 1-10: ")
        if guessed == int(entry):
            print("Congratulations!.\nYou've guessed it right")
            break
        print(f"Ouch!,the number is -> {guessed}\nYou may guess again\n")


guess()
```

```
=========================================================

Enter a number between 1-10: 3
Ouch!,the number is -> 5
You may guess again

Enter a number between 1-10: 6
Congratulations!.
You've guessed it right
```

Calendar Module

The **calendar** module is essential for working with dates and time in a system. It allows you to display the calendar for any given year, past or future. Additionally, it provides various methods for checking leap years, retrieving the number of days in a month, and working with months and weekdays.

Calendar Methods

Function	Definition
calendar.calendar	The main module used for handling date-related functionalities.
calendar.day_abbr	A list of abbreviated weekday names (e.g., ['Mon', 'Tue', 'Wed', ...]).
calendar.day_name	A list of full weekday names (e.g., ['Monday', 'Tuesday', ...]).
calendar.different_locale	Returns the current setting for the first day of the week (default is Monday).
calendar.firstweekday()	Sets the first day of the week (e.g., setfirstweekday(calendar.SUNDAY)).
calendar.format(formatstring)	Used for formatting calendar outputs.
calendar.formatstring	A string pattern used for formatting calendar output.
calendar.isleap(year)	Checks if a given year is a leap year (returns True or False).
calendar.leapdays(y1, y2)	Returns the number of leap years between two years (exclusive).
calendar.mdays	A list where the index represents a month (1-12), and the value is the number of days in that month.
calendar.month(year, month)	Returns a string representation of a month's calendar.
calendar.month_abbr	A list of abbreviated month names (e.g., ['', 'Jan', 'Feb', 'Mar', ...]).
calendar.month_name	month_name: A list of full month names (e.g., ['', 'January', 'February', ...]).
calendar.monthcalendar(yr, m)	Returns a list of weeks for the specified month. Each week is a list of seven integers, where 0 represents days outside the month.
calendar.monthrange(year, month)	Returns a tuple (start_day, num_days), where start_day is the weekday index of the first day of the month, and num_days is the total number of days in that month.
calendar.prcal(year,w, l, c)	Prints a formatted calendar for a full year.
calendar.prmonth(yr, m, w, l)	Prints a formatted calendar for a single month.
calendar.setfirstweekday(weekday)	Sets the first day of the week (e.g., setfirstweekday(calendar.SUNDAY)).
calendar.timegm(tuple)	Converts a time tuple (like one returned by time.gmtime()) into a Unix timestamp (seconds since epoch).
calendar.weekday(year, month,day)	Returns the weekday index for a given date (Monday = 0, Sunday = 6).
weekheader	Returns a header string with abbreviated weekday names up to n characters per name.

Table 4.6

calendar(theyear = int, w = int , l=int, c=int, m=int) **, prcal(yr, m, w, l)**

```
Python
from calendar import calendar

cal = calendar(theyear=2026, m=4)
print(cal)
```

```
#Output
                                                  2026

      January                   February                   March                     April
Mo Tu We Th Fr Sa Su      Mo Tu We Th Fr Sa Su      Mo Tu We Th Fr Sa Su      Mo Tu We Th Fr Sa Su
          1  2  3  4                         1                         1             1  2  3  4  5
 5  6  7  8  9 10 11       2  3  4  5  6  7  8       2  3  4  5  6  7  8       6  7  8  9 10 11 12
12 13 14 15 16 17 18       9 10 11 12 13 14 15       9 10 11 12 13 14 15      13 14 15 16 17 18 19
19 20 21 22 23 24 25      16 17 18 19 20 21 22      16 17 18 19 20 21 22      20 21 22 23 24 25 26
26 27 28 29 30 31         23 24 25 26 27 28         23 24 25 26 27 28 29      27 28 29 30
                                                    30 31

        May                       June                      July                     August
Mo Tu We Th Fr Sa Su      Mo Tu We Th Fr Sa Su      Mo Tu We Th Fr Sa Su      Mo Tu We Th Fr Sa Su
             1  2  3       1  2  3  4  5  6  7             1  2  3  4  5                      1  2
 4  5  6  7  8  9 10       8  9 10 11 12 13 14       6  7  8  9 10 11 12       3  4  5  6  7  8  9
11 12 13 14 15 16 17      15 16 17 18 19 20 21      13 14 15 16 17 18 19      10 11 12 13 14 15 16
18 19 20 21 22 23 24      22 23 24 25 26 27 28      20 21 22 23 24 25 26      17 18 19 20 21 22 23
25 26 27 28 29 30 31      29 30                     27 28 29 30 31            24 25 26 27 28 29 30
                                                                              31

     September                  October                   November                  December
Mo Tu We Th Fr Sa Su      Mo Tu We Th Fr Sa Su      Mo Tu We Th Fr Sa Su      Mo Tu We Th Fr Sa Su
    1  2  3  4  5  6                1  2  3  4                         1          1  2  3  4  5  6
 7  8  9 10 11 12 13       5  6  7  8  9 10 11       2  3  4  5  6  7  8       7  8  9 10 11 12 13
14 15 16 17 18 19 20      12 13 14 15 16 17 18       9 10 11 12 13 14 15      14 15 16 17 18 19 20
21 22 23 24 25 26 27      19 20 21 22 23 24 25      16 17 18 19 20 21 22      21 22 23 24 25 26 27
28 29 30                  26 27 28 29 30 31         23 24 25 26 27 28 29      28 29 30 31
```

month(year, month) **, prmonth**(yr, m)

```
Python
>>> from calendar import *
>>>
>>> month(2026, 6)
...  June 2026
Mo Tu We Th Fr Sa Su
 1  2  3  4  5  6  7
 8  9 10 11 12 13 14
15 16 17 18 19 20 21
22 23 24 25 26 27 28
29 30

>>> prmonth(2026, 12)
...  December 2026
Mo Tu We Th Fr Sa Su
```

```
    1  2  3  4  5  6
 7  8  9 10 11 12 13
14 15 16 17 18 19 20
21 22 23 24 25 26 27
28 29 30 31
```

monthcalendar(year, month**)**

●●● Python

```
>>> from calendar import monthcalendar
>>> monthcalendar(2026, 3)
... [[0, 0, 0, 0, 0, 0, 1], [2, 3, 4, 5, 6, 7, 8], [9, 10, 11, 12, 13, 14,
15], [16, 17, 18, 19, 20, 21, 22], [23, 24, 25, 26, 27, 28, 29], [30, 31,
0, 0, 0, 0, 0]]
```

isleap(year = int**)**

●●● Python

```
>>> from calendar import isleap
>>> isleap(2025)
... False
>>> isleap(2024)
... True
```

leapdays(year, year**)**

●●● Python

```
>>> from calendar import leapdays
>>> leapdays(2014, 2026)
... 3
```

monthrange(year, month**)**

●●● Python

```
>>> from calendar import monthrange
>>> monthrange(2026, 9)
... (1, 30)
```

Datetime Module

The datetime module in Python is used to work with **dates and times** based on the system's current settings. It provides several methods for handling months, years, time zones, and formatting date-time values.

Datetime Methods

Function	Definition
astimezone	Converts the given datetime object to the specified time zone (tz). It is useful for handling time zones when working with global applications.
combine(date, time)	Combines a date object and a time object into a single datetime object.
ctime	Returns a string representation of the date-time in a human-readable format.
date	Extracts and returns the date portion from a datetime object.
day	Returns the day of the month as an integer (1-31).
dst	Returns the daylight saving time (DST) offset for time zones that observe DST.
fold	Used when dealing with ambiguous times in time zones that observe DST transitions.
fromisocalendar(yr,wk,d)	Converts an ISO calendar (year, week number, weekday) into a datetime object.
fromisoformat	Converts an ISO 8601 formatted string into a datetime object.
fromordinal(ordinal)	Converts a Gregorian ordinal (days since 01-01-0001) into a date object.
fromtimestamp	Converts a timestamp (seconds since epoch) into a datetime object.
hour	Returns the hour of the day (0-23).
isocalendar	Returns a tuple representing the year, week number, and weekday.
isoformat	Returns an ISO 8601 formatted string of the datetime object.
isoweekday	Returns the weekday as an integer (1=Monday, 7=Sunday).
max, min	datetime.max → The maximum representable date-time (9999-12-31 23:59:59.999999). datetime.min → The minimum representable date-time (0001-01-01 00:00:00).
microsecond	Returns the microsecond component of the datetime object (0-999999).
minute	Returns the minute of the hour (0-59).
month	Returns the month of the year (1-12).
now	Returns the current local date-time. If a time zone (tz) is provided, it returns the date-time in that time zone.
replace	Returns a new datetime object with modified values.
resolution	Returns the smallest time unit (datetime can measure microseconds).
second	Returns the second component (0-59).
strftime(format)	Converts a datetime object into a formatted string.
strptime(string, format)	Parses a string and converts it into a datetime object based on the given format.
time()	Extracts the time portion from a datetime object.
timestamp()	Returns the timestamp (seconds since epoch) for a datetime object.
timetuple()	Returns a time.struct_time object representing the date-time.
timetz()	Extracts the time and time zone from a datetime object.
today()	Returns the current local date.

toordinal()	Converts the datetime object to a Gregorian ordinal (days since 01-01-0001).
tzinfo()	Returns information about the time zone of the datetime object.
tzname()	Returns information about the time zone of the datetime object.
utcfromtimestamp()	Converts a timestamp into a UTC datetime object.
utcnow()	Returns the current UTC date-time.
utcoffset()	Returns the time zone offset from UTC.
utctimetuple()	Converts a datetime object to a UTC time.struct_time.
weekday()	Returns the day of the week (0=Monday, 6=Sunday).
year	Returns the year as integer

Table 4.7

now() , today()

Python

```
>>> from datetime import datetime
>>> today = datetime.now()
>>> print(today)
... 2026-01-22 22:31:30.810541

>>> #date()
>>> today = datetime.now()
>>> print(today.date())
... 2026-01-22

>>> #day
>>> today = datetime.now()
>>> print(today.day)
... 22

>>> #weekday()
>>> today = datetime.now()
>>> print(today.weekday())
... 2

>>> #month
>>> today = datetime.now()
>>> print(today.month)
... 1

>>> #year
>>> today = datetime.now()
>>> print(today.year)
... 2026
```

```
>>> #time()
>>> today = datetime.now()
>>> print(today.time())
... 22:43:42.802373

>>> #hour
>>> today = datetime.now()
>>> print(today.hour)
... 22

>>> #minute
>>> today = datetime.now()
>>> print(today.minute)
... 43

>>> #microsecond / second
>>> today = datetime.now()
>>> print(today.microsecond)
... 802373
```

date(year, month, day **)**

```
Python
import datetime

date = datetime.date(2027,4,22)
print(f"day->{date.day} month->{date.month} year->{date.year}")
```

```
#Output
day->22 month->4 year->2027
```

time(hour, minute, second, microsecond **)**

```
Python
import datetime

time = datetime.time(4,16,5,489)
print(f"hour-> {time.hour} minute-> {time.minute}")
```

strftime(format)

Format	Definition	Example
%Y	Four-digit year	2025
%y	Two-digit year	25 (for 2025)
%m	Month	01 to 12
%B	Full month name	March
%b / %h	Abbreviated month name	Mar
%d	Day of the month	01 to 31
%j	Day of the year	001 to 366
%H	Hour (24 hour format)	00 to 23
%I	Hour (12 hour format)	01 to 12
%p	AM/PM notation	AM or PM
%M	Minutes	00 to 59
%S	Seconds	00 to 59
%f	Microseconds	000000 to 999999
%z	UTC offset	+0000, -0400
%Z	Timezone name	UTC, EST, IST
%A	Full weekday name	Monday
%a	Abbreviated weekday name	Mon
%w	Weekday as a number (Sun =0, Mon =1)	0 to 6
%W	Week number of the year (Monday start)	00 to 53
%U	Week number of the year (Sunday start)	00 to 53
%c	Full date and time representation	Sat Mar 31 14:30:45 2025
%x	Date representation	03/31/2025
%X	Time representation	14:30:45

Table 4.8

Python

```
>>> from datetime import datetime
>>> today = datetime.now()
>>> print(today)
... 2026-01-22 22:31:30.810541
>>> date = today.strftime("%d - %m - %Y")
>>> print(date)
... 22 - 01 - 2026
>>> date = today.strftime("%d  %B,  %Y")
>>> print(date)
... 22  January, 2026
>>> date_time = today.strftime("%d  %B,  %Y %H: %M:%S")
>>> print(date_time)
... 22  January, 2026 23: 32:01
>>> date_time = today.strftime("%c")
>>> print(date_time)
... Thu Jan 22 23:40:46 2026
```

Key Terms

randint
shuffle
sample
strftime
timedelta

Review Questions

1. Which method returns a random integer between two given values (inclusive)?
a) random()
b) randint()
c) uniform()
d) choice()
Answer: b

2. Which calendar method returns the weekday index of the first day of a given month and the total number of days?
a) monthcalendar()
b) month()
c) monthrange()
d) prmonth()
Answer: c

3. Which method in datetime gives the current local date and time?
a) datetime.today()
b) datetime.now()
c) datetime.time()
d) datetime.date()
Answer: b

4. Which random method returns multiple unique elements from a sequence?
a) choice()
b) choices()
c) sample()
d) shuffle()
Answer: c

5. What does %B represent in strftime format strings?
a) Abbreviated month name
b) Full month name
c) Day of the year
d) Hour (24-hour format)
Answer: b

Review Exercises

1. **Random Module Exercise**:
   Write a Python program to simulate rolling a six-sided dice 10 times using randint(), and print the results.

2. **Calendar Module Exercise**:
   Using the calendar module, print the calendar for July 2026 and check if 2024 is a leap year.

3. **Datetime Module Exercise**:
   Write a program that prints today's date in the format: Friday, January 22, 2026 using strftime().

OS and SYS Module

OS (Operating System) Module

The OS module is a crucial library in Python programming as it provides direct access to the underlying operating system. It allows users to create and rename files, manage system resources, and retrieve system information. Its functionalities are broadly categorized into the following groups:

File and Directory Management
Handling file creation, deletion, and renaming.

Process Management
Managing system processes and execution.

System Information Retrieval
Fetching system details such as OS type, environment variables, and user information.

Path and Directory Navigation
Working with file paths, directories, and symbolic links.

Permissions and Security
Managing file access permissions and inheritance.

OS Methods

File and Directory Management

Function	Definition
mkdir	Creates a directory.
makedirs	Creates a directory along with any necessary parent directories.
rmdir	Removes an empty directory.
removedirs	Removes multiple nested directories.
rename	Renames a file or directory.
renames	Renames a file, creating any needed intermediate directories.
replace	Replaces a file or directory.
remove	Deletes a file.
unlink	Alias for remove(), used to delete a file.
listdir	Lists files and directories in a specified path.
scandir	Returns an iterator for directory entries.
walk	Generates file names in a directory tree.

Table 4.9

mkdir(path, mode) , makedirs(path, mode)

```
••• Python
import os

#Creates mydocument directory
os.mkdir("mydocument")

#Creates download then mydocument directory
os.makedirs("download/mydocument")
```

listdir()

```
••• Python
import os

for folder in os.listdir():
    print(folder)
```

```
#Output
download
mydocument
```

rename(src, dst)

```
••• Python
import os
os.rename("download", "fetched")
os.rename("mydocument", "docs")

#list dirs
print(os.listdir())
```

```
#Output
['docs', 'fetched']
```

renames(old, path)

```
••• Python
import os
os.renames("music/mysong.mp3", "songs/myaudio.mp3")
```

replace(src, dst)

```python
import os
os.replace("mydocs", "newdocs")
```

remove(path) , unlink(path)

```python
import os
os.remove("docs/myfile.docx")
os.unlink("fetched/image.png")
```

scandir(path)

```python
import os
for file in os.scandir("docs"):
    print(file)
```

```
#Output
<DirEntry 'classic_music.mp3'>
<DirEntry 'flower.png'>
<DirEntry 'mytext.txt'>
```

walk(path)

```python
import os
for file in os.walk("."):
    print(file)
```

```
#Output
('.\\docs', [], ['classic_music.mp3', 'flower.png', 'mytext.txt'])
('.\\music', [], ['cool.mp3', 'favorite.mp3', 'great_movie.mp4'])
```

Process Management

Function	Definition
abort	Immediately terminates the process.
kill	Sends a signal to terminate a process by its PID.
waitpid	Waits for a child process to terminate.
system	Executes a command in the system shell.
spawnl, spawnle, spawnv, spawnve	Starts a new process.
execl, execle, execlp, execlpe, execv, execve, execvp, execvpe	Replaces the current process with a new one.
popen	Opens a pipe to a command.

Table 5.0

system("command")

Python

```
>>> import os
>>> version = os.system("Python --version")
>>> print(version)
... Python 3.13.0

>>> os.system("ipconfig/all")
...Windows IP Configuration
   Host Name . . . . . . . . . . . . : MyPC
   Primary Dns Suffix . . . . . . . :
   Node Type . . . . . . . . . . . . : Mixed
   IP Routing Enabled. . . . . . . . : No
   WINS Proxy Enabled. . . . . . . . : No
```

Note

os.system() requires native OS commands, which are specific to the operating system platform. The examples above use Windows OS commands, which differ from those used in Linux or macOS.

getpid( ) , getppid( ) , kill(pid, signal)

Python

```
>>> import os
>>> import signal
```

```
>>> pid = os.getpid()
>>> print(pid)
... 18572

>>> pid = os.getppid()
>>> print(pid)
... 32008

>>> pid = 32008
os.kill(pid, signal.SIGTERM)
```

System Information

Function	Definition
getcwd	Returns the current working directory.
getcwdb	Returns the current working directory as bytes.
getpid	Returns the process ID of the current process.
getppid	Returns the parent process ID.
getlogin	Returns the username of the logged-in user.
uname	Retrieves system-related information like OS name and version.
environ	Returns environment variables.
getenv	Fetches the value of an environment variable.
putenv	Sets an environment variable.
unsetenv	Removes an environment variable.

Table 5.1

```
Python
>>> import os

>>> #getcwd()
>>> cwd = os.getcwd()
>>> print(cwd)
... D:\Project\document

>>> #getpid()
>>> pid = os.getpid()
>>> print(pid)
... 25448
```

```
>>> #getlogin()
>>> user = os.getlogin()
>>> print(user)
... Asiedu

>>> #getenv()
>>> env = os.getenv("JAVA_HOME")
>>> print(env)
... C:\Program Files\Java\jdk-21

>>> #putenv()
>>> os.putenv("JAVA_HOME", "D:/Project/Java/jdk-21")
...
>>> #environ()
>>> env = os.environ
>>> print(env)
... []
```

Path and Direction Navigation

Function	Definition
chdir	Changes the current working directory.
curdir	Represents the current directory (".").
pardir	Represents the parent directory ("..").
altsep	Alternate path separator.
pathsep	Separator used for file paths in PATH environment variable.
sep	The OS-specific file path separator (/ for Linux, \ for Windows).
extsep	Extension separator (.).

Table 5.2

Python

```
>>> import os
>>> #chdir()
>>> os.chdir("media/video")

>>> #curdir
>>> cur = os.curdir
>>>  print(cur)
... .
```

```
>>> #pathsep
>>> print(os.pathsep)
... ;

>>> #sep
>>> print(os.sep)
... \
```

Permissions and Security

Function	Definition
chmod	Changes the permissions of a file.
lchmod	Changes the permissions of a symbolic link.
fchmod	Changes file permissions using a file descriptor.
access	Checks user permissions for a file or directory.
umask	Sets the file mode creation mask.

Table 5.3

System Utilities

Function	Definition
open	Opens a file descriptor.
close	Closes a file descriptor.
dup, dup2	Duplicates file descriptors.
fsync	Flushes file data to disk.
truncate	Truncates a file to a given size.
read	Reads data from a file descriptor.
write	Writes data to a file descriptor.
lseek	Moves the file pointer to a specific position.
cpu_count	Returns the number of CPU cores available.
get_terminal_size	Returns the terminal window size.
isatty	Checks if a file descriptor refers to a terminal.
urandom	Generates secure random bytes.
linesep	Returns the OS-specific line separator (\n for Linux/macOS, \r\n for Windows).
error	Contains error-related exception classes.
strerror	Returns error message strings based on error codes.

Table 5.4

SYS Module

The **sys** module is a powerful utility in Python used to interact with and retrieve abstract information about the system. It provides access to details about the operating system, the Python runtime environment, and interpreter configuration. This module is widely used for handling system-level functionalities, command-line arguments, runtime configuration, and process management.

Key Functionalities of the sys Module

The sys module's functionality can be broadly categorized into the following areas:

📌 System & Environment Information
Retrieve system-related details like OS, version, and execution environment.

📌 Python Runtime Configuration
Access interpreter settings, execution parameters, and runtime limits.

📌 Memory & Performance Management
Optimize memory allocation and manage recursion limits.

📌 Input/Output Handling
Redirect standard input, output, and error streams.

📌 Module & Path Management
Modify the Python module search path and interact with the import system.

SYS Methods

System & Environment Information

Method	Definition
argv	Retrieves command-line arguments passed to the script.
executable	Returns the path of the Python interpreter binary.
platform	Returns the name of the operating system.
winver	Retrieves the Windows version (Windows only).
getwindowsversion	Returns version information about Windows OS (Windows only).
hexversion	Returns Python's version as a hexadecimal number.
version	Returns the Python version.
version_info	Provides version details as a tuple.
copyright	Displays Python's copyright information.
dllhandle	Returns the DLL handle of the Python process (Windows).
orig_argv	Retrieves the original command-line arguments.

flags	Displays command-line flags passed to the interpreter.
prefix	Returns the installation directory of Python.
base_prefix	Similar to base_exec_prefix, returns the base directory.
base_exec_prefix	Gets the base directory of the Python installation.
platlibdir	Retrieves the directory for platform-specific libraries.

Table 5.5

Command-Line Arguments with sys.argv

The **sys.argv** list, provided by the sys module, allows a Python program to access command-line arguments passed during execution. These arguments are supplied when the script is run from the command line and are automatically stored as a list of strings.

The first element, **sys.argv[0]**, represents the name of the script itself, while the subsequent elements (**sys.argv[1]**, **sys.argv[2]**, etc.) contain the arguments entered by the user, separated by whitespace.

Note

All command-line arguments are received as **strings**. You can explicitly convert them to other data types (such as int or float) when needed.

Example 1 (sample.py),

Python
```
#sample.py

import sys

filename = sys.argv[0]
first_item = sys.argv[1]
all_items = sys.argv[1:]

print(f"Filename -> {filename}")
print(f"First Item -> {first_item}")
print(f"Items -> {all_items}")
```

Command Line Execution:

```
PS D:\Project\Document> python  sample.py  lion crocodile antelope
Filename -> sample.py
First Item -> lion
Items -> ['lion', 'crocodile', 'antelope']
```

Explanation
In this example:

- The **sys.argv** list captures all the inputs provided after the script name.
- The command **python sample.py lion crocodile antelope** passes three arguments (lion, crocodile, and antelope) to the script.
- Since **sys.argv** always returns string values, you can use type casting functions like int(), float(), or bool() to convert them as needed.

Example 2 (mymath.py)

```python
#mymath.py

import sys

def math():
    entries = [int(x) for x in sys.argv[1:]]
    size = len(entries)
    total = sum(entries)

    average = total/size
    return f"Data->{entries}\nTotal->{total}\nAverage-> {average}"


print(math())
```

Command Line Execution:

```
PS D:\Project\Document> python  mymath.py  10 20 30
Data-> [10, 20, 30]
Total-> 60
Average-> 20.0
```

Python

```
>>> import sys

>>> #executable
>>> print(sys.executable)
... C:\Program Files\Python\python.exe

>>> #platform
>>> print(sys.platform)
... win32

>>> #version
>>> print(sys.version)
... 3.13.0 (tags/v3.13.0:60403a5, Oct  7 2024, 09:38:07) [MSC v.1941 64 bit
(AMD64)]

>>> #version_info
>>> print(sys.version_info)
... sys.version_info(major=3, minor=13, micro=0, releaselevel='final',
serial=0)
```

Python Runtime Configuration

Method	Definition
dont_write_bytecode	Prevents Python from generating .pyc files.
pycache_prefix	Specifies the location for storing .pyc files.
meta_path	Lists meta path finders used for importing modules.
path	Lists directories where Python looks for modules.
path_hooks	Contains hooks for path-based module importers.
path_importer_cache	Caches module importers.
modules	Displays all currently loaded modules.
stdlib_module_names	Lists standard library module names.
builtin_module_names	Lists all built-in modules compiled into Python.
implementation	Provides details about the Python implementation (e.g., CPython, PyPy).
exec_prefix	Retrieves the path of platform-specific libraries.
warnoptions	Lists warning options set by the interpreter.

Table 5.6

```python
Python
>>> import sys

>>> #path
>>> print(sys.path)
... [.........]

>>> #modules
>>> print(sys.modules)
... [.........]
```

Memory and Performance Management

Method	Definition
getsizeof()	Returns the memory size of an object in bytes.
getallocatedblocks()	Returns the number of allocated memory blocks.
getrefcount()	Returns the reference count of an object.
getprofile()	Retrieves the profiling function set by sys.setprofile().
setprofile()	Sets a profiling function for debugging.
gettrace()	Returns the trace function set for debugging.
settrace()	Sets a debugging trace function.
getrecursionlimit()	Gets the maximum recursion depth.
setrecursionlimit()	Sets the maximum recursion depth.
get_int_max_str_digits()	Returns the maximum number of digits allowed in an integer.
set_int_max_str_digits()	Sets the maximum allowed digits in an integer.
setswitchinterval()	Configures the thread switch interval.
getswitchinterval()	Gets the interval for thread switching.
maxsize	Retrieves the maximum size of a Python object.
maxunicode	Returns the largest Unicode code point supported.
int_info	Returns system-specific integer properties.
float_info	Returns system-specific float precision and limits.
float_repr_style	Indicates how floating-point numbers are represented.
hash_info	Provides details about Python's hash function.

Table 5.7

Input/Output Handling

Method	Definition
stdin	Standard input stream.
stdout	Standard output stream.
stderr	Standard error output stream.
displayhook	Controls how output is displayed in interactive mode.
excepthook	Holds the last exception object.
unraisablehook	Handles unraisable exceptions.

Table 5.8

Process, Debugging, Module, Execution and Exception Handling

Method	Definition
exit()	Terminates the program with an optional exit status.
exc_info()	Retrieves information about the last exception.
exception	Holds the last exception object.
breakpointhook()	Defines the behavior when calling breakpoint().
audit()	Reports security-sensitive operations to the auditing system.
addaudithook()	Adds an auditing hook for security checks.
monitoring	Provides monitoring hooks for the interpreter.
activate_stack_trampoline()	Activates stack trampolining for optimization.
deactivate_stack_trampoline()	Deactivates stack trampolining.
is_stack_trampoline_active()	Checks if stack trampolining is enabled.
call_tracing()	Runs a function with tracing enabled for debugging.
is_finalizing()	Checks if Python is in the process of shutting down.
thread_info	Retrieves threading implementation details.
byteorder	Indicates the byte order (endianness) of the system.
getfilesystemencoding()	Returns the encoding used for file system operations.
getfilesystemencodeerrors()	Retrieves the error handling strategy for filesystem encoding.
getunicodeinternedsize()	Returns the memory usage of interned Unicode strings.

Table 5.9

Key Terms

Process
Kill
Runtime
Debugging
Permission

Review Questions

1. Which function creates nested directories if parent directories don't exist?
   a) mkdir()
   b) makedirs()
   c) rmdir()
   d) walk()
   Answer: b

2. Which os module method deletes a file?
   a) remove()
   b) rmdir()
   c) unlink()
   d) Both a & c
   Answer: d

3. What does sys.argv[0] represent?
   a) First command-line argument
   b) Python interpreter path
   c) Script filename
   d) All arguments as list
   Answer: c

4. Which function changes the current working directory?
   a) getcwd()
   b) chdir()
   c) curdir()
   d) pathsep()
   Answer: b

5. Which sys module function returns the Python version as a tuple of major, minor, and micro?
   a) version
   b) hexversion
   c) version_info
   d) executable
   Answer: c

Review Exercises

1. **OS Module Exercise:**
   Write a program to create a folder named ProjectFiles with subfolders Docs and Media, then list all files and directories in the current working directory.

2. **Process Management Exercise:**
   Using os.system(), write a script to check the Python version on the system and print it.

3. **SYS Module Exercise:**
   Create a Python script that accepts multiple integers via command-line arguments and prints the maximum, minimum, and sum of the numbers using sys.argv.

Pathlib and Glob

Pathlib Module

Programming across multiple operating systems (Windows, Linux, macOS) presents challenges, especially when working with file paths. Each OS follows different path conventions, which can lead to compatibility issues. Python provides a unified way to handle file paths seamlessly across different operating systems using the **pathlib** module.

With **pathlib**, a file path written for Windows can work on Linux without modification, reducing the likelihood of path-related errors. However, **pathlib** is not just for handling paths—it also allows you to search for files, create directories, check file existence, rename, replace files, and even read or write text and bytes efficiently.

Pathlib Classes

Class	Description
Path	Represents a file system path and provides methods for working with files and directories.
PosixPath	A subclass of Path used for Unix-like operating systems (Linux/macOS).
WindowsPath	A subclass of Path designed for Windows paths.
PurePath	A version of Path that handles paths in a platform-independent manner but doesn't interact with the file system.
PurePosixPath	A subclass of PurePath that represents Unix-style paths.
PureWindowsPath	A subclass of PurePath that represents Windows-style paths.

Table 6.0

Path Methods

Path Representation and Properties

Method	Definition
absolute()	Returns the absolute path of the file/directory.
anchor	Returns the root part of the path (C:\ on Windows, / on Unix).
drive	Returns the drive letter (Windows) or an empty string (Linux).
home()	Returns the home directory of the current user.
root	Returns the root of the path (e.g., / on Unix, C:\ on Windows).
name	Returns the filename or last part of the path.
stem	Returns the filename without the extension.
suffix	Returns the file extension (e.g., .txt).
suffixes	Returns all file extensions if there are multiple (eg., .tar.gz).
parents	Returns a sequence of parent directories.

parent	Returns the immediate parent directory.
parts	Returns a tuple representing different components of the path.

Table 6.1

Python

```
>>> import pathlib

>>> #home()
>>> home = pathlib.Path.home()
>>> print(home)
... C:\Users\John

>>> #root
>>> root = pathlib.Path("C:/Users/Asiedu/file.docx").root
>>> print(root)
... \

>>> #name
>>> name = pathlib.Path("C:/Users/Asiedu/file.docx").name
>>> print(name)
... file.docx

>>> #stem
>>> stem = pathlib.Path("C:/Users/Asiedu/file.docx").stem
>>> print(stem)
... file

>>> #suffix
>>> suffix = pathlib.Path("C:/Users/Asiedu/file.docx").suffix
>>> print(suffix)
... .docx

>>> #suffixes
>>> suffixes = pathlib.Path("C:/Users/Asiedu/file.tar.gz").suffixes
>>> print(suffixes)
... ['.tar', '.gz']

>>> #parts
>>> parts = pathlib.Path("C:/Users/Asiedu/file.tar.gz").parts
>>> print(parts)
... ('C:\\', 'Users', 'Asiedu', 'file.tar.gz')
```

File and Directory Operations

Method	Definition
joinpath(paths)	Adds paths to create a single path
mkdir(parents, exist_ok)	Creates a new directory.
rmdir()	Removes an empty directory.
unlink(missing_ok)	Deletes a file.
rename(target)	Renames the file or directory to a new location.
replace(target)	Renames a file or directory, overwriting if necessary.
touch(mode, exist_ok)	Creates an empty file or updates its timestamp.
symlink_to(target)	Creates a symbolic link to the target file/directory.
hardlink_to(target)	Creates a hard link to the target file.

Table 6.2

Python

```
>>> import pathlib

>>> #joinpath()
>>> paths = pathlib.Path.home().joinpath("Desktop", "mydoc")
>>> print(paths)
... C:\Users\John\Desktop\mydoc

>>> #mkdir()
>>> pathlib.Path("Document/mydoc").mkdir()

>>> #rmdir()
>>> pathlib.Path("mydoc").rmdir()

>>> #unlink()
>>> pathlib.Path("Document/file.docx").unlink()

>>> #rename()
>>> pathlib.Path("file.txt").rename('mydoc.txt')

>>> #replace()
>>> pathlib.Path('files/doc.pdf').replace('book.pdf')

>>> #touch()
>>> pathlib.Path("newfile.pdf").touch()
```

File and Directory Status

Method	Definition
exists()	Returns True if the path exists.
is_absolute()	Returns True if the path is absolute.
is_relative_to(other)	Returns True if the path is relative to other.
is_reserved()	Returns True if the path is reserved (Windows only).
is_dir()	Returns True if the path is a directory.
is_file()	Returns True if the path is a file.
is_symlink()	Returns True if the path is a symbolic link.
is_mount()	Returns True if the path is a mount point.
is_fifo()	Returns True if the path is a FIFO (named pipe).
is_socket()	Returns True if the path is a socket.
is_junction()	Returns True if the path is a junction (Windows only).

Table 6.3

Python

```
>>> from pathlib import Path

>>> #exists()
>>> file = Path("/Document/book.pdf").exists()
>>> print(file)
... True

>>> #is_file()
>>> file = Path("/Document/book.pdf").is_file()
>>> print(file)
... True

>>> #is_absolute()
>>> file = Path("music/favorite.mp3").is_absolute()
>>> print(file)
... False

>>> #is_dir()
>>> file = Path("media/music").is_dir()
>>> print(file)
... True
```

File and Directory Searching

Method	Definition
glob(pattern)	Finds all files matching the pattern (e.g., "*.txt").
rglob(pattern)	Recursively searches for files matching the pattern.
match(pattern)	Checks if the path matches a given pattern ("*.txt").
walk()	Iterates through the directory tree.
iterdir()	Iterates over files and directories in the current directory.

Table 6.4

glob(pattern, case_sensitive **)**

case_sensitive → If True, the search will distinguish between uppercase and lowercase letters.

Python
```
from pathlib import Path

files = Path("Document/files").glob('*docx')

for file in files:
    print(file)
```

```
#Output
file.docx
template.docx
letter.docx
resume.docx
```

Insight

"*" → Lists all files in the specified path.
"*docx" → Lists all files that end with "docx" in the path.
"sample*" → Lists all files that start with "sample" in the path.
"sample*docx" → Lists all files that start with "sample" and end with "docx" in the path.

iterdir()

```python
from pathlib import Path

files = Path.home().iterdir()

for file in files:
    print(file)
```

```
#Output
C:\Users\Marrie\Desktop
C:\Users\Marrie\Documents
C:\Users\Marrie\Downloads
C:\Users\Marrie\Music
C:\Users\Marrie\OneDrive
C:\Users\Marrie\royal.png
C:\Users\Marrie\Saved Games
C:\Users\Marrie\Templates
C:\Users\Marrie\user.txt
```

walk()

```python
from pathlib import Path

desk = Path.home().joinpath("Desktop").walk()

for file in desk:
    print(file)
```

```
#Output
(WindowsPath('C:/Users/Marrie/Desktop'), ['mydoc'], user.txt', 'story.pdf',
'Chrome.lnk','desktop.ini', 'Documents.lnk', 'Downloads.lnk', 'Gmail.lnk',
'Yahoo Mail.lnk'])
(WindowsPath('C:/Users/Marrie/Desktop/mydoc'), [], ['cools.mp3',
"favorite.mp3", 'computer.pdf'])
```

File Reading and Writing

Method	Definition
open(mode, encoding)	Opens the file for reading or writing.
read_bytes()	Reads the file as bytes.
read_text(encoding)	Reads the file as a string.
write_bytes(data)	Writes bytes to the file.
write_text(data,encoding)	Writes a string to the file.

Table 6.5

open(mode, buffering, encoding)

Python
```
from pathlib import Path

lines = Path('recipe.txt').open().readlines()
for line in lines:
    print(line)
```

```
#Output
--Pepperoni Pizza Recipe--

Items: oven, spoon, knife, roller

Ingredient set1: pepper, carrot, flour, meat, onion

Ingredient set2: tuna, tomato, garlic, mushroom
```

Note

The use of **Pathlib** for reading and writing files is explored in more detail in the next chapter on *File Handling and Byte Operations*.

Path Modification and Construction

Method	Definition
as_posix()	Returns a POSIX-style (Unix-like) string representation of the path.
as_uri()	Converts the path into a file URI (file:///C:/Users/...).
expanduser()	Expands ~ to the user's home directory.
joinpath(*other)	Joins multiple path components (p.joinpath("subdir", "file.txt")).
relative_to(*other)	Returns a relative path based on the given base path.
resolve()	Returns the absolute path, resolving any symbolic links.
with_name(new_name)	Returns a new path with the same directory but a different filename.
with_stem(new_stem)	Returns a new path with the same directory but a different filename without changing the extension.
with_suffix(new_suffix)	Returns a new path with the same directory but a different file extension.

Table 6.6

Python
```
>>> from pathlib import Path

>>> paths = Path('Document/media') / "music"
>>> print(paths)
... Document\media\music

>>> #joinpath()
>>> paths = Path.home().joinpath("Desktop", "mydoc")
>>> print(paths)
... C:\Users\John\Desktop\mydoc

>>> paths = Path("Document").joinpath("video.mp4")
>>> print(paths)
... Document\video.mp4

>>> #as_posix()
>>> paths = Path('C:\\Users\\John\\Document').as_posix()
>>> print(paths)
... C:/Users/John/Document

>>> #as_uri()
>>> paths = Path.home().as_uri()
>>> print(paths)
```

```
... file:///C:/Users/Oliver

>>> #with_name()
>>> file = Path("media/music.mp3").with_name("audio.mp3")
>>> print(file)
... media\audio.mp3

>>> #with_suffix()
>>> file = Path("document/ebook.docx").with_suffix(".pdf")
>>> print(file)
... document\ebook.pdf

>>> #with_stem()
>>> file = Path("document/ebook.docx").with_stem("myfile")
>>> print(file)
... document\myfile.docx
```

File Metadata and Permissions

Method	Definition
chmod(mode)	Changes the file's permissions.
lchmod(mode)	Changes the file's permissions but doesn't follow symbolic links.
owner()	Returns the owner of the file.
group()	Returns the group owner of the file.
stat()	Returns file metadata (size, creation date, etc.).
lstat()	Like stat(), but doesn't follow symbolic links.
samefile(other_path)	Returns True if both paths point to the same file.
chmod(mode)	Changes the file's permissions.

Table 6.7

glob.glob()

The **glob.glob()** function works similarly to **pathlib.Path.glob()**, both being used to search for files that match a specified pattern.

Key Difference

- *glob.glob(pattern, path)* → The path is passed as a parameter to the glob function.
- *pathlib.Path(path).glob(pattern)* → The path is specified inside the Path class before calling glob().

Example ,

```python
from pathlib import Path
from glob import glob

music_path = Path.home().joinpath("Downloads/media")
pdf_path = Path("D:\\Library")

music = glob(pathname="*.mp3", root_dir = music_path)
pdf = glob(pathname="*.pdf", root_dir = pdf_path, recursive= True)
doc = glob(pathname="*letter*docx", root_dir = "Document")


print(f"Music Files -> {music}")
print(f"PDF Files -> {pdf}")
print(f"Doc Files -> {doc}")
```

```
#Output
Music Files -> ['lucky_dube.mp3','Hillsong.mp3','westlife.mp3']
PDF Files -> ['Adobe Scan.pdf','resume.pdf', 'demo.pdf']
Doc Files -> ['2026 letter.docx', 'approved_letter.docx']
```

Other glob Methods

Method	Definition
iglob(pattern, recursive)	Works like glob() but returns an iterator instead of a list, which is more memory-efficient.
escape(pathname)	Escapes special characters (*, ?, [) in a given pathname so they are treated as literal characters instead of wildcards.

fnmatch(filename, pattern)	Checks if a filename matches a given pattern, considering case sensitivity based on the OS.
fnmatchcase(filename, pattern)	Similar to fnmatch(), but case-sensitive regardless of the OS.
has_magic(pattern)	Returns True if the pattern contains wildcard characters (*, ?, [ ]).
glob0(dirname, basename)	Helper function that performs non-recursive matching within a directory.
glob1(dirname, pattern)	Similar to glob0(), but specifically for non-recursive wildcard expansion in a directory.
translate(pattern)	Converts a glob pattern into a regular expression (re) pattern for use in filtering.
contextlib	Used for context management (e.g., safely handling file access).
functools	Provides higher-order functions like caching and function composition.
itertools	Supports efficient looping constructs and iteration utilities.
operator	Provides efficient operations for function-based comparisons.
os	Used to interact with the filesystem (e.g., listing directories).
re	Used for translating wildcard patterns into regex for pattern matching.
stat	Retrieves file status and metadata.
sys	Provides access to system-specific parameters.
magic_check(pattern)	Validates if the given pattern contains wildcard characters.
magic_check_bytes(pattern)	Similar to magic_check(), but works on byte strings instead of text.

Table 6.8

Key Terms

Pathlib
Glob
PurePath
resolve

Review **Questions**

1. What is the main purpose of the pathlib module?
A. To compress files
B. To handle file paths and directories in an OS-independent way
C. To manipulate URLs
D. To create graphical interfaces
Answer: B

2. Which of the following pathlib classes is platform-independent and does *not* touch the filesystem?
A. Path
B. WindowsPath
C. PurePath
D. PosixPath
Answer: C

3. What does Path.home() return?
A. The desktop directory
B. The current working directory
C. The system root directory
D. The user's home directory
Answer: D

4. What is the main difference between glob.glob() and Path.glob()?
A. glob() only works on Windows
B. Path.glob() is object-oriented; glob.glob() is function-based
C. Path.glob() returns a list
D. They are identical in functionality
Answer: B

5. Which method can be used to create a new empty file or update its timestamp?
A. write_text()
B. mkdir()
C. touch()
D. create_file()
Answer: C

Review Exercises

1. Write a Python program that lists all .pdf files in the user's "Documents" folder using Path.glob().

2. Using pathlib, create a directory named **"projects"**, then inside it, create an empty file named **"notes.txt"**.

3. Write a script that reads the text of info.txt using read_text(), converts it to uppercase, and saves it as info_copy.txt using write_text().

Handling Errors and Exceptions

Programming inherently involves errors or **bugs**. Writing code requires applying human logic while adhering to the programming language's **structure**, **syntax** and **semantic** rules. However, mistakes in logic, incorrect syntax, or unforeseen runtime conditions can lead to errors or exceptions.

Errors in a program are commonly referred to as *bugs*. Regardless of a programmer's experience, encountering bugs is inevitable, making error handling an essential part of software development. Errors can cause programs to behave unexpectedly, produce incorrect results, or fail to run entirely.

Python is an **interpreted** language, meaning it executes code line by line. When an error occurs, execution stops immediately, preventing further code from running. To ensure smooth execution and prevent abrupt program crashes, error handling is crucial.

Reasons for Handling Errors in Programming

To prevent program crashes: Proper error handling ensures that a single error does not cause the entire program to terminate unexpectedly.

To allow a program to continue running despite encountering an error: Handling exceptions gracefully allows a program to recover from errors and continue execution.

To display user-friendly error messages: Instead of showing cryptic system-generated messages, developers can provide clear error messages to guide users on what went wrong.

To use errors as conditions for executing alternative tasks: Some exceptions may indicate an expected situation that can be handled by executing a fallback solution.

To log errors for debugging and future reference: Logging errors helps developers identify issues and improve the software over time.

To enhance security: Some unhandled errors can expose sensitive information or allow attackers to exploit vulnerabilities in the software.

To improve software reliability and maintainability: Well-structured error handling ensures that software remains stable and easy to maintain in the long run.

Errors in Python Programming

In Python, errors can arise due to several factors. They may be caused by logic mistakes, syntax violations, structural misconfigurations, incorrect data handling, incompatible data types, or missing dependencies.

Python errors are broadly categorized into two main types:

1. **Syntax Errors**
2. **Runtime Errors**

Syntax Errors

Every programming language follows a strict set of structural rules for using **variables, objects, functions, keywords, operators, punctuation, and mnemonics**. When these elements are not used correctly, or the required syntax is not followed, Python raises a *syntax error*. Syntax errors occur during the parsing stage and prevent the program from running.

Common Causes of Syntax Errors:

Incorrect indentation – Python enforces indentation to structure code blocks properly.

```python
def sample():
    #Wrong Indentation
print("Hello World")
```

```
#Output
IndentationError: expected an indented block after function definition on
line 15
```

Missing colons (:) – Required for defining functions, loops, and conditionals.

```python
def sample()
    pass
```

```
#Output
SyntaxError: expected ':'
```

Empty code blocks without the pass keyword – Python does not allow empty function or loop bodies.

```python
def sample():
```

```
#Output
IndentationError: expected an indented block after function definition on line 15
```

Misspelled keywords or function names – Example: writing prnt() instead of print().

```python
prit("Hello World")
```

```
#Output
NameError: name 'prit' is not defined. Did you mean: 'print'?
```

Mismatched parentheses, brackets, or braces – Example: print("Hello World" (missing closing parenthesis).

```python
print("Hello World"
```

```
#Output
SyntaxError: '(' was never closed
```

Incorrect use of assignment (=) instead of comparison (==) – Example: if x = 5: instead of if x == 5:.

```python
if x = 5:
    pass
```

```
#Output
SyntaxError: invalid syntax. Maybe you meant '==' or ':=' instead of '='?
```

Unclosed string literals – Example,

```python
var = "Hello
```

```
#Output
SyntaxError: unterminated string literal (detected at line 15)
```

Using reserved words as variable names – Example: class = "Hello" (since class is a keyword).

```python
class = "Hello"
```

```
#Output
SyntaxError: invalid syntax
```

Runtime Exception

Runtime errors occur during the execution of a program rather than during **compilation** or syntax checking. These errors are not caused by violations of the language's syntax or structure but rather by logical mistakes, incorrect operations, invalid data handling, or unexpected conditions. Unlike *syntax errors*, which prevent the program from running, *runtime errors* appear while the program is running and may cause it to crash or behave unexpectedly.

Common Causes of Runtime Errors:

Runtime Exception	Description
ZeroDivisionError	Occurs when a number is divided by zero
KeyError	Attempting to access a dictionary key that does not exist.
NameError	Trying to use a variable that has not been declared.
IndexError	Attempting to access a list, tuple, or string index that does not exist.

TypeError	Performing operation on incompatible types. For example, trying to add a string and an integer.
IndentationError	Wrong indentation in program
FloatingPointError	Operations on floating point fail
LookupError	Base class for errors raised when a key or index lookup fails in mappings or sequences.
ImportError	Imported module is not found
AssertionError	Assertion statements fail
RecursionError	Occurs when the maximum recursion depth is exceeded — usually due to a function calling itself infinitely.
FileNotFoundError	Trying to open a non-existent file
ValueError	Occurs when a function receives an argument of the correct type but inappropriate
AttributeError	An invalid attribute reference or assignment is attempted
MemoryError	Raised when an operation runs out of memory, such as when trying to create a very large object.
TabError	Raised when indentation in the code uses a mix of tabs and spaces inconsistently.
UnicodeError	An encoding or decoding operation fails
EOFError	The input() function reaches the end-of-file condition
SystemError	Raised when the interpreter itself detects an internal error, but the situation is not fatal enough to stop execution.
TimeoutError	Raised when a system operation times out, usually in I/O or network connections.

Table 6.9

Handling Errors and Exceptions

Errors and exceptions can be addressed in a program during debugging, allowing developers to correct them before deployment. However, some errors may only occur under specific conditions, such as user input errors, file access issues, or network failures. These types of errors are unpredictable and can arise during the production stage of an application. To prevent a program from crashing and to ensure it continues running smoothly, **error handling** is necessary.

Python provides **two main ways** to handle errors and exceptions:

1. **try-except** Block – Used to catch and handle specific errors, preventing the program from crashing when an exception occurs.
2. **try-finally** or **try-except-finally** Block – Ensures that certain cleanup operations (e.g., closing files or releasing resources) are executed, regardless of whether an exception occurs.

try-except

In this approach, the code that is likely to raise an exception is placed inside the **try block**. If an exception occurs, the **except block** is executed to handle the error. However, if no exception occurs, the statements inside the **except block** will not run.

Syntax

```
try:
    #Statement or Code runs when no errors occur

except ErrorType:
    #Statement or Code runs when errors occur
```

📖 **Note**

The ErrorType is optional and can be any of the runtime errors listed above. It allows the execution of specific statements when multiple statements are likely to raise different types of errors. However, the program will still handle errors properly even without specifying an ErrorType.

Example 1 – A simple program to handle exceptions

```python
try:
    var = 1 / 0
except:
    print('Error')
```

```
#Output
Error
```

Unhandled Exception

```python
var = 1 / 0
```

```
#Output
    var = 1 / 0
          ~~^~~
ZeroDivisionError: division by zero
```

Example 2 – A program likely to raise **TypeError**

Python

```
try:
    var = "10" + 20

except TypeError:
    print("Error-> Program may have type error")
```

```
#Output
Error-> Program may have type error
```

Example 3 – A program to handle a **ZeroDivisionError**,

Python

```
def division():
    try:
        x = int(input("Enter first number: "))
        y = int(input("Enter second number: "))
        result = x/y
        print(f"{x}/{y} -> {result}")
    except ZeroDivisionError:
        print("Sorry!, error has occurred,try again")
        division() #call the function again

division()
```

```
#Output
Enter first number: 5
Enter second number: 0
Sorry!, error has occurred, try again
Enter first number: 5
Enter second number: 10
5/10 -> 0.5
```

Example 4 - A program to handle selective exceptions,

```
Python

def sample(data):
    try:
        total = sum(data)
        divi = total / data[0] #dividing by the first index
        item = data[3]         #getting item at 3

    except ZeroDivisionError:
        print("Error-> number is divided by zero")

    except IndexError:
        print("Error-> index is out of range")

    except:
        print("Program has error")


sample([0, 5, 10]) #Likely to raise exception: data[0]= 0
sample([6, 2])     #Likely to raise exception: data[3]= null
```

```
#Output
Error-> number is divided by zero
Error-> index is out of range
```

Explanation

This example demonstrates that:

- ZeroDivisionError is raised when dividing by zero (data[0] = 0).
- IndexError occurs when trying to access an index that doesn't exist (data[3]).
- The generic **except** block acts as a final safety net for any other unexpected errors.

try-finally

The **try-finally** approach is useful in situations where certain statements or functions must execute regardless of whether an error occurs.

The code that might raise an error is placed inside the **try** block. The **except** block is optional and can be used to handle specific exceptions. The **finally** block always executes, whether an error occurs or not. The **finally** block is mainly used for cleanup operations, such as closing files, releasing resources, or disconnecting from databases.

Syntax

```
try:
    #Statement or Code runs when no errors occur
finally:
    #Statement or Code must run
```

Or

```
try:
    #Statement or Code runs when no errors occur
except:
    #Statement or Code when error occurs
finally:
    #Statement or Code must run
```

Note

Errors
These are issues that arise due to incorrect code structure, syntax, or system limitations, making the program unable to execute.

Exceptions
These occur during the execution of a program when an unexpected condition is encountered, such as dividing by zero or accessing an invalid index.

Example 1,

Python

```python
try:
    var = int("abc")
finally:
    print("Execution is completed!")
```

```
#Output
Execution is completed!
    var = int("abc")
ValueError: invalid literal for int() with base 10: 'abc'
```

Example 2,

Python

```
try:
    var = 6.3 + "2.5"
    print(var)

except:
    print("Error!")

finally:
    print("Execution is completed!")
```

```
#Output
Error!
Execution is completed!
```

Key Terms

Bug
except
Semantic
Interpreted
Structure
Syntax
try
finally
Exception
Traceback
ZeroDivisionError
IndentationError

Review Questions

1. Which of the following is a syntax error?
   a) print("Hello"
   b) x = 10 / 2
   c) len([1,2,3])
   d) x = int("5")
   Answer: a

2. Which exception is raised when accessing a dictionary key that does not exist?
   a) IndexError
   b) KeyError
   c) TypeError
   d) ValueError
   Answer: b

3. What type of error occurs if a variable is used before assignment?
   a) SyntaxError
   b) TypeError
   c) NameError
   d) ZeroDivisionError
   Answer: c

4. Which error will Python raise for mixing tabs and spaces inconsistently?
   a) TabError
   b) IndentationError
   c) SyntaxError
   d) ValueError
   Answer: a

5. Dividing a number by zero will raise:
   a) ValueError
   b) ZeroDivisionError
   c) TypeError
   d) ArithmeticError
   Answer: b

Review Exercises

1. Identify the type of error in the following code:

   ```
   print("Python)
   ```

2. Write a program that attempts to divide a number by zero and handle the error using a try-except block.

3. Create a list nums = [1,2,3] and write code that attempts to access nums[5]. Use exception handling to display a custom error message.

File Handling (File I/O Operations)

A **file** is a collection of data stored on a computer that can be accessed and manipulated by programs. Files can contain various types of data, including:

- **Text-based content** (e.g., .txt, .csv, .json, .xml, .docx)
- **Binary data** (e.g., images: .jpg, .png, videos: .mp4, .avi, audio: .mp3, .wav)
- **Executable files** (.exe, .bin, .sh)
- **Compressed archives** (.zip, .tar, .rar)
- **Database files** (.sqlite, .db)

In Python, before accessing or modifying a file, it must first be opened. Python provides built-in support for file handling, allowing files to be read, written, modified, and even converted between different formats.

File Operations

Python offers several methods for handling files, including:

1. Opening a file
2. Reading a file
3. Writing to a file
4. Appending data to a file (a mode)
5. Accessing file attributes
6. Closing a file

Opening Files

Python is a flexible language that provides multiple ways to open a file. However, in this book, we will explore two of the most commonly used methods.

open(file, mode="r", buffering=-1, encoding=None, newline=None, errors=None)

The **open()** function is the standard way to open files in Python. It allows you to specify various parameters, including the file path, mode, encoding, and more.

Parameters:

file → The path to the file (can be a string or Path object).

mode → Specifies how the file should be opened. (See the table below for available modes.)

buffering	→	Controls buffering: 0 for no buffering (binary mode), 1 for line buffering (text mode), >1 for a custom buffer size, and -1 (default) lets Python decide.
encoding	→	Specifies the encoding (e.g., "utf-8", "ascii"). Only applicable in text mode.
newline	→	Determines how newlines are handled (None, '\n', '\r', '\r\n'). Useful when working with different operating systems
errors	→	Defines how errors in encoding/decoding are handled (e.g., "strict", "ignore", "replace").
closefd	→	If True (default), the file descriptor is closed when the file is closed. Should be False only when working with file descriptors instead of file paths.

File Modes

Mode	Description
'r'	Read mode (default). Fails if the file does not exist
'w'	Write mode. Overwrites the file if it exists; creates a new file if it doesn't.
'a'	Append mode. Adds new content to the end of the file. Creates the file if it doesn't exist.
'x'	Exclusive creation mode. Fails if the file already exists.
'rb', 'wb'	Binary mode (e.g., for images, videos, and executables). 'rb' for reading bytes and 'wb' for writing bytes.
'rt', 'wt'	Text mode (default). 'rt' for reading and 'wt' for writing the txt
'+'	Read and write mode (e.g., 'r+', 'w+', 'a+', 'rb+', 'wb+').

Table 7.0

Example,

Python
```python
#open for reading
text = open("Document\\myfile.txt")

#open for writing
docx = open("Document\\letter.docx", mode='w')

#open for reading bytes
bytes = open("image.jpg", mode='rb')

#open for writing bytes
bytes = open("audio.mp3", mode='wb')
```

Reading Files

After opening a file using either the built-in **open()** function or the **pathlib** module, the file can be read from or written to.

Reading Methods

Method	Description
read	Reads the entire content
readline	Reads a single line
readlines	Reads all lines into a list

Table 7.1

Example 1 – Reading the entire content of a text file

Python

```python
file   = open("Document/letter.txt")
content = file.read()
print(content)
file.close()
```

```
#Output
Hi Buddy,
I'm very happy to be a Pythonista.
Well, don't doubt me - I can print anything using print("Hello World").
I know everything from variables to file I/O, and I can handle exceptions
perfectly.
Python is truly a great course to begin with.
I think I'm already in love with Python.
```

Insight

It is good practice to explicitly call the **close()** method to close an opened file and release system resources. However, using the **with** statement is recommended, as it automatically handles file closing once the block is exited.

Example 2 – Reading all lines of a file into a list,

```
Python

with open("letter.txt") as file:
    content = file.readlines()

print(content)
```

```
#Output
['Hi Buddy,\n', "I'm very happy to be a Pythonista.\n", 'Well, don\'t doubt me - I can print anything using print("Hello World").\n', 'I know everything from variables to file I/O, and I can handle exceptions perfectly.\n', 'Python is truly a great course to begin with.\n', "I think I'm already in love with Python.\n", '\n']
```

Example 3 – Reading a single line from a file,

```
Python

with open("letter.txt") as f:
    text = f.readline()

print(text)
```

```
#Output
Hi Buddy,
```

Reading with Pathlib

Example 1

```
Python

from pathlib import Path

content = Path("sales.txt").read_text()
print(content)
```

```
#Output
====================Today's Sales ==================
--------Item --------------Unit ---------------Amount
1.      shoes : ----------- 4 pairs  ----------$ 600
2.      bags :   ---------- 6   ---------------$ 250
3.      perfume : --------- 10   --------------$ 450
4.      dress : ------------4    --------------$ 800
5.      jeans : ------------12   --------------$ 1,200

total : $3,300
```

Example 2 – Reading a single line,

```python
from pathlib import Path

text = Path("mybiology.txt").open().readline()
print(text)
```

```
#Output
====================Today's Sales ==================
```

Note

The **read(size)**, **readline(size)**, and **readlines(size)** methods can take an optional **size** parameter that limits how much data is read from the file. When a size is specified, only that number of bytes or characters is returned instead of the full file content. For example,

```
with open("letter.txt") as f:
     text = f.read(150)
print(text)

#Output
====================Today's Sales ==================
--------Item --------------Unit ---------------Amount
1.      shoes : ----------- 4 pairs  ----------$ 600
2.      ba
```

Writing Files

File I/O operations in Python also support writing data to files or creating new ones. Creating a new file typically involves writing fresh content to a file that does not yet exist, or copying data from an existing file into a new one. During the process of copying or rewriting, it is also possible to convert the file's format—this is especially common with binary or image files, where byte-level operations are performed.

Writing Methods

Method	Description
write	Writes an entire content to a file
writelines	Writes a list of content to a file

Table 7.2

Example 1,

Python
```
text = """Pizza Recipe Ingredient:
--------------------------------------
1. Two cups of flour
2. onion, pepper and tomato
3. meat, tuna and mushroom
4. oil and salad
"""
file =  open("my_recipe.txt", 'w')
file.write(text)
file.close()
```

Explanation

When this code is executed, a new file named **my_recipe.txt** is created in the current working directory (or in a specified directory if a path is provided). The content of the text variable is then written into the file. After writing, the **close()** method is called to ensure that the file is properly saved and system resources are released.

Example 2,

Python
```
cars = ["Audi\n", "Ford\n", "Tesla\n", "Toyota"]

with open("favorite_cars.txt", 'w') as file:
    file.writelines(cars)
```

Appending Data to a File

Appending data to a file means adding new content to an existing file without overwriting its original content—typically used with text files. This is done using the write methods in append mode ('**a**').

Example

●●● Python

```
with open("myfile.txt", "a") as file:
    file.write("Hello World!")
```

Writing with Pathlib

Example

●●● Python

```
from pathlib import Path

message = """Hello Pythonista!
I just want to wish you a happy coding...
Enjoy a coffee too!
"""
Path("message.txt").write_text(message)
```

Reading and Writing Bytes

In the previous examples, the focus was on reading from and writing to text files. However, to handle non-text files such as images, audio, video, PDFs, or Word documents, file operations must be performed in **binary mode**.

This is achieved by specifying the file mode as '**rb**' (read binary) for reading and '**wb**' (write binary) for writing. In binary mode, data is read and written as **bytes objects** rather than strings, which allows Python to correctly process file types that do not contain plain text data.

Example 1 – Reading a Word document,

●●● Python

```python
file = open("template.docx", 'rb')
file_byte = file.read()
file.close()
```

Example 2 – Converting image in one format to another format,

●●● Python

```python
#Reading image file (png)
with open("flower.png", 'rb') as file:
    image = file.read()

#Writing image file (jpg)
with open("media/flower.jpg", 'wb') as file:
    file.write(image)
```

Example 3 – Converting audio into another format

●●● Python

```python
#Reading audio file (mp3)
with open("westlife.mp3", 'rb') as file:
    audio_bytes = file.read()

#Writing audio file (wav)
with open("westlife.wav", 'wb') as file:
    file.write(audio_bytes)
```

Reading and Writing Bytes with Pathlib

Example 1 – Reading video file,

●●● Python

```python
from pathlib import Path

video_bytes = Path("monster.mp4").read_bytes()
```

Example 2 – Reading and writing pdf file to different location,

```
Python

#Reading PDF
pdf = Path("Document/ebook.pdf").read_bytes()

#Writing PDF
Path.home().joinpath("Downloads","mydoc.pdf").write_bytes(pdf)
```

Accessing File Attributes

File attributes provide metadata and useful information about a file object. Once a file is opened, you can access several of its attributes to learn about the file's name, mode, encoding, and more.

Attribute	Description
file.name	Returns the name of the file.
file.mode	Returns the mode used to open the file ('r', 'w', 'a', etc.).
file.closed	Returns True if the file is closed; otherwise, False.
file.encoding	Returns the encoding used (for text files only).
file.fileno()	Returns the file descriptor (an integer) used by the operating system.
file.readable()	Returns True if the file was opened in a readable mode.
file.writable()	Returns True if the file was opened in a writable mode.
file.seekable()	Returns True if the file supports random access (seeking).
file.tell()	Returns the current position of the file pointer (in bytes).
file.seek(offset)	Moves the file pointer to a specified position.
file.encoding	Returns the encoding used (for text files only).

Table 7.3

```
Python

>>> file = open("recipe.txt", "r")
>>> #name
>>> print(file.name)
... recipe.txt

>>> #mode
>>> print(file.mode)
... r
```

```
>>> #readable()
>>> print(file.readable())
... True

>>> #writable()
>>> print(file.writable())
... False

>>> #close
>>> print(file.close)
... False

>>> #encoding
>>> print(file.encoding)
... cp1252

>>> #tell()
>>> print(file.tell())
... 0

>>> #seekable()
>>> print(file.seekable())
... True

>>> #fileno()
>>> print(file.fileno())
... 3
```

Key Terms

File Descriptor
Read Mode ('r')
Write Mode ('w')
Binary Mode ('rb', 'wb')
Context Manager

Review Questions

1. Which error occurs when trying to open a non-existent file?
   a) IOError
   b) FileNotFoundError
   c) PermissionError
   d) UnsupportedOperation
   Answer: b

2. What happens if you try to write to a file opened in read mode ('r')?
   a) FileNotFoundError
   b) IsADirectoryError
   c) UnsupportedOperation
   d) PermissionError
   Answer: c

3. Which of the following errors may occur when trying to access a file without proper permissions?
   a) PermissionError
   b) NameError
   c) EOFError
   d) TabError
   Answer: a

4. Which error is raised when trying to open a directory as a file?
   a) IOError
   b) IsADirectoryError
   c) FileNotFoundError
   d) ValueError
   Answer: b

5. What does the with statement prevent?
   a) Syntax errors
   b) File descriptor leaks
   c) Index errors
   d) Memory overflow
   Answer: b

Review Exercises

1. Write Python code to open a file "data.txt" and handle the error if the file does not exist using try-except.

2. Attempt to write "Hello World" to a file "read_only.txt" opened in read mode and catch the exception.

3. Create a program that reads a binary file "image.png" and handles PermissionError if the file is not accessible.

HTTP Requests

Python's **requests** library is one of the most popular and user-friendly tools for making HTTP requests. It allows your Python program to interact with web services, download content from the internet, submit data via forms, communicate with APIs, and more.

Key Features

- Supports all HTTP methods (GET, POST, PUT, DELETE, etc.)
- Easy access to response content in various formats
- Handles cookies, headers, sessions, and authentication
- Works well with JSON APIs
- Simplifies error handling and redirects

Installation

Installation can be done using the pip install command in the terminal or command line interface.

```
pip install requests
```

Common Requests Methods

Method	Description
get()	Retrieve information from the server
post()	Submit data to the server
put()	Replace existing data on the server
patch()	Partially update data
delete()	Remove data from the server
head()	Return headers without the body
options()	Returns server-supported methods
auth()	Contains support for HTTP Basic/Digest Auth.
cookies	Manage and inspect HTTP cookies.
ssl	Internal SSL utilities.
session	Manage cookies and connections across multiple requests:

Table 7.4

GET Requests

The get() method is used to make an HTTP request to a web server. It returns a response, which can be either successful (positive) or unsuccessful (negative). A negative response typically results from an HTTP error (such as 404 or 500), while a positive response contains data from the server.

The response can be accessed in various formats, such as:

- .text – returns the response body as a string
- .json() – returns the response in JSON format (if applicable)
- .content – returns the response as raw bytes
- .status_code – provides the HTTP status code of the response

Parameters

url	→	The URL you are making a GET request to.
params	→	(dict or bytes) — Appends query string to the URL.
headers	→	(dict) — Custom headers like user-agent, auth token, etc.
cookies	→	(dict or CookieJar) — Send cookies with the request.
auth	→	(tuple) — For basic authentication: ('username', 'password').
timeout	→	(float or tuple) — How long to wait for a response. Prevents hanging.
allow_redirects	→	(bool) — Whether to follow redirects (default is True).
proxies	→	(dict) — Use a proxy server for the request.
stream	→	(bool) — If True, doesn't download the response immediately.
verify	→	(bool or str) — SSL certificate verification. Set to False to ignore SSL (not recommended).
cert	→	(str or tuple) — Client-side SSL certs, if required.

Example 1

```
Python
import requests

response  =  requests.get(url= "https://google.com/")
print(f"url-> {response.url}" )
print(f"response code-> {response.status_code}")
```

```
#Output
url-> https://www.google.com/
response code-> 200
```

Example 2

```python
import requests

url = "https://google.com/"
params = {"search": "python"}
headers = {"User-Agent": "MyApp"}
cookies = {"session": "123abc"}

response  =  requests.get(
     url= url,
     params = params,
     headers = headers,
     cookies = cookies,
     timeout = 5,
     allow_redirects = True
)

print( response.text )
```

```
#Output
<!doctype html>.......</html>
```

Common HTTP Status Codes

Code	Meaning	Code	Meaning
200	OK	400	Bad Request
201	Created	401	Unauthorized
204	No Content	403	Forbidden
301	Moved Permanently	404	Not Found
304	Not Modified	500	Internal Server Error

Table 7.5

Downloading a File

```python
import requests
response  =  requests.get(url= "https://example.com/image.png")

with open("downloadedImage.png", "wb") as file:
      file.write( response.content )
```

POST Requests

The **post()** method is commonly used to send data to a server, typically through a form or an API. Unlike **get()**, which is used for retrieving data, post() is designed for submitting data (e.g., creating a new resource).

Although post() can also return a response, it is not primarily used for retrieving content like get(). The returned response can still be accessed using ***.text***, ***.json()***, or ***.status_code*** just like with get().

Parameters

url	→	(str) The endpoint you're sending the request to.
data	→	(dict, bytes, or file-like) Data to send in the body (form-encoded).
headers	→	(dict) — Custom headers like user-agent, auth token, etc.
json	→	(dict) A JSON payload to send (sets Content-Type: application/json).
cookies	→	(dict or CookieJar) — Send cookies with the request.
auth	→	(tuple) — For basic authentication: ('username', 'password').
timeout	→	(float or tuple) — How long to wait for a response. Prevents hanging.
files	→	(dict) Used for file upload. Format: {'file': open('filename', 'rb')}.
allow_redirects	→	(bool) — Whether to follow redirects (default is True).
proxies	→	(dict) To route the request through a proxy.
stream	→	(bool) — If True, doesn't download the response immediately.
verify	→	(bool or str) SSL cert verification. Set to False to skip (not recommended).
cert	→	(str or tuple) — Client-side SSL certs, if required.

Example 1 - Sending Form Data,

```
Python
import requests
payload = {'username': 'user', 'password': 'pass'}
response = requests.post('https://httpbin.org/post', data=payload)
print(response.text)
```

Example 2 - Sending JSON Data,

```
Python
import requests
json_data = {'id': 101, 'name': 'John'}
response=requests.post('https://httpbin.org/post',json=json_data)
print(response.json())
```

Uploading a File

```python
import requests

file = open('myImage.jpg', 'rb')
data = {'file': file }
response = requests.post('https://httpbin.org/post', files = data)
print(response.text)
```

PUT Requests

- Replaces the entire resource with new data.
- Often used when you know the **full structure** of the resource.

Example,

```python
import requests

url = "https://api.example.com/user/123"
data = {"name": "Alice", "email": "alice@example.com"}
response = requests.put(url = url, json = data)
print(response.status_code)
```

PATCH Requests

- Updates **only part** of the resource.
- Useful when you want to **change one or two fields**.

Example,

```python
import requests

url = "https://api.example.com/user/123"
data = {"email": "newemail@example.com"}
response = requests.patch(url = url, json = data)
print(response.status_code)
```

DELETE Requests

- Deletes the specified resource from the server.
- Usually doesn't require a body.

Example,

```python
import requests

url = "https://api.example.com/user/123"
response = requests.delete( url )
print(response.status_code)
```

Insight

PUT, PATCH, and DELETE methods accept the same arguments as POST and GET, such as headers, params, data, json, auth, and timeout. The difference lies in the type of action each method performs on the server.

Key Terms

Timeout Parameter
Status Codes
Raise for Status
SSL Verification
Exception Handling
GET
PUT
POST
PATCH
DELETE

Review Questions

1. Which exception occurs when the server is unreachable?
   a) Timeout
   b) ConnectionError
   c) HTTPError
   d) TooManyRedirects
   Answer: b

2. What does response.raise_for_status() do?
   a) Retries the request
   b) Raises an HTTPError for bad responses
   c) Ignores redirects
   d) Converts JSON to Python dict
   Answer: b

3. Which error occurs when a request exceeds the allowed number of redirects?
   a) Timeout
   b) ConnectionError
   c) TooManyRedirects
   d) RequestException
   Answer: c

4. Which exception can catch all requests-related errors?
   a) HTTPError
   b) RequestException
   c) Timeout
   d) ValueError
   Answer: b

5. What error is raised when a request takes longer than the specified time?
   a) ConnectionError
   b) Timeout
   c) HTTPError
   d) TooManyRedirects
   Answer: b

Review Exercises

1. Write a Python program using requests.get() to fetch a URL and handle ConnectionError and Timeout.

2. Use requests.post() to send JSON data to https://httpbin.org/post and handle HTTPError if the response is not successful.

3. Create a script that requests https://httpbin.org/redirect/5 with allow_redirects=True and handles TooManyRedirects exception.

Msoffcrypto-tool

The **msoffcrypto-tool** library provides Python-based tools for working with encrypted Microsoft Office documents. It can be used to decrypt supported Microsoft Office files using passwords or other supported keys and can also encrypt OOXML documents such as Word (.docx), Excel (.xlsx), and PowerPoint (.pptx) files.

The library is particularly useful when an application needs to process protected Office documents programmatically. Instead of manually opening a document and entering a password, Python code can be used to provide the required credentials and read, decrypt, or create protected Office files.

The library supports several Microsoft Office encryption formats and key types. For password-based operations, the OfficeFile interface can be used to load a password before decrypting a document. For OOXML encryption, the OOXMLFile class provides an encrypt() method.

Installation
msoffcrypto-tool is not included in Python's standard library. It can be installed from the Python Package Index (PyPI) using pip:

```
pip install msoffcrypto-tool
```

After installation, the library can be imported into a Python program using:
import msoffcrypto

Encrypting Microsoft Office Files

Encryption involves protecting a document with a password so that unauthorized users cannot open or access its contents without the required credentials.
The msoffcrypto-tool library provides OOXML encryption through the OOXMLFile class. OOXML is the document format used by modern Microsoft Office applications, including Word (.docx), Excel (.xlsx), and PowerPoint (.pptx).

The encryption process generally involves the following steps:

1. Open the original Office document in binary mode.
2. Create an OOXMLFile object from the opened file.
3. Specify a password and an output destination.
4. Save the encrypted data to a new file.

Note

The encryption functionality is currently documented as **experimental** by the msoffcrypto-tool project. The examples in this section demonstrate the API and should be tested carefully before being incorporated into production systems.

Example 1 — Encrypting a Word Document

The following example encrypts a .docx file and stores the encrypted result in memory before writing it to a new file.

```python
import msoffcrypto
from io import BytesIO
from pathlib import Path

outfile = BytesIO()  # Creates an in-memory buffer for the encrypted file

with open("document.docx", "rb") as file:
    msfile = msoffcrypto.OfficeFile(file)
    msfile.encrypt("my_password", outfile=outfile)

Path("encrypted_document.docx").write_bytes(
    outfile.getvalue()
)  # Writes the encrypted data to a new Word document
```

The **BytesIO** object creates an in-memory binary buffer. Instead of immediately writing the encrypted document to disk, the encrypted data is temporarily stored in this buffer. The **getvalue()** method then retrieves the resulting bytes, which can be written to a file.

The **with open(...)** statement automatically closes the source file when the block finishes, so an explicit **file.close()** call is unnecessary.

Example 2 — Encrypting a Word Document with OOXMLFile

The OOXMLFile class can be used directly when working with OOXML documents:

```python
from msoffcrypto.format.ooxml import OOXMLFile

# Creates an OOXMLFile object from the document
with open("document.docx", "rb") as file:
    msfile = OOXMLFile(file)

    # Encrypts the document into the output file
    with open("encrypted_document.docx", "wb") as outfile:
        msfile.encrypt("my_password123", outfile)
```

Here, the source document is opened in binary-read mode ("rb"), while the destination document is opened in binary-write mode ("wb"). The ***encrypt()*** method receives the password and the output file where the encrypted document will be stored.

Example 3 – Encrypting an Excel Workbook
The same approach can be applied to an Excel workbook because .xlsx files are also OOXML documents:

```python
from msoffcrypto.format.ooxml import OOXMLFile

# Creates an OOXMLFile object for the workbook
with open("records.xlsx", "rb") as file:
    msfile = OOXMLFile(file)

    # Encrypts the workbook with the password
    with open("encrypted_records.xlsx", "wb") as outfile:
        msfile.encrypt("mypass_123", outfile)
```

The original workbook remains unchanged, while the encrypted version is written to encrypted_records.xlsx.

Decryption

Decryption is the process of removing encryption from a protected file so that its contents can be accessed normally. In the case of password-protected Microsoft Office documents, the correct password is required to decrypt the file.

The decryption process is similar to the encryption process. The protected document is first opened in binary mode, an appropriate msoffcrypto file object is created, and the password is supplied using the **load_key()** method. The **decrypt()** method then writes the decrypted document to an output destination.

Example 1 – Decrypting a Password-Protected .docx File
The following example decrypts a password-protected Word document and saves the decrypted result as a new .docx file.

```python
from msoffcrypto.format.ooxml import OOXMLFile
from io import BytesIO

outfile = BytesIO() # Creates an in-memory buffer for the decrypted document
```

```
with open("encrypted_document.docx", "rb") as file:
    msfile = OOXMLFile(file)
    msfile.load_key("mypass_123")  #Password for the file
    msfile.decrypt(outfile=outfile)

with open("decrypted_document.docx", "wb") as file:
    file.write(outfile.getvalue())
```

In this example, *encrypted_document.docx* is the encrypted source document, while *decrypted_document.docx* is the decrypted output.

The **BytesIO** object is used as an in-memory binary buffer. The decrypted document is first written into this buffer by **decrypt()**. The **getvalue()** method then retrieves the resulting binary data, which is written to the new file using binary-write mode ("wb").

The **load_key()** method supplies the password required for decryption. If the supplied password is incorrect, the document cannot be successfully decrypted.

Key Terms

Encryption
Decryption
OOXMLFile
load_key
io
ByteIO

Review Questions

1. What is msoffcrypto-tool primarily designed to work with?
A. Image files
B. Microsoft Office files
C. Audio files
D. Database files
Answer: B
2. Which command installs the package?
A. pip install msoffcrypto
B. pip install msoffcrypto-tool
C. pip install officecrypto
D. python install msoffcrypto
Answer: B
3. Which Office file format can be processed by msoffcrypto-tool?
A. .docx
B. .xlsx
C. .pptx
D. All of the above
Answer: D
4. Which Python class can be used to work with an Office file?
A. OfficeFile
B. OfficeDocument
C. MSFile
D. DocumentFile
Answer: A
5. What is the purpose of BytesIO in the examples?
A. To store data in memory as a file-like binary stream
B. To encrypt Python source code
C. To create a database
D. To convert text to speech
Answer: A
6. Which method is used to provide a password before decrypting an Office file?
A. set_password()
B. load_key()
C. decrypt_key()
D. password()
Answer: B
7. Which method performs the decryption operation?
A. unlock()
B. decode()
C. decrypt()
D. open()
Answer: C
8. Which module contains the OOXMLFile class used in the examples?
A. msoffcrypto.format.ooxml
B. msoffcrypto.office.ooxml
C. msoffcrypto.ooxml.file
D. msoffcrypto.tools
Answer: A
9. Why is BytesIO useful when encrypting or decrypting files?
A. It provides an in-memory binary destination
B. It automatically creates passwords
C. It installs Office applications
D. It converts PDFs to Word documents
Answer: A
10. What is required to decrypt a password-protected Office file?
A. The original filename only
B. The file extension only
C. The appropriate password/key
D. An Internet connection
Answer: C

Review Exercises

1. Install msoffcrypto-tool and write a program that encrypts a .docx file with a password.
2. Modify the encryption program to process an .xlsx file.
3. Write a program that decrypts a password-protected Office document when the correct password is supplied.
4. Create a program that reads an Office file into memory using BytesIO, encrypts it, and writes the encrypted result to a new file.
5. Create a small utility that allows the user to select between encrypting and decrypting a supported Office document

Pikepdf

pikepdf is a powerful Python library for reading, inspecting, manipulating and transforming PDF documents. It provides an interface for working with the internal structure of PDF files and can be used for tasks such as opening and saving PDFs, creating blank PDF documents, merging and splitting pages, modifying PDF objects, working with metadata, handling encrypted documents, and optimizing PDF content.

Unlike libraries designed primarily for creating PDF documents from scratch, pikepdf is particularly well suited to working with existing PDF files. It is built on the QPDF library and provides Python-friendly access to many of the structures and operations found inside a PDF document.

pikepdf is not included in Python's standard library and must be installed separately.

Installation
Install pikepdf using the following command:

```
pip install pikepdf
```

1. Creating a PDF

pikepdf can create a new, empty PDF document using the **new()** method of the **Pdf** class. Although pikepdf can create a blank PDF and add pages to it, its primary strength is manipulating and transforming existing PDF documents.

The **add_blank_page()** method adds an empty page to the newly created document.

Example:

```python
from pikepdf import Pdf

new_pdf = Pdf.new()            # Create a new PDF document
new_pdf.add_blank_page()       # Add a blank page

new_pdf.save("new_document.pdf")
```

The Pdf.new() method creates an empty PDF object in memory, while add_blank_page() adds a blank page to the document. The **save()** method then writes the PDF to a file.

By default, add_blank_page() creates a page using US Letter dimensions unless another page size is specified.

2. Opening a PDF

Before performing operations such as reading, inspecting, modifying, splitting, merging, or saving an existing PDF, the document must first be opened.

pikepdf provides the *Pdf.open()* method for opening a PDF file. The method accepts the path to the PDF file and returns a Pdf object representing the document.

Example:

```
Python
from pikepdf import Pdf

pdf = Pdf.open("hello.pdf")
print(pdf.filename)
```

Once the PDF has been opened, its pages and other internal structures can be accessed through the returned Pdf object.

pikepdf also provides pikepdf.open() as a convenient alias for pikepdf.Pdf.open().

3. Opening and Saving a PDF

A common pattern is to open an existing PDF, perform an operation, and save the result as another PDF file.

```
Python
from pikepdf import Pdf

with Pdf.open("document.pdf") as pdf:
    pdf.save("new_document.pdf")
```

The **with** statement is recommended when working with PDF files because it ensures that the PDF object is properly closed when the block finishes executing.

4. Opening a Password-Protected PDF

Some PDF documents are encrypted and require a password before their contents can be accessed. pikepdf supports opening encrypted PDFs by supplying the password through the password parameter of Pdf.open().

Example:

```python
from pikepdf import Pdf

with Pdf.open("document.pdf", password="mypass") as pdf:
    print(pdf.docinfo)
```

If the document requires a password and the correct password is not supplied, the PDF may not be opened successfully.

pikepdf supports opening most encrypted PDF files by supplying the appropriate password.

5. Getting PDF Information

A PDF document contains more than the visible pages displayed by a PDF reader. Internally, it contains dictionaries, streams, objects, page trees, metadata, and other structures that describe how the document is organized.

pikepdf provides several properties and methods that allow you to inspect these structures.

For example, the **objects** property provides an iterable collection of the objects contained in the PDF. These objects may represent pages, fonts and other internal PDF structures.

Example:

```python
from pikepdf import Pdf

pdf = Pdf.open("document.pdf")
print(pdf.objects)
```

Other PDF Attributes

pikepdf provides several useful properties for obtaining information about a PDF document.

Method	Definition
pdf_version	Returns the version of the PDF specification used by the document, such as 1.7.
filename	Returns the source filename associated with the PDF when available.

docinfo	Provides access to the older PDF Document Information dictionary containing metadata such as title, author, creator, producer, creation date, and modification date.
objects	Provides an iterable collection of the PDF objects contained in the document.
pages	Provides access to the pages contained in the PDF.
Root	Provides access to the document's root dictionary, which represents the main catalog of the PDF.
get_warnings()	Retrieves warnings generated while opening or processing a PDF.

Table 7.6

```python
Python
from pikepdf import Pdf

with Pdf.open("mydocument.pdf") as pdf:
    print(f"Filename -> { pdf.filename}")
    print(f"PDF Version -> { pdf.pdf_version}")
    print(f"PDF Info -> { pdf.docinfo}")
```

```
Output
Filename -> mydocument.pdf
PDF Version -> 1.7
PDF Info -> pikepdf.Dictionary({
  "/Author": "Asiedu Williams",
  "/CreationDate": "D:20260516115345+00'00'",
  "/Creator": "Microsoft® Word for Microsoft 365",
  "/ModDate": "D:20260516115345+00'00'",
  "/Producer": "Microsoft® Word for Microsoft 365"
})
```

6. Getting Pages

A PDF document consists of one or more pages organized within a single PDF file. In pikepdf, pages are accessed through the pages property of a Pdf object. The pages follow Python's standard zero-based indexing system: the first page has an index of 0, the second page has an index of 1, the third page has an index of 2 and so on.

The pages property behaves similarly to a Python list, allowing you to access, add, remove, insert, and rearrange pages.

Example:

```python
from pikepdf import Pdf

file = Pdf.open("document.pdf")
pages = file.pages

# Get the total number of pages
print(f"Total pages -> {len(pages)}")

# Access the underlying PDF object of the first page
print(f"First page object -> {pages[0].obj}")
```

```
Output
Total pages -> 4
First page object -> <pikepdf.Dictionary(Type="/Page")({
  "/Contents": pikepdf.Stream(owner=<...>, data=b' /Span <</MCID
    0/Lan'..., {
    "/Filter": "/FlateDecode",
    "/Length": 450
  }),
  "/Group": {
   ...
```

Insight

Page indexes start at 0, not 1. Therefore, pages[0] refers to the first page, while pages[1] refers to the second page.

Methods and Operations of the pages Object

Because pdf.pages follows the Python list protocol, many familiar list operations can be used to manipulate PDF pages.

append(page)

The append() method adds a page to the end of a PDF document.

For example, the following code opens two PDF documents and appends the second page of file1 to file2:

```python
from pikepdf import Pdf

file1 = Pdf.open("document1.pdf")
file2 = Pdf.open("document2.pdf")

# Add the second page of file1 to file2
file2.pages.append(file1.pages[1])
file2.save("new_document.pdf")
```

extend(pages)

The extend() method adds multiple pages to the end of a PDF document.

```python
from pikepdf import Pdf

first_file = Pdf.open("document1.pdf")
second_file = Pdf.open("document2.pdf")

# Add all pages from first_file to the second_file
second_file.pages.extend(first_file.pages)
second_file.save("new_document.pdf")
```

In this example, all pages from file1 are appended to file2.

insert(index, page)

The insert() method adds a page at a specified position.

```python
from pikepdf import Pdf

file1 = Pdf.open("document1.pdf")
file2 = Pdf.open("document2.pdf")

# Insert the first page of file1 at the third page of file2
file2.pages.insert(2, file1.pages[0])
file2.save("new_document.pdf")
```

The first argument, 2, specifies the position at which the page should be inserted. Since PDF pages use zero-based indexing, position 2 represents the third page of the document.

remove(page)

The remove() method removes a specified page from the page list.

```python
from pikepdf import Pdf

file = Pdf.open("document.pdf")

file.pages.remove(file.pages[0])  # Remove the first page
file.pages.remove(file.pages[3])  # Remove the fourth page

file.save("edited_document.pdf")
```

> **Note**
>
> Be careful when removing multiple pages in succession. Once a page is removed, the indexes of the remaining pages may change.
>
> For example, after removing pages[0], the page that was previously at index 1 becomes the new page at index 0.

reverse()

The reverse() method reverses the order of the pages in the document. For example, a document arranged as:

Page 1 → Page 2 → Page 3 → Page 4

becomes:

Page 4 → Page 3 → Page 2 → Page 1

The operation does not sort the pages into ascending or descending numerical order; it simply reverses their existing order.

```python
from pikepdf import Pdf

file = Pdf.open("document.pdf")

file.pages.reverse()  # Reverse the order of all pages
file.save("new_document.pdf")
```

index(page)

The index() method returns the position of a specified page in the page list.

7. Deleting Pages

pikepdf allows unwanted pages to be removed from a PDF document. Pages can be deleted using normal Python list operations, including the **remove()** method and the **del** statement.

Using remove()

The remove() method is useful when you have a reference to the page you want to remove.

```python
from pikepdf import Pdf

file = Pdf.open("document.pdf")
page = file.pages[0]
file.pages.remove(page)
file.save("new_file.pdf")
```

This removes the first page from the document.

Using the del Statement

Python's built-in **del** statement can also be used to remove a page or a range of pages.

```python
from pikepdf import Pdf

del file.pages[2]      # Delete the third page
del file.pages[1:4]    # Deletes from the second page to the third page
file.save("new_file.pdf")
```

8. Splitting a PDF

Splitting a PDF involves separating a document into multiple PDF files. A common approach is to create a new PDF for each page of the original document.

The following example loops through all pages, creates a new PDF for each page, adds the current page to it, and saves the page as a separate PDF file.

```python

from pikepdf import Pdf
```

```
file = Pdf.open("document.pdf")

for index, page in enumerate(file.pages):
    new_file = Pdf.new()                # Create a new empty PDF
    new_file.pages.append(page)         # Add the current page to the new PDF
    new_file.save(f"file_{index}.pdf") # Save the page as a separate PDF
```

If the original document contains four pages, the program produces files similar to:
file_0.pdf
file_1.pdf
file_2.pdf
file_3.pdf

9. Merging PDFs

Merging PDFs involves combining pages from multiple PDF documents into a single PDF file. This is sometimes referred to as concatenating PDF documents.

One simple approach is to create a new PDF and extend its pages with the pages from each source document.

Example 1 – Merging a List of PDF Files

```python
from pikepdf import Pdf

new_file = Pdf.new()

files = ["file1.pdf", "file2.pdf", "file3.pdf"]

for filename in files:
    doc = Pdf.open(filename)
    new_file.pages.extend(doc.pages)

new_file.save("new_document.pdf")
```

The program opens each PDF in the files list and adds all of its pages to new_file. The resulting document contains the pages in the same order as the files appear in the list.

Example 2 – Merging PDFs Using glob

Python's glob module can be used to locate files matching a particular pattern. This is useful when several PDF files are stored in the same directory.

```python
from glob import glob
from pikepdf import Pdf

new_file = Pdf.new()

for filename in glob("*.pdf"):
    doc = Pdf.open(filename)
    new_file.pages.extend(doc.pages)

new_file.save("new_document.pdf")
```

The pattern *.pdf matches every PDF files in the current directory.

Insight

The order in which files are returned by **glob()** should not be relied upon when a specific document order is important. If the order matters, it is better to provide an explicitly ordered list of filenames or sort the results before merging.

10. Encryption and Decryption

PDF documents can contain sensitive or restricted information. pikepdf provides support for PDF encryption, allowing developers to protect documents with passwords and configure certain document permissions.

Encryption can be applied when saving a PDF by supplying a **pikepdf.Encryption** object to the **save()** method. Permissions can be configured using **pikepdf.Permissions**.

Encryption

Encryption is the process of protecting a PDF so that access to its contents can require a password. The Encryption class provides settings for configuring PDF encryption.

```
pikepdf.Encryption(
    owner = "owner_password",
    user = "user_password",
    allow = pikepdf.Permissions(...),
)
```

The principal parameters include:

Parameter	Description
owner	Specifies the owner password used to control permissions and security settings.
user	Specifies the user password required to open the encrypted document when one is set.
allow	Specifies the operations that users are permitted to perform on the document through a pikepdf.Permissions object.

Table 7.7

pikepdf's current versions select a strong encryption method by default when creating encrypted PDFs. The exact encryption algorithm and security handler depend on the settings and capabilities of the PDF specification supported by the installed version.

Encrypting a PDF with a Password

The following example creates a password-protected copy of a PDF:

```python
from pikepdf import Pdf, Encryption

file = Pdf.open("document.pdf")

file.save(
    "encrypted.pdf",    #the new filename
    encryption = Encryption(
        user="user123",
        owner="owner456"
    )
)
```

When the resulting PDF is opened, the user password can be required to access the document.

Restricting PDF Operations

The **pikepdf.Permissions** class can be used to specify operations that should be restricted.

```python
from pikepdf import Pdf, Encryption, Permissions

file = Pdf.open("document.pdf")
permission = Permissions(
    print_lowres=True,        #default->True
    print_highres=True,       #default->True
    accessibility= True,      #default->True
    extract=False,            #default -> False
    modify_annotation=True, #default->True
```

```
    modify_assembly= True,  #default -> False
    modify_form= True,      #default->True
    modify_other=True,      #default->True
)

file.save(
    "encrypted.pdf",
    encryption = Encryption(
        user="user123",
        owner="mypass123",
        allow=permission,
        aes= True,
    )
)
```

Decryption

Decryption is the process of opening an encrypted PDF with the appropriate credentials and saving an unencrypted copy.

For example,

```
Python
from pikepdf import Pdf

with Pdf.open("encrypted.pdf", password="user123") as pdf:
    pdf.save("decrypted.pdf")
```

The resulting **decrypted.pdf** is saved without the encryption applied to the source document.

Insight

The **is_encrypted** property can be used to determine whether a PDF is encrypted. If the document is encrypted, the result is True; otherwise, it is False.

The **encryption** method also provides information about the document's encryption configuration when available. For example:

```
>>> from pikepdf import Pdf
>>> pdf = Pdf.open("document.pdf")
>>> print(pdf.is_encrypted)
... True
```

Key Terms

save
new
Permissions
is_encrypted
owner
user

Review Questions

1. What is pikepdf primarily used for?
A. Working with PDF files
B. Creating databases
C. Automating the mouse
D. Processing audio
Answer: A
2. Which command installs pikepdf?
A. pip install pdf
B. pip install pikepdf
C. pip install python-pdf
D. python install pikepdf
Answer: B
3. Which class is commonly used to create and manipulate PDF documents with pikepdf?
A. PDFFile
B. Document
C. Pdf
D. PDFDocument
Answer: C
4. Which method creates a new PDF document?
A. Pdf.create()
B. Pdf.new()
C. Pdf.make()
D. Pdf.create_new()
Answer: B
5. Which method opens an existing PDF?
A. Pdf.read()
B. Pdf.load()
C. Pdf.open()
D. Pdf.import()
Answer: C
6. What does add_blank_page() do?
A. Deletes a PDF page
B. Adds an empty page to a PDF
C. Encrypts a page
D. Extracts text from a page
Answer: B
7. Which object provides access to the pages of a PDF?
A. pages
B. documents
C. pdfpages
D. page_list
Answer: A
8. Which method can be used to add several pages **to a PDF?**
A. extend()
B. expand()
C. append_all()
D. add_pages()
Answer: A
9. Which Python operation can remove a page or range of pages from the pages collection?
A. del
B. remove_page
C. delete
D. erase
Answer: A
10. What is one common purpose of PDF encryption?
A. To protect a PDF from unauthorized access
B. To convert a PDF to an image
C. To increase the number of pages
D. To change Python syntax
Answer: A

Review Exercises

1. Create a new PDF document with pikepdf and add several blank pages to it.
2. Open an existing PDF and write a program that displays the total number of pages.
3. Create a program that removes selected pages from a PDF and saves the result as a new file.
4. Write a program that splits a multi-page PDF into separate PDF files, with each output file containing one page.
5. Create a PDF-merging utility that accepts several PDF filenames and combines them into a single PDF document.

Yt-dlp (Video and Audio Downloader)

The **yt-dlp** module is an advanced, open-source Python library and command-line utility designed for downloading videos, audios, subtitles, and metadata from YouTube and over 1,000 other supported websites.

It is a fork of the popular youtube-dl project and is actively maintained with improved performance, better site compatibility, and enhanced options for customization.

yt-dlp can:

- Extract media files in various formats (e.g., MP4, MP3, WebM).
- Download and merge separate video and audio streams using **FFmpeg**.
- Automatically handle playlists, subtitles, and metadata.
- Support cookies, authentication, and post-processing like audio conversion.

Why Use yt-dlp?

1. **High Performance** – Optimized for faster downloads and multi-threaded fragment fetching.
2. **Wider Site Support** – Works on over a thousand platforms, including YouTube, Vimeo, Facebook, and TikTok.
3. **Simple Syntax** – Easy-to-use Python interface and command structure.
4. **Extensive Options** – Customize video quality, subtitles, file naming, and post-processing.
5. **Metadata Extraction** – Extracts rich metadata such as title, channel, upload date, and duration.
6. **Actively Maintained** – Regular updates by contributors ensure compatibility and performance.
7. **Community Driven** – Open-source and supported by an active Python developer community.Installation

yt-dlp can be installed via pip:

```
pip install yt-dlp
```

Dependencies and System Requirements

yt-dlp depends on FFmpeg, a multimedia framework used to process, convert, and merge audio or video streams. Without FFmpeg, yt-dlp can still download media, but merging or post-processing (like embedding thumbnails or metadata) will fail.

Installing FFmpeg:

Windows

1. Download FFmpeg from ffmpeg.org.
2. Extract the package.
3. Add the bin directory to your system PATH.

macOS

```
brew install ffmpeg
```

Linux

```
sudo apt update
sudo apt install ffmpeg
```

Downloading Videos or Audio

The main interface for programmatic downloads is the **YoutubeDL()** class. The downloading process should be managed with the **with** statement, ensuring that resources are properly opened and released.

Example,

```python
import yt_dlp
url = "https://www.youtube.com/watch?v=abcd1234"
options = {
    "format": "bestvideo+bestaudio/best",    # Best video+audio
    "merge_output_format": "mp4",            # Merge format
    "outtmpl": "%(title)s.%(ext)s",          # File naming
}

with yt_dlp.YoutubeDL(options) as ydl:
    ydl.download([url])
```

Key Points

📌 **url** → The video or playlist link copied from YouTube or another supported site.

📌 **format** → Defines which quality to download. Examples:

- "bestvideo+bestaudio/best" → best quality video & audio merged.
- "bestaudio/best" → best audio only (ideal for songs or podcasts).

📌 **merge_output_format** → Specifies the final file format (e.g., mp4, webm).

📌 **outtmpl** → Controls file naming:

- %(title)s → Video title
- %(uploader)s → Channel name
- %(ext)s → File extension

Additional Options

Subtitles Options

📌 "**writesubtitles**": True → download subtitles if available
📌 "**writeautomaticsubtitles**": True → auto-generated captions
📌 "**subtitleslangs**": ["en"] → language(s) to download
📌 "**subtitlesformat**": "srt" → save as .srt

Metadata / Thumbnail

📌 "**writeinfojson**": True → save metadata JSON
📌 "**writethumbnail**": True → download thumbnail
📌 "**embedthumbnail**": True → embed thumbnail (needs FFmpeg)
📌 "**embedmetadata**": True → embed metadata

Performance

📌 "**retries**": 5 → retry failed downloads
📌 "**fragment_retries**": 5 → retry failed fragments
📌 "**concurrent_fragment_downloads**": 5 → download multiple fragments at once

Playlists

📌 "**yesplaylist**": True → download playlist if URL is playlist
📌 "**playlist_items**": "1-5,10" → download only specific videos

Error Handling

- 📌 "**ignoreerrors**": True → skip failed videos
- 📌 "**no_warnings**": True → suppress warnings

Extracting Metadata

yt-dlp can also fetch video information only, such as title, duration, uploader, and formats, without actually downloading the media:

Example,

Python

```
import yt_dlp

url = "https://www.youtube.com/watch?v=example"

with yt_dlp.YoutubeDL() as ydl:
    info = ydl.extract_info(url, download=False)
    print(info.get('title'))
    print(info.get('duration'))
    print(info.get('uploader'))
    print(info.get('view_count'))
```

Insight

This is particularly useful when you only need video details such as title, uploader, duration, or view count without saving the file.

Key Terms

YoutubeDL
merge_output_format
outtmpl
FFmpeg
extract_info
metadata

Review Questions

1. Which error occurs if a video is removed or private?
   a) DownloadError
   b) UnavailableVideoError
   c) ExtractorError
   d) PostProcessingError
   Answer: b

2. What is required for merging video and audio streams in yt-dlp?
   a) Python standard library
   b) FFmpeg
   c) curl
   d) Requests library
   Answer: b

3. Which method fetches video metadata without downloading the file?
   a) download()
   b) extract_info(download=False)
   c) write_text()
   d) open()
   Answer: b

4. If a URL is unsupported or invalid, which error is raised?
   a) GeoRestrictedError
   b) ExtractorError
   c) PostProcessingError
   d) TimeoutError
   Answer: b

5. What option allows skipping failed videos in a playlist?
   a) "ignoreerrors": True
   b) "retries": 5
   c) "yesplaylist": True
   d) "outtmpl": "%(title)s.%(ext)s"
   Answer: a

Review Exercises

1. Write a Python script using yt-dlp to download a YouTube video and handle DownloadError if the video cannot be retrieved.

2. Use yt-dlp to extract metadata (title, uploader, duration) from a video URL without downloading it and handle ExtractorError.

3. Download a playlist of videos but skip unavailable videos using "ignoreerrors": True, and ensure FFmpeg is used to merge audio and video streams

JSON and Pickle

JSON

The **json** (JavaScript Object Notation) module in Python plays a crucial role in data exchange, especially between systems or applications. It allows for:

Encoding (serialization): Converting Python objects into JSON-formatted strings.

Decoding (deserialization): Converting JSON-formatted strings back into Python objects.

JSON is commonly used when:

- Receiving data from web servers (APIs).
- Communicating with applications written in other languages (e.g., JavaScript, Java, PHP).
- Storing lightweight configuration files or settings.
- Persisting structured data in a human-readable format.

Insight

JSON data is structured as key-value pairs, much like Python dictionaries.
{ key : value }

Why Use JSON?

1. Supports structured data like objects, arrays, numbers, strings, booleans, and null.
2. Easy to read and write for both humans and machines.
3. Lightweight format with small size — great for transmitting over the web.
4. Language-independent but supported in almost every programming language.
5. Fast parsing and generation.
6. Ideal for RESTful APIs.
7. Easily integrates with HTTP requests and responses.

Common JSON Methods

Method	Description
json.dump()	Serialize Python object and write to file
json.dumps()	Serialize Python object to JSON string
json.load()	Deserialize JSON content from a file
json.loads()	Deserialize JSON string to Python object

Table 7.8

Encoding (Serializing)

dump() and dumps()

Common Parameters

Parameter	Type	Description	Example
obj	Any	The Python object to serialize (e.g., dict, list). Required.	json.dumps({"name": "John"})
fp	File object	File-like object with a .write() method where the output is written. Used only in json.dump().	json.dump(data, open("file.json", "w"))
skipkeys	bool	If True, skips non-string dictionary keys instead of raising a TypeError.	skipkeys=True
ensure_ascii	bool	If True, escapes non-ASCII characters using \uXXXX sequences.	ensure_ascii=False
check_circular	bool	If False, disables circular reference checks. Defaults to True.	check_circular=True
allow_nan	bool	If True, allows NaN, Infinity, and -Infinity. Defaults to True.	allow_nan=True
cls	Class	A custom JSONEncoder subclass for custom serialization.	cls=CustomEncoder
indent	int or str	When None, output is compact; an int provides spacing; a str (like "\t") allows custom indent characters.	indent=4 , indent="\t"
separators	tuple	Controls how items are separated: (item_separator, key_separator). Defaults to (', ', ': ').	separators=(',', ':')
default	Function	A function called for objects that can't be serialized by default.	default=str
sort_keys	bool	If True, the output will be sorted by dictionary keys.	sort_keys=True

Table 7.9

Method	Description
json.dump()	Serialize Python object and write to file
json.dumps()	Serialize Python object to JSON string
json.load()	Deserialize JSON content from a file
json.loads()	Deserialize JSON string to Python object

Table 8.0

Example 1- dump()

```
Python
import json

data = {
    "firstname" : "George",
     "lastname" : "Wood",
     "country" :  "Canada",
     "age" : 25,
     "id" : 68392
}

with open("data.json", "w") as file:
      json.dump(data, file)
```

Key Points

- The code above saves a file named data.json that contains JSON-formatted data.
- JSON files use the .json file extension.

Insight

Reading and writing files with **open()** were covered in the previous chapter under File Handling and Byte Operations.

Example 2 - dump()

```
Python
import json

profile = {"name" : "Bob",
           "email" : "bob@gmail.com",
           "profession" :  "Data Scientist"}

file_Obj = open("profile.json", "w")
json.dump( profile, file_Obj)
```

Example 3 - dumps(),

```python
import json

student = {
    "name" : "John",
     "college" : "Harvard",
     "year" : 2,
     "course" : "Computer Science"
}

#serialize string to JSON
jsonString =  json.dumps(student)

print( jsonString )
```

```
#Output
{"name": "John", "college": "Harvard", "year": 2, "course": "Computer Science"}
```

Key Points

- json.dumps() takes a Python object (commonly a dictionary) as a required argument.
- json.dumps() serializes (encodes) the object into a JSON-formatted string.
- The resulting JSON string can then be sent over a network, written to a file, or passed to other systems or languages.
- json.dumps() ensures the data is converted into a text format that complies with the JSON standard.

Decoding (Deserializing)

load() and loads()

Common Parameters

Parameter	Type	Description	Example
fp	File object	A file-like object containing a JSON document.	json.load(open("data.json"))
s	str	JSON string to decode.	json.loads('{"name": "Alice"}')
cls	Class	Custom JSONDecoder subclass.	cls=MyDecoder

object_hook	function	Custom function to convert dicts into custom objects.	object_hook=my_converter
parse_float	function	Custom function to parse float values (e.g., to use Decimal).	parse_float=Decimal
parse_int	function	Custom function to parse integer values.	parse_int=lambda x: int(x) * 2
parse_constant	function	Handles constants like NaN, Infinity, and -Infinity.	parse_constant=my_handler
object_pairs_hook	function	Similar to object_hook but called with a list of key-value pairs.	object_pairs_hook=OrderedDict
strict	bool	If False, allows control characters in strings. Defaults to True.	strict = False

Table 8.1

Example 1 - load(),

```
Python
import json

file =  open("data.json")

#deserialize JSON file content
json_string = json.load( file)
print( json_string )
```

```
#Output
{'firstname': 'Alice', 'lastname': 'Wood', 'country': 'Canada', 'age': 25, 'id': 68392}
```

Example 2 - load(),

```
Python
import json

#deserialize JSON String
with open("profile.json") as file:
     json_string = json.load( file )

print( json_string )
```

```
#Output
{'name': 'Bob', 'email': 'bob@gmail.com', 'profession': 'Data Scientist'}
```

Example 3 - loads(),

```
••• Python
import json

json_string = '{"name": "box", "color": "red", "size": 10 }'
decoded = json.loads(  json_string )
print( decoded )
```

```
#Output
{'name': 'box', 'color': 'red', 'size': 10}
```

Key Points

- json.loads() decodes (deserializes) a JSON **string** into a Python object.
- json.load() loads and decodes a JSON **file** (or file-like object) into a Python object.
- The decoded JSON content is returned as native Python types like dict, list, str, int, float, bool, or None.
- The json.load() method is typically used when working with .json files stored on disk.
- json.loads() is best used when you have JSON data in **string format** (e.g., from an API or text stream).

Pickle

The pickle module in Python is used for serializing and deserializing Python objects. While it serves a similar purpose to the json module in that both can save and load data, pickle is specific to Python and can handle a much wider range of Python objects, not just dictionaries or **key-value** pairs.

Unlike JSON (which is a text-based format readable across many programming languages), pickle saves data in a binary format. This makes it more powerful for internal use in Python applications, but also less portable.

Key Features of pickle

- Allows you to serialize (pickle) and deserialize (unpickle) complex Python objects (e.g., classes, functions, sets, custom objects).
- Offers fast and efficient storage and retrieval of Python objects.
- Supports almost all Python data types, including those that JSON cannot handle like tuples, sets, and class instances.
- Stores data in a **.pkl** or **.pickle** binary file format.
- It is Python-specific — data pickled in Python can't be easily read in other languages.

Common Pickle Methods

Method	Description
pickle.dump()	Serializes (pickles) a Python object and writes it to a binary file.
pickle.dumps()	Serializes a Python object and returns it as a byte string.
pickle.load()	Reads a pickled object from a binary file and deserializes it.
pickle.loads()	Deserializes a pickled object from a byte string.
pickle.pickler	A class used to create a custom pickle writer with more control.
pickle.unpickler	A class used to create a custom pickle reader for deserialization.

Table 8.2

Writing to a Pickle File (Serializing)

pickle.dump() and pickle.dumps()

Common Parameters

Parameter	Description
obj	The Python object you want to serialize (convert to binary format).

file	A file-like object opened in binary write mode (wb) where the data will be written.
protocol	(Optional) The protocol version to use. 0–5. By default, it uses the highest supported protocol.
fix_imports	If True (default), makes Python 2-to-3 compatible pickles (mainly useful when writing Python 3 pickles that should be readable in Python 2).
buffer_callback	(Optional) For out-of-band buffers (used in advanced scenarios with protocol 5+). Typically not needed unless working with binary data efficiently.

Table 8.3

Example 1 - dump(),

```python
import pickle

profile = {
    "name" : "Winifred",
    "profile_id": 205,
    "birthday": "10th April, 1998",
    "email": "wini@gmail.com",
    "favorite" : ["nature", "music", "programming"]
}

with open("profile.pickle", "wb") as file:
      pickle.dump(profile, file)
```

Example 2 - dumps(),

```python
import pickle

profile = {
    "name" : "Winifred",
    "profile_id": 205,
    "birthday": "10th April, 1998",
    "email": "wini@gmail.com",
    "favorite" : ["nature", "music", "programming"]
}

byte_data = pickle.dumps(profile)
```

Reading from a Pickle File (Deserializing)

pickle.load() and pickle.loads()

Common Parameters

Paramter	Description
file	A file-like object opened in binary read mode (rb) containing pickled data.
data	A bytes-like object containing pickled data (e.g., from a file, network, etc.)
fix_imports	For Python 2 compatibility. When True, attempts to map old module names to new ones.
encoding	Only used if the pickled data is from Python 2. Common options: 'ASCII', 'latin1', 'bytes'.
errors	Error handling for decoding non-ASCII bytes. Same as in standard text decoding.
buffers	Optional. Sequence of out-of-band buffers if the object uses pickle.PickleBuffer. Used for efficient memory handling in complex objects.

Table 8.4

Example 1 - load(),

Python
```
import pickle

file = open("profile.pickle", "rb")
data = pickle.load(file)
name = data.get('name')
birthday = data.get('birthday')
email = data.get('email')
favorites = data.get('favorite')

print(name)
print(birthday)
print(email)
print(favorites)
```

```
#Output
Winifred
10th April, 1998
wini@gmail.com
['nature', 'music', 'programming']
```

Insight

The **profile.pickle** file was created using **pickle.dump()**. To view its contents, refer to the explanation of **pickle.dump()**.

Example 2 - loads(),

Python
```
import pickle

from pathlib import Path

filebytes = Path('profile.pickle').read_bytes()

data = pickle.loads(filebytes)

name = data.get('name')
id = data.get('profile_id')
birthday = data.get('birthday')
email = data.get('email')
favorites = data.get('favorite')

print(name)
print(id)
print(birthday)
print(email)
print(favorites)
```

```
#Output
Winifred
205
10th April, 1998
wini@gmail.com
['nature', 'music', 'programming']
```

Key Terms

Serialization
Deserialization
Encoding
Decoding
dump
load
loads

Review Questions

1. Which error occurs when JSON is invalid?
   a) TypeError
   b) JSONDecodeError
   c) EOFError
   d) FileNotFoundError
   Answer: b

2. Which method serializes a Python object into a JSON-formatted string?
   a) json.load()
   b) json.dumps()
   c) pickle.load()
   d) pickle.loads()
   Answer: b

3. What is the main difference between JSON and Pickle?
   a) JSON is binary; Pickle is text
   b) JSON is Python-specific; Pickle is language-independent
   c) JSON is text-based and cross-language; Pickle is binary and Python-specific
   d) Both are identical in functionality
   Answer: c

4. Which Pickle error occurs when reading a corrupted file?
   a) EOFError
   b) PickleError / UnpicklingError
   c) FileNotFoundError
   d) JSONDecodeError
   Answer: b

5. Which Python type is NOT JSON-serializable by default?
   a) dict
   b) list
   c) set
   d) int
   Answer: c

Review Exercises

1. Create a Python script to serialize a dictionary containing user information into a JSON file, then read it back and print the content. Handle JSONDecodeError.

2. Use Pickle to serialize a Python list of custom objects into a .pkl file and then deserialize it. Handle EOFError and PickleError.

3. Compare serialization with json.dumps() and pickle.dumps() for a Python dictionary containing integers, strings, and a set. Explain why Pickle succeeds where JSON fails.

SQLite3

Data is a crucial part of any software application. It often works hand in hand with the logic of a program, which makes it essential to store data persistently for continued use and reference. This process goes beyond just saving data—it involves organizing it in a structured manner and managing it efficiently. This is where database systems come into play.
Almost every application that processes or stores data utilizes a Database Management System (DBMS)—either built into the app or connected externally. In Python, several database modules are available to work with both client-server databases and standalone (embedded) databases.
Examples of Python-compatible database modules include:

- sqlite3 (built-in, embedded)
- mysql-connector-python (for MySQL)
- psycopg2 (for PostgreSQL)
- sqlalchemy (ORM that supports multiple DBMS)
- pyodbc (for Microsoft SQL Server and others)

Some database modules require external server software (e.g., MySQL, PostgreSQL), while others like sqlite3 work without any additional dependencies.

What is SQLite3?

sqlite3 is a lightweight, embedded database engine included in the Python Standard Library. It doesn't require a separate server or installation. Data is stored in a local file with the **.db** or **.sqlite** extension, making it an ideal choice for desktop, mobile, or embedded applications where ease of use and simplicity are a priority.

Key Feature of SQLite3?

- No installation required (bundled with Python)
- Cross-platform compatibility
- Lightweight and fast for small to medium datasets
- Great for prototyping and local storage
- SQL-compliant with support for standard SQL syntax
- Integrated with Python via the sqlite3 module
- Data persistence between program executions
- File-based storage (no need for a server)

📖 **Note**

Before using a database, it's important to design your data model or structure in advance. This helps ensure efficient data storage and retrieval. See the sample model below for reference. For example

Social Media

Profile

ID (Primary Key)	Name	Country	Date of Birth	Profile Picture

Metrics

ID (Foreign Key)	Comments	Likes	Favorites	Followers

SQLite3 Methods

Parameter	Description
sqlite3.connect(database)	Connects to a SQLite database file. Creates the file if it doesn't exist.
connection.cursor()	Returns a Cursor object used to execute SQL commands.
cursor.execute(sql, params)	Executes a single SQL statement. Can use placeholders for parameters.
cursor.executemany(sql, seq)	Executes the same SQL statement for a sequence of parameters.
cursor.executescript(script)	Executes multiple SQL statements at once separated by semicolons.
cursor.fetchone()	Fetches the next row of a query result set. Returns a single tuple or None.
cursor.fetchall()	Fetches all (remaining) rows of a query result. Returns a list of tuples.
cursor.fetchmany(size)	Fetches the next set of rows (up to size) from a query result.
connection.commit()	Saves (commits) all changes made in the current transaction.
connection.rollback()	Rolls back the current transaction.
cursor.close()	Closes the cursor object.
connection.close()	Closes the connection to the database.
sqlite3.connect(':memory:')	Creates a temporary in-memory database instead of a file.
sqlite3.Row	A row factory that enables name-based access to columns (like a dictionary).
sqlite3.version	Returns the version of the sqlite3 module.
sqlite3.sqlite_version	Returns the version of the SQLite engine itself.

Table 8.5

Creating and Connecting to a SQLite Database File

Before data can be stored or accessed, it must be saved in a database file. This file acts as the data source for your application. Losing the database file means losing the stored data, so it's crucial to keep it in a secure location—ideally within your application folder or a protected storage path.

Syntax

```
object = sqlite3.connect("path")
```

Example,

```python
import sqlite3
object = sqlite3.connect("document/database.db")
```

Key Points

- The above code creates a new SQLite database file if it doesn't already exist.
- If the specified file already exists, the code connects to the existing database.
- The ***database.db*** file stores the database in a binary format, including tables, records, and other objects.

Creating a Cursor

Once you've successfully connected to a database file, the next step is to create a **cursor**. A cursor is used to execute SQL commands and interact with the database—such as inserting, retrieving, updating, and deleting records

Syntax

```
cursor = object.cursor()
```

Example,

```python
import sqlite3

object = sqlite3.connect("document/database.db")
cursor = object.cursor()
```

Key Points

- A cursor is an object created from the database connection.
- It acts as a control structure that allows you to execute SQL commands and fetch data from the result set.
- A cursor should be closed (optional but recommended) when no longer needed, using cursor.close().
- You can create multiple cursors from the same connection if needed.

Note

After making changes to a table or records in the database, it's important to save those changes and properly close the database connection. This is done using **connection.commit()** to save the changes and **connection.close()** to close the connection to the database.

Querying Records

To interact with a SQLite3 database, you must write SQL (Structured Query Language) statements. These statements instruct the database on how to store, update, retrieve, or delete data. They function much like keywords in Python—predefined commands that SQLite understands and executes.

Syntax

```
#Execute a single statement
cursor.execute("sql statement", param)

#Execute same statement with different param
cursor.executemany("sql statement", [param] )

#Execute multiple statements
cursor.executescript( script )
```

Example,

```
Python
import sqlite3
object = sqlite3.connect("database.db")
cursor = object.cursor()
cursor.execute("SELECT something FROM data_table")
```

Creating a Table

A database table is similar to a grid consisting of rows and columns. Before data can be stored, a table must be created with a unique name and structured columns, each having its own data type.

```
CREATE TABLE IF NOT EXISTS table_name (
  column_name1 DATATYPE PRIMARY KEY AUTOINCREMENT,
  column_name2 DATATYPE,
  column_name3 DATATYPE NOT NULL,
  column_name4 DATATYPE UNIQUE,
  column_name5 DATATYPE CHECK(column_name6 > 0),
  column_name6 DATATYPE DEFAULT 'value',
  FOREIGN KEY(column_name1) REFERENCES table(column)
);
```

Explanation

- IF NOT EXISTS is optional but helps prevent errors if the table already exists.
- **table_name** can be in any case format—uppercase, lowercase, camelCase, or Capitalized.
- The column definitions must be enclosed within parentheses ().
- **column_name** can be any valid string identifier. It should describe the type of data the column will hold.
- Each column definition ends with a comma, except the last one.
- Data types in SQLite3 include:
    - INTEGER → Whole numbers
    - TEXT → Strings of any length
    - VARCHAR(n) → Strings with a maximum length n
    - REAL → Floating-point numbers
    - BLOB → Binary Large Objects (e.g., images, audio, files)
    - BOOLEAN → True/False (stored as 0/1 internally)
    - DATE → Date values
    - DATETIME → Date and time values

- **PRIMARY KEY** is optional but helps uniquely identify each record.
- **NOT NULL** means that a column must contain a value and cannot be left empty.
- **UNIQUE** prevents duplicate entries in a column or group of columns.
- **AUTOINCREMENT** guarantees strictly increasing numbers (no reuse even after deletion).
- **DEFAULT** sets a default value if none is provided during insertion.
- **CHECK** validates that values meet a given condition before insertion.
- **FOREIGN KEY** creates a relationship between two tables. Links a column in one table to the **PRIMARY KEY** of another.

Note

- Use **AUTOINCREMENT** only when you need guaranteed monotonic IDs. AUTOINCREMENT must follow INTEGER PRIMARY KEY in SQLite. eg. (column_name INTEGER PRIMARY KEY AUTOINCREMENT)
- Always prefer **NOT NULL** and **CHECK** for data integrity.
- Use **FOREIGN KEY** constraints to maintain relationships between tables.

Example 1 – Creating a student table

COLUMN	ID	Firstname	Lastname	Year	Department	Course
ROW1						
ROW2						
ROW3						
ROW4						

Table Structure

Python

```python
import sqlite3
```

```
conn = sqlite3.connect("datafile.db")
cursor = conn.cursor()

cursor.execute('''
            CREATE TABLE IF NOT EXISTS student (
                    id INTEGER PRIMARY KEY,
                    firstname VARCHAR(100),
                    lastname VARCHAR(100),
                    year INTEGER NOT NULL,
                    department VARCHAR(100),
                    course VARCHAR(100)
                   );
         ''')
```

Insight

An SQLite database file can contain multiple tables, which may be either related or independent. A relationship between tables is typically established through **keys**—most commonly a **Primary Key** in one table and a corresponding **Foreign Key** in another. The **Primary Key** uniquely identifies each record in a table, while the **Foreign Key** creates a link to the Primary Key of another table, enabling data integrity and relational mapping.

Altering Tables

As your application grows, you might need to make changes to your database structure—such as adding new columns, renaming existing ones, or changing column data types. SQLite provides the **ALTER TABLE** command to make such modifications without recreating the entire table.

Syntax

```
#--Add a new column
ALTER TABLE table_name ADD COLUMN column_name DATA_TYPE;

#--Rename an existing table
ALTER TABLE old_table_name RENAME TO new_table_name;

#--Rename a column (SQLite 3.25.0+)
ALTER TABLE table_name RENAME COLUMN old_column_name TO new_column_name;
```

Key Points

- **ALTER TABLE** is used to modify the structure of an existing table.
- You can add columns, rename tables, and rename columns.
- You cannot drop a column directly in SQLite.
- When adding a column, it must have a default value or allow **NULL** unless values are provided for existing rows.
- Column types must be valid SQLite data types (e.g., TEXT, INTEGER, REAL, BLOB, NUMERIC).

> **Note**
>
> To delete the entire table, use
>
> **DROP TABLE** table_name;
>
> **Effect**: Deletes the entire table including its structure and data.

Example 1 – Adding new column,

```python
import sqlite3

conn = sqlite3.connect("datafile.db")
cursor = conn.cursor()

cursor.execute(" ALTER TABLE student ADD COLUMN email  TEXT ")
```

This adds a new column called **email** to the student table.

Example 2 - Renaming a table

```python
import sqlite3

conn = sqlite3.connect("datafile.db")
cursor = conn.cursor()

cursor.execute("ALTER TABLE student RENAME TO student_profile")
```

This renames the **student** table to **student_profile**.

Example 3 – Renaming a column,

```python
import sqlite3

conn = sqlite3.connect("datafile.db")
cursor = conn.cursor()

cursor.execute("ALTER TABLE student RENAME COLUMN lastname  TO  surname")
```

This changes the column name **lastname** to **surname**.

Adding Records to a Database

After creating the table(s), you can begin inserting records. The **INSERT INTO** statement specifies the target table and the corresponding columns where values should be stored. Each value must match the data type and order of the specified columns. If a value is not provided for a column, **NULL** is automatically inserted—unless the column has a **NOT NULL** constraint.

Syntax

```
INSERT INTO table (column1, column2, ...)  VALUES (value1, value2, ...);
```

Using Parameters(recommended)

```
"INSERT INTO table (column1, column2, ...)  VALUES(?, ? ...)", (value1, value2 ... );
```

Reference Table

```python
cursor.execute("""CREATE TABLE IF NOT EXISTS student(
      ID INTEGER NOT NULL,
      FIRSTNAME VARCHAR(100),
      LASTNAME VARCHAR(100),
      YEAR INT,
      COURSE VARCHAR(100)
     );"""
)
```

Example 1 – Using the simple approach,

```python
import sqlite3

connection = sqlite3.connect("datafile.db")
cursor = connection.cursor()

cursor.execute("""
      INSERT INTO student (ID, FIRSTNAME, LASTNAME, YEAR, COURSE)
      VALUES (489, "John", "Diego", 2, "Computer Science")
   """)

cursor.execute("""
      INSERT INTO student (ID, FIRSTNAME, LASTNAME, YEAR, COURSE)
      VALUES (785, "Marvin", "Delson", 4, "Optometry")
   """)

connection.commit()  #Saves the record
connection.close()
```

Example 2 – Using parameters (recommended approach),

```python
import sqlite3

connection = sqlite3.connect("datafile.db")
cursor = connection.cursor()

cursor.execute("""
   INSERT INTO student (ID, FIRSTNAME, LASTNAME, YEAR, COURSE)
   VALUES(?,?,?,?,?)""",
   (268, "Marrie", "Bridge", 2, "Electrical Engineering")
  )

cursor.execute("""
   INSERT INTO student (ID, FIRSTNAME, LASTNAME, YEAR, COURSE)
   VALUES(?,?,?,?,?)""",
   (925, "Gloria", "Olivet", 3, "Biological Science")
  )

connection.commit()  #Saves the record
connection.close()
```

Example 3 - Adding many records at once,

●●● Python

```python
import sqlite3

connection = sqlite3.connect("datafile.db")
cursor = connection.cursor()

data = [
    (489, "John", "Diego", 2, "Computer Science"),
    (785, "Marvin", "Delson", 4, "Optometry"),
    (268, "Marrie", "Bridge", 2, "Electrical Engineering"),
    (925, "Gloria", "Olivet", 3, "Biological Science")
]

cursor.executemany("""
   INSERT INTO student (ID, FIRSTNAME, LASTNAME, YEAR, COURSE)
   VALUES(?,?,?,?,?)""",
   data
  )

connection.commit()  #Saves the record
connection.close()
```

Insight

The **executemany()** method is ideal for inserting multiple records at once. Unlike **execute()**, which adds a single record per call, ***executemany()*** takes a list of data tuples and executes the same SQL statement for all of them in one operation. This approach is faster and more efficient for bulk data insertion.

Updating Records

If an existing record in the database needs to be changed, the **UPDATE** statement is used. You specify the table name, the column(s) to update, the new values, and a condition (**WHERE**) to select which rows should be updated.

Syntax

```
UPDATE table_name
SET column1 = new_value1, column2 = new_value2
WHERE condition;
```

Using Parameters(recommended)

```
UPDATE table_name
SET column1 = ?, column2 = ?
WHERE condition = ?
(value1, value2, condition)
```

Reference Table

ID	FIRSTNAME	LASTNAME	YEAR	COURSE
489	John	Diego	2	Computer Science
785	Marvin	Delson	4	Optometry
268	Marrie	Bridge	2	Electrical Engineering
925	Gloria	Olivet	3	Biological Science

Example 1 – Using the simple approach,

```python
import sqlite3
conn = sqlite3.connect("datafile.db")
cursor = conn.cursor()

cursor.execute("""
    UPDATE student
    SET lastname = "Wood"
    WHERE firstname = "John"
    """,
)

cursor.execute("""
    UPDATE student
    SET course = "Communication Design", id = 642, year = 1
    WHERE lastname = "Bridge"
    """,
)
```

```
conn.commit()  #Updates the records
conn.close()
```

Updates

ID	FIRSTNAME	LASTNAME	YEAR	COURSE
489	John	**Wood**	2	Computer Science
785	Marvin	Delson	4	Optometry
642	Marrie	Bridge	**1**	**Communication Design**
925	Gloria	Olivet	3	Biological Science

Example 2 – Using parameters (recommended approach),

```
Python
import sqlite3

connection = sqlite3.connect("datafile.db")
cursor = connection.cursor()

cursor.execute("""
    UPDATE student
    SET firstname = ?
    WHERE id = ?""",
    ("Diana", 925)
)

cursor.execute("""
    UPDATE student
    SET firstname = ?, lastname = ?, course = ?
    WHERE id = ?""",
    ("George", "Kingston", "Biochemistry", 785)
)

connection.commit()  #Updates the records
connection.close()
```

Updates

ID	FIRSTNAME	LASTNAME	YEAR	COURSE
489	John	Diego	2	Computer Science
785	**George**	**Kingston**	4	**Biochemistry**
268	Marrie	Bridge	2	Electrical Engineering
925	**Diana**	Olivet	3	Biological Science

Deleting Records from the Database

Sometimes, records stored in a database may contain errors, become outdated, or no longer be relevant to the application. SQL provides a simple and powerful command to delete such records from a table.

Syntax

```
#Deleting an entire records from the table
DELETE FROM table_name

#Deleting a single or specified record from the table
DELETE FROM table_name WHERE condition
```

Reference Table

TYPE	CATEGORY	NUTRIENT	DEFICIENCY	VALUE
fish	Animal	Protein	Poor vision	5
carrot	Plant	Vitamin B	Dry skin	8
beans	Plant	Protein	Poor growth	4
tomato	Plant	Vitamin A	Night blindness	10

Example 1 ,

```
Python
import sqlite3

connection = sqlite3.connect("datafile.db")
cursor = connection.cursor()

cursor.execute(""" DELETE FROM food WHERE type = 'beans' """)

connection.commit()  #Saves the records
connection.close()
```

Results

TYPE	CATEGORY	NUTRIENT	DEFICIENCY	VALUE
fish	Animal	Protein	Poor vision	5
carrot	Plant	Vitamin B	Dry skin	8
tomato	Plant	Vitamin A	Night blindness	10

Example 2 ,

```
••• Python
cursor.execute(""" DELETE FROM food WHERE category = 'Plant' """)

connection.commit()  #Saves the records
connection.close()
```

Results

TYPE	CATEGORY	NUTRIENT	DEFICIENCY	VALUE
fish	Animal	Protein	Poor vision	5

Example 3 ,

```
••• Python
cursor.execute(""" DELETE FROM food WHERE value > 5 """)

connection.commit()  #Saves the records
connection.close()
```

Results

TYPE	CATEGORY	NUTRIENT	DEFICIENCY	VALUE
fish	Animal	Protein	Poor vision	5
beans	Plant	Protein	Poor growth	4

Example 4 ,

```
••• Python

cursor.execute(""" DELETE FROM food """)

connection.commit()  #Saves the records
connection.close()
```

Results

TYPE	CATEGORY	NUTRIENT	DEFICIENCY	VALUE

Fetching Data from a Database

Fetching data refers to retrieving records stored in a database for use within a program. This process is essential, as most applications rely on stored data for displaying information, applying configurations, providing feedback, and general application logic. Depending on the requirement, you can retrieve all records at once, a specified number of records, or just a single record.

Record Fetching Methods

Method	Description
fetchone	Fetches the next single row
fetchmany(size)	Fetches the next 'size' number of rows
fetchall	Fetches all rows from the last executed query

Table 8.6

Syntax

```
records = cursor.fetchall()
records = cursor.fetchmany(size)
record  = cursor.fetchone()
```

Key Points

- These methods are used after executing a **SELECT** query with **cursor.execute()**.
- **fetchall()** retrieves all results at once and stores them in a list of tuples.
- **fetchmany(size)** retrieves the next set of rows (as specified by size) and is memory-efficient for large datasets.
- **fetchone()** returns the next single row and is useful when expecting only one result or reading results one at a time.
- If no more rows are available, fetchone() and fetchmany() return None and an empty list respectively.

SQL Commands for Fetching Records

SQL provides several commands for retrieving data from a database. These commands fall under the **Data Query Language (DQL)** category and are mainly used with the **SELECT** statement. Below are grouped and described commands commonly used for fetching records:

Reference Model

Title: Zoo Management System

animals

id	name	category	feed	location
1	Lion	Mammal	Carnivore	Savannah Zone
2	Monkey	Mammal	Omnivore	Jungle Habitat
3	Crocodile	Reptile	Carnivore	Swamp Area
4	Python	Reptile	Carnivore	Snake House
5	Elephant	Mammal	Herbivore	Grassland
6	Eagle	Bird	Carnivore	Aviary

animal_stats

id	weight_kg	age_years	care_cost	health_status
1	190.5	8	350.00	Good
2	35.0	5	120.00	Good
3	420.0	12	400.00	Fair
4	75.2	6	200.00	Good
5	5400.0	20	600.00	Good
6	6.5	4	180.00	Excellent

Basic SELECT Commands

Command	Description
SELECT * FROM table_name;	Fetches all columns and rows from the specified table.
SELECT column1, column2 FROM table_name;	Fetches specific columns from the table.
SELECT DISTINCT column FROM table_name;	Fetches unique (non-duplicate) values from a column.

Table 8.7

Example 1 – Getting an entire records,

Python
```python
import sqlite3

conn = sqlite3.connect("database.db")
cursor = conn.cursor()

cursor.execute("SELECT * FROM animals")
records = cursor.fetchall()
print(records)
```

```
#Output
[(1, 'Lion', 'Mammal', 'Carnivore', 'Savannah Zone'), (2, 'Monkey', 'Mammal', 'Omnivore', 'Jungle Habitat'), (3, 'Crocodile', 'Reptile', 'Carnivore', 'Swamp Area'), (4, 'Python', 'Reptile', 'Carnivore', 'Snake House'), (5, 'Elephant', 'Mammal', 'Herbivore', 'Grassland'), (6, 'Eagle', 'Bird', 'Carnivore', 'Aviary')]
```

Note

The results returned from an SQL query in Python are typically presented as a list of tuples. While these results can be used for various purposes in your program, they may not be visually appealing when printed directly. To improve readability and present the data in a clean, table-like format, you can use the ***tabulate*** or the ***pandas*** module.
You can install it using the command: **pip install tabulate pandas**

Example 2 - Extracting id, name and location,

```python
import sqlite3
from tabulate import tabulate

conn = sqlite3.connect("database.db")
cursor = conn.cursor()

cursor.execute("SELECT id, name, location FROM animals")
records = cursor.fetchall()
columns = [x[0] for x in cursor.description ]

table = tabulate(records, headers=columns, tablefmt="grid")
print(table)
```

```
#Output
+------+-----------+----------------+
|   id | name      | location       |
+======+===========+================+
|    1 | Lion      | Savannah Zone  |
+------+-----------+----------------+
|    2 | Monkey    | Jungle Habitat |
+------+-----------+----------------+
|    3 | Crocodile | Swamp Area     |
+------+-----------+----------------+
|    4 | Python    | Snake House    |
```

```
+------+-----------+---------------+
|    5 | Elephant  | Grassland     |
+------+-----------+---------------+
|    6 | Eagle     | Aviary        |
+------+-----------+---------------+
```

Example 3 - Extracting distinctive records,

```
Python

cursor.execute("SELECT DISTINCT name FROM animals")
records = cursor.fetchall()
```

Select with Conditions(Filtering Data)

Command	Description
SELECT * FROM table_name WHERE column = value;	Fetches rows where the column matches a value.
SELECT * FROM table_name WHERE column IN (val1, val2);	Fetches rows where column matches any value in a list.
SELECT * FROM table_name WHERE condition;	Fetches rows that meet a specified condition.
SELECT * FROM table_name WHERE column BETWEEN val1 AND val2;	Fetches rows with values within a range.
SELECT * FROM table_name WHERE column LIKE pattern;	Fetches rows using pattern matching (e.g., 'A%' for names starting with 'A').

Table 8.8

Example 1 – Selecting a single record,

```
Python
import sqlite3
from tabulate import tabulate

conn = sqlite3.connect("database.db")
cursor = conn.cursor()

cursor.execute("SELECT * FROM animals WHERE name = 'Elephant' ")
records = cursor.fetchall()
columns = [x[0] for x in cursor.description ]

table = tabulate(records, headers=columns, tablefmt="grid")
print(table)
```

```
#Output
+------+----------+------------+-----------+------------+
|   id | name     | category   | feed      | location   |
+======+==========+============+===========+============+
|    5 | Elephant | Mammal     | Herbivore | Grassland  |
+------+----------+------------+-----------+------------+
```

Example 2 – Selecting individual records using **IN**

```python
cursor.execute("""
    SELECT id, name, location FROM animals
    WHERE name IN ('Lion','Eagle','Python')
 """)
records = cursor.fetchall()
columns = [x[0] for x in cursor.description ]

table = tabulate(records, headers=columns, tablefmt="grid")
print(table)
```

```
#Output

+======+========+============+===============+
|    1 | Lion   | Mammal     | Savannah Zone |
+------+--------+------------+---------------+
|    4 | Python | Reptile    | Snake House   |
+------+--------+------------+---------------+
|    6 | Eagle  | Bird       | Aviary        |
+------+--------+------------+---------------+
```

Example 3 – Selecting records based on condition,

```python
cursor.execute("SELECT * FROM animal_stats WHERE care_cost > 300")
rows = cursor.fetchall()
columns = [ x[0] for x in cursor.description ]

table = tabulate(rows, headers=columns, tablefmt="grid")
print(table)
```

```
#Output
+------+-------------+-------------+-------------+-----------------+
|   id |   weight_kg |   age_years |   care_cost | health_status   |
+======+=============+=============+=============+=================+
|    1 |       190.5 |           8 |         350 | Good            |
+------+-------------+-------------+-------------+-----------------+
|    3 |       420   |          12 |         400 | Fair            |
+------+-------------+-------------+-------------+-----------------+
|    5 |      5400   |          20 |         600 | Good            |
+------+-------------+-------------+-------------+-----------------+
```

Example 4 – Selecting records between ranges using **BETWEEN**,

```python
cursor.execute("""
       SELECT * FROM animal_stats
       WHERE age_years BETWEEN 1 AND 6
""")

rows = cursor.fetchall()
columns = [ x[0] for x in cursor.description ]

table = tabulate(rows, headers=columns, tablefmt="grid")
print(table)
```

```
#Output
+------+-------------+-------------+-------------+-----------------+
|   id |   weight_kg |   age_years |   care_cost | health_status   |
+======+=============+=============+=============+=================+
|    2 |        35   |           5 |         120 | Good            |
+------+-------------+-------------+-------------+-----------------+
|    4 |        75.2 |           6 |         200 | Good            |
+------+-------------+-------------+-------------+-----------------+
|    6 |         6.5 |           4 |         180 | Excellent       |
+------+-------------+-------------+-------------+-----------------+
```

Pattern Matching in SQLite

SQLite supports pattern matching mainly through two operators — **LIKE** (case-insensitive by default) and **GLOB** (case-sensitive and Unix shell–style). These patterns help you filter rows based on specific string matches.

LIKE Operator Patterns

Pattern	Meaning	Example
'A%'	Strings starting with "A"	Antelope, Anaconda
'%A'	Strings ending with "A"	Panda, Anaconda
'%A%'	Strings containing "A" anywhere	Cat, Bat
'A_t'	"A" followed by any single character, then "t"	Ant
'A__%'	"A" followed by two characters or more	Alligator, Anaconda
'____'	Exact number of characters (here: 4 letters)	Lion, Tiger

Table 8.9

Wildcards:

- % → any sequence of zero or more characters
- _ → any single character

GLOB Operator Patterns

Pattern	Meaning	Example
'A*'	Strings starting with "A"	'Antelope', 'Alligator'
'*A'	Strings ending with "A"	'Cobra', 'Panda'
'*A*'	Strings containing "A"	'Camel', 'Panther'
'A?C'	"A" followed by one character, then "C"	'ABC', 'AXC'
'[A-C]*'	Strings starting with A, B, or C	'Bear', 'Cat', 'Ant'
'A*'	Strings starting with "A"	'Antelope', 'Alligator'

Table 9.0

Wildcards:

- * → matches zero or more characters
- ? → matches exactly one character
- [abc] → matches any single character in the set
- [A-Z] → matches any single character in the range

Example 5 – Getting all animals starting with '**E**' using **LIKE**

Python

```python
cursor.execute(" SELECT * FROM animals WHERE name LIKE 'E%' ")
rows = cursor.fetchall()
columns = [ head[0] for head in cursor.description ]

table = tabulate(rows, headers=columns, tablefmt="grid")
print(table)
```

```
#Output
+------+----------+-----------+-----------+------------+
|   id | name     | category  | feed      | location   |
+======+==========+===========+===========+============+
|    5 | Elephant | Mammal    | Herbivore | Grassland  |
+------+----------+-----------+-----------+------------+
|    6 | Eagle    | Bird      | Carnivore | Aviary     |
+------+----------+-----------+-----------+------------+
```

Example 6 – Fetching all animals with letter '**o**' using **GLOB**

```python
cursor.execute(" SELECT * FROM animals WHERE name GLOB '*o*' ")
rows = cursor.fetchall()
columns = [ head[0] for head in cursor.description ]

table = tabulate(rows, headers=columns, tablefmt="grid")
print(table)
```

```
#Output
+------+-----------+------------+-----------+-----------------+
|   id | name      | category   | feed      | location        |
+======+===========+============+===========+=================+
|    1 | Lion      | Mammal     | Carnivore | Savannah Zone   |
+------+-----------+------------+-----------+-----------------+
|    2 | Monkey    | Mammal     | Omnivore  | Jungle Habitat  |
+------+-----------+------------+-----------+-----------------+
|    3 | Crocodile | Reptile    | Carnivore | Swamp Area      |
+------+-----------+------------+-----------+-----------------+
|    4 | Python    | Reptile    | Carnivore | Snake House     |
+------+-----------+------------+-----------+-----------------+
```

SELECT with Sorting and Limiting

Command	Description
SELECT * FROM table_name ORDER BY column ASC;	Fetches data sorted by a column in ascending order.
SELECT * FROM table_name ORDER BY column DESC;	Fetches data sorted by a column in descending order.
SELECT * FROM table_name LIMIT number;	Limits the number of rows returned. Useful for pagination or previewing results.
SELECT * FROM table_name ORDER BY column ASC;	Fetches data sorted by a column in ascending order.

Table 9.1

Example 1 – Fetch and sort data in descending order using **ORDER BY**, **DESC**

```
Python
import sqlite3
import pandas

connection = sqlite3.connect("database.db")

data = pandas.read_sql_query(
    "SELECT * FROM animals ORDER BY id DESC", connection
)

print(data)
```

```
#Output
   id       name category       feed        location
0   6      Eagle     Bird  Carnivore          Aviary
1   5   Elephant   Mammal  Herbivore       Grassland
2   4     Python  Reptile  Carnivore     Snake House
3   3  Crocodile  Reptile  Carnivore      Swamp Area
4   2     Monkey   Mammal   Omnivore  Jungle Habitat
5   1       Lion   Mammal  Carnivore   Savannah Zone
```

Example 2 – Fetch records with limited number of rows using **LIMIT**,

```
Python
import sqlite3
import pandas

connection = sqlite3.connect("database.db")

data = pandas.read_sql_query(
    "SELECT * FROM animals LIMIT 3", connection
)

print(data)
```

```
#Output
   id       name category       feed        location
0   1       Lion   Mammal  Carnivore   Savannah Zone
1   2     Monkey   Mammal   Omnivore  Jungle Habitat
2   3  Crocodile  Reptile  Carnivore      Swamp Area
```

SELECT with Aggregates(Summarizing Data)

Command	Description
SELECT COUNT(*) FROM table_name;	Returns the total number of rows.
SELECT MAX(column) FROM table_name;	Returns the maximum value in a column.
SELECT MIN(column) FROM table_name;	Returns the minimum value in a column.
SELECT AVG(column) FROM table_name;	Returns the average value of a column.
SELECT SUM(column) FROM table_name;	Returns the sum of a numeric column.

Table 9.2

Example

Python
```
import sqlite3
import pandas

conn = sqlite3.connect("database.db")

total_animal = pandas.read_sql_query("""
    SELECT COUNT(*) FROM animals """, conn)

max_weight = pandas.read_sql_query("""
    SELECT MAX(weight_kg) FROM animal_stats """, conn)

min_weight = pandas.read_sql_query("""
    SELECT MIN(weight_kg) FROM animal_stats """, conn)

average_age = pandas.read_sql_query("""
    SELECT AVG(age_years) FROM animal_stats """, conn)

total_cost = pandas.read_sql_query("""
    SELECT SUM(care_cost) FROM animal_stats """, conn)

print(total_animal)
print(max_weight)
print(min_weight)
print(average_age)
print(total_cost)
```

```
#Output
COUNT(*)
0        6
   MAX(weight_kg)
0          5400.0
   MAX(weight_kg)
0          5400.0
   AVG(age_years)
0        9.166667
   SUM(care_cost)
0          1850.0
```

SELECT with Grouping

Command	Description
SELECT column, COUNT(*) FROM table_name GROUP BY column;	Groups records and applies aggregate functions.
SELECT column, COUNT(*) FROM table_name GROUP BY column HAVING COUNT(*) > 1;	Filters groups using aggregate condition (like WHERE but for groups).

Table 9.3

Example 1 – Fetch records grouped by feed type column using GROUP BY,

```python
import sqlite3
from tabulate import tabulate

conn = sqlite3.connect("database.db")
cursor = conn.cursor()

cursor.execute("SELECT * FROM animals GROUP BY feed")
records = cursor.fetchall()
columns = [x[0] for x in cursor.description ]

table = tabulate(records, headers=columns, tablefmt="grid")
print(table)
```

```
#Output
+------+----------+------------+-----------+-----------------+
|   id | name     | category   | feed      | location        |
+======+==========+============+===========+=================+
|    1 | Lion     | Mammal     | Carnivore | Savannah Zone   |
+------+----------+------------+-----------+-----------------+
|    5 | Elephant | Mammal     | Herbivore | Grassland       |
+------+----------+------------+-----------+-----------------+
|    2 | Monkey   | Mammal     | Omnivore  | Jungle Habitat  |
+------+----------+------------+-----------+-----------------+
```

Key Terms

Primary Key
Foreign Key
Cursor
Connection
Transaction
AUTOINCREMENT
fetchone
fetchmany
fetchall
LIKE
GLOB
Commit

Review Questions

1. Which method is used to save changes in SQLite?
a) cursor.commit()
b) connection.commit()
c) cursor.save()
d) connection.save()
Answer: b

2. What happens if DELETE FROM table is executed without a WHERE clause?
a) Deletes one record
b) Deletes all records
c) Throws an error
d) Deletes only rows with NULL values
Answer: b

3. Which method fetches all rows of a query result?
a) fetchone()
b) fetchmany()
c) fetchall()
d) execute()
Answer: c

4. In SQLite, what is the effect of UPDATE student SET id = 642 if id is a PRIMARY KEY?
a) Safe operation
b) May break foreign key constraints
c) Converts id to TEXT
d) Auto-increments id
Answer: b

5. Which operator is case-sensitive in SQLite?
a) LIKE
b) GLOB
c) BETWEEN
d) IN
Answer: b

6. Which SQL statement retrieves unique values from a column?
a) SELECT column FROM table
b) SELECT DISTINCT column FROM table
c) SELECT UNIQUE column FROM table
d) SELECT column GROUP BY column
Answer: b

7. What is returned by fetchone() when no rows remain?
a) Empty tuple
b) None
c) Empty list
d) Zero
Answer: b

8. Which method is recommended for inserting multiple records efficiently?
a) execute()
b) executemany()
c) executescript()
d) fetchall()
Answer: b

9. To rename a column in SQLite 3.24.0, which statement is correct?
a) ALTER TABLE table_name RENAME COLUMN old TO new
b) RENAME COLUMN table_name old TO new
c) ALTER COLUMN table_name old RENAME TO new
d) ALTER TABLE table_name CHANGE COLUMN old new
Answer: a

Review Exercises

1. Database Setup:
Create a SQLite database company.db and a table employees with columns: emp_id INTEGER PRIMARY KEY AUTOINCREMENT, name TEXT, department TEXT, salary REAL. Insert 5 sample records.

2. Update Records:
Update the department of one employee and increase the salary of another using parameterized queries. Fetch all records to verify changes.

3. Delete Records:
Delete employees with salary less than 50000. Ensure deletion does not affect other records.

4. Fetching & Filtering:
Retrieve all employees in the "IT" department. Then fetch employees with names starting with "A" using LIKE. Display results in a tabular format using tabulate.

Pyttsx3 (Text -to-Speech)

Text-to-speech (TTS) has become an essential feature in mobile, web, and desktop applications, offering accessibility, user convenience, and automation. This functionality is based on the concept of converting written text into spoken audio. Its counterpart, speech-to-text, converts spoken words into written text and typically relies on machine learning or AI-powered models.

In Python, **pyttsx3** is a popular offline module used for text-to-speech conversion. Unlike cloud-based solutions, pyttsx3 works without an internet connection, making it ideal for local applications.

Installation

The pyttsx3 module is not included in the standard Python library. You can install it via pip:

```
$ pip install pyttsx3
```

Why Use Text-to-Speech in Applications

- Enhances accessibility for visually impaired users.
- Improves user interaction through voice-enabled responses.
- Useful in virtual assistants and chatbots.
- Can generate audio for learning tools or audiobooks.
- Allows dynamic content to be voiced without pre-recorded audio.
- Supports multiple voices and adjustable speech rate for customization.
- Works offline, ensuring privacy and speed in local applications.

Text-to-Speech Methods

Methods	Description
pyttsx3.speak(text)	Method to queue text to be spoken
pyttsx3.init()	Function used to initialize the TTS engine
pyttsx3.engine	Controls voice, speech rate, volume, and queues text for speaking
pyttsx3.driver	Manages speech synthesis under the hood (e.g., 'sapi5', 'espeak', 'nsss')
pyttsx3.weakref	Used internally in pyttsx3 for memory management without affecting object lifecycle

Table 9.4

speak(text)

pyttsx3.speak(text) takes the provided text and converts it into spoken audio using the system's speech engine.

```python
import pyttsx3 as sp
text = "Hello World"
sp.speak(text)
```

The above code generates either a male or female voice that reads the text aloud when executed. The speech can be heard through your device's speakers.

init

The **init()** function initializes the text-to-speech engine and returns an engine object. This object can be used not only to generate speech from text, but also to customize the speech experience—such as changing the voice, adjusting the pitch and volume, saving audio to a file, and more.

The init Methods

Method	Definition
connect()	Registers a callback function for specific engine events like started-utterance
disconnect()	Unregisters a callback from the event loop
endLoop()	Ends the event loop started by startLoop()
getProperty()	Gets properties such as 'rate', 'volume', or 'voice'
isBusy()	Returns True if the engine is still processing speech
iterate()	Yields the next event (used internally in async speech synthesis)
proxy()	Internal use for proxying engine method calls (less commonly used directly)
runAndWait()	Starts speech processing and waits for all queued commands to finish
save_to_file()	Saves spoken text to an audio file (e.g., .mp3 or .wav)
say()	Queues text to be spoken
setProperty()	Sets speech properties like 'rate', 'volume', or 'voice'
startLoop()	Starts a non-blocking event loop for speech synthesis
stop()	Stops current speech and clears the queue

Table 9.5

say(text)

```
●●● Python
import pyttsx3 as sp

engine = sp.init()      #Initialize the engine
text = "There is nothing much better than coding in silence"
engine.say(text)        #Set the text to be spoken
engine.runAndWait()     #Run the engine
```

📌 **runAndWait()** → Runs the speech engine until all commands are processed.

Getting Properties

The **getProperty()** method in pyttsx3 allows you to access different attributes of the speech engine. These include voice settings, speech rate, and volume, among others.

Voices

getProperty("voices")

```
●●● Python
import pyttsx3 as sp

engine = sp.init()
voices = engine.getProperty("voices")

print(f"first_voice_name = {voices[0].name}")
print(f"second_voice_name = {voices[1].name}")
print(f"first_voice_id = {voices[0].id}")
print(f"second_voice_id = {voices[1].id}")
```

```
#Output
first_voice_name = Microsoft David Desktop - English (United States)
second_voice_name = Microsoft Zira Desktop - English (United States)
first_voice_id =
HKEY_LOCAL_MACHINE\SOFTWARE\Microsoft\Speech\Voices\Tokens\TTS_MS_EN-
US_DAVID_11.0
second_voice_id =
HKEY_LOCAL_MACHINE\SOFTWARE\Microsoft\Speech\Voices\Tokens\TTS_MS_EN-
US_ZIRA_11.0
```

This returns a list of available voice objects on the system. Each voice has properties such as id, name, languages, and gender. On Windows, pyttsx3 typically comes with two default voices: one male and one female (e.g., Microsoft David and Microsoft Zira).

Volume

getProperty("volume")

Python

```
import pyttsx3 as sp
engine = sp.init()
volume = engine.getProperty("volume")
print(f"Volume level :{volume}")
```

```
#Output
Volume level :1.0
```

This returns the current volume level of the speech engine. Volume is a floating-point number between 0.0 (mute) and 1.0 (maximum).

Rate

getProperty("rate")

Python

```
import pyttsx3 as sp

engine = sp.init()
rate = engine.getProperty("rate")
print(f" rate :{rate}")
```

```
#Output
rate : 200
```

This returns the current speech rate (words per minute). The default value typically ranges between 150 and 200.

Setting Properties

After retrieving the engine's properties using getProperty(), you can customize them using engine.**setProperty**(name, value)

setProperty(name, value)

```
Python
import pyttsx3 as sp

engine = sp.init()

# Set voice
voices = engine.getProperty("voices")
engine.setProperty("voice", voices[1].id)

# Set volume
engine.setProperty("volume", 0.9)

# Set rate
engine.setProperty("rate", 180)

# Speak
engine.say("Hello, this is a customized voice!")
engine.runAndWait()
```

Saving Speech to an Audio File

pyttsx3 allows you to convert text to speech and save the spoken audio directly to a file. This is useful for generating voice messages, narrations, or offline audio files from written content.

Supported Audio Formats

pyttsx3 typically supports **WAV** format by default, as it uses the underlying text-to-speech engine of the system (such as SAPI5 on Windows). Other formats like **MP3** or **OGG** are not natively supported directly by pyttsx3. If you need other formats, consider saving as .wav and converting later using external libraries like **pydub** or **ffmpeg**.

save_to_file(text, filename)

```
••• Python
import pyttsx3

engine = pyttsx3.init()

text = "Heya! Hope you're loving it. Keep Pythonizing."

# Save speech to WAV audio file
engine.save_to_file( text, "output.wav")

engine.runAndWait()
```

📌 Always call *engine.runAndWait()* after *save_to_file()* to ensure the audio is properly written.

Key Terms

pyttsx3
Engine
say
runAndWait()
getProperty()
setProperty()
save_to_file

Review Questions

1. Which pyttsx3 function initializes the TTS engine?
a) init()
b) speak()
c) save_to_file()
d) setProperty()
Answer: a

2. Which method queues text for speech in pyttsx3?
a) runAndWait()
b) say()
c) speak()
d) startLoop()
Answer: b

3. What is the valid range for pyttsx3 engine volume?
a) 0–100
b) -1.0–1.0
c) 1–10
d) 0.0–1.0
Answer: d

4. Which audio format is natively supported by pyttsx3 for saving speech?
a) MP3
b) WAV
c) OGG
d) FLAC
Answer: d

What does runAndWait() do in pyttsx3?
a) Stops the engine
b) Queues text to speech
c) Processes all queued commands and waits until finished
d) Saves speech to a file
Answer: c

Review Exercises

1. **Basic TTS:**
Write a Python program using pyttsx3 that reads aloud the sentence: "Python programming is fun!".

2. **Customizing Voice:**
Initialize the pyttsx3 engine, list available voices, and set the engine to use the second voice. Adjust the rate to 150 words per minute and volume to 0.8, then read the sentence "Welcome to the world of Python!".

Save Speech to File:
Create a Python script that converts the text "This is a generated audio file using pyttsx3" into a WAV file named sample.wav. Ensure that the file is properly written

QR Code

A **QR Code (Quick Response Code)** is a type of matrix barcode (or two-dimensional barcode) that stores information as a pattern of black-and-white squares. While the pattern may look random, it is a structured visual code that can hold various types of data such as:

- URLs or website links
- Text messages
- Contact details (vCards)
- Wi-Fi login credentials
- Emails and phone numbers
- Calendar events
- Geolocation (latitude and longitude)
- App download links
- Product or payment information

This information can be quickly retrieved by scanning the QR Code using a smartphone camera, QR scanner, or barcode reader. Python provides a handy library called **qrcode** to easily generate QR codes from custom content.

Installation

```
pip install qrcode
```

Why Use QR Codes?

- To embed URLs or web links
- To store and share plain text messages
- For secure authentication (e.g., two-factor authentication codes)
- To share Wi-Fi network credentials without typing
- To store contact information (e.g., name, phone number, email)
- For event invitations or calendar scheduling
- In product packaging for more information or support
- For quick app downloads or installation instructions

The qrcode Methods

Method	Definition
qrcode.make(data)	A shortcut function that takes data (string) and returns a QR Code image. Useful for quick QR code generation.
qrcode.image	Provides different backends for generating image outputs like PIL (Pillow). You can subclass it to use a custom image factory.
qrcode.main	The primary module with user-friendly functions like make() that simplifies creating QR codes with just one line of code.
qrcode.run_example()	A built-in demonstration function that generates a sample QR code when run. Useful for testing and seeing default behavior.
qrcode.base	Contains the core QRCode class used for creating and configuring QR codes. It handles the data input, version, error correction level, box size, and border.
qrcode.compat	Provides compatibility functions between Python 2 and 3. This is mainly used internally and not commonly accessed directly.
qrcode.constants	Holds constants used by the QRCode generator such as error correction levels (e.g., ERROR_CORRECT_L, ERROR_CORRECT_M, ERROR_CORRECT_Q, ERROR_CORRECT_H).
qrcode.exceptions	Defines custom exceptions used in the QR code process. Helps catch specific QR code generation-related errors.
qrcode.util	Contains utility functions used internally like matrix creation, bit buffer handling, and version checks. Typically not used directly by most users.

Table 9.6

make()

The make() method is a high-level convenience function provided by the qrcode module. It is used to quickly generate a QR code from simple data such as a string, URL, or message. This method is ideal when you don't need to customize the QR code's appearance or settings extensively. It automatically chooses the best-fit version and error correction level for the data.

Parameters

data	The main content (text, URL, etc.) to encode into the QR code. This is a required parameter.
image_factory	*(Optional)* A custom image factory used to generate the image. For example, qrcode.image.pil.PilImage (default) or SVG-based factories.
version	*(Optional)* Specifies the size/version of the QR code. Ranges from 1 to 40. If not provided, it's auto-calculated.
error_correction	*(Optional)* Sets the error correction level. Values can be qrcode.constants.ERROR_CORRECT_L, M, Q, or H.
box_size	*(Optional)* The number of pixels for each box of the QR code grid. Affects the image resolution.
border	*(Optional)* The thickness of the border (number of boxes thick). Default is 4, which is the minimum required.

Table 9.7

Example,

```python
import qrcode
image = qrcode.make("https://google.com")
image.save("mycode.png")
```

```
#Output
```

Example 2 - Changing size of the box,

```python
import qrcode

image=qrcode.make("Hello, fellow Pythonist-this is my page", box_size= 50)
image.save("mycode.jpg")
```

```
#Output
```

Example 3 - Adding colors to the image,

```python
import qrcode

data = "https://www.example.com"

# Create a QRCode object
qr = qrcode.QRCode(
    version=1,
    box_size=10,
    border=5
)
```

```
qr.add_data( data )
qr.make(fit=True)

# Generate an image with custom fill and background colors
img = qr.make_image(fill_color="orange", back_color="white")

# Save the image
img.save("myqrcode.jpg")
```

```
#Output
```

- fill_color → The color of the actual QR code (default is black).
- back_color → The background color (default is white).
- You can use color names ("red", "green"), hex codes ("#ff5733"), or RGB tuples ((255, 0, 0))

Key Terms

qrcode.QRCode
add_data
make
make_image
fill_color
back_color

Review Questions

1. Which Python library is commonly used for generating QR codes?
   a) pyttsx3
   b) matplotlib
   d) pillow
   d) qrcode
   Answer: d

2. Which method adds content to a QRCode object?
   a) add_data()
   b) make_image()
   c) save()
   d) run_example()
   Answer: a

3. How do you generate a QR code image after adding data?
   a) QRCode.save()
   b) make_image()
   c) init()
   d) runAndWait()
   Answer: b

4. What is the default color of a QR code's squares?
   a) Black
   b) White
   c) Red
   d) Blue
   Answer: a

5. Which class allows specifying box size, border, and error correction in QR codes?
   a) qrcode.make()
   b) qrcode.QRCode
   c) qrcode.constants
   d) qrcode.image
   Answer: b

Review Exercises

1. **Basic QR Code:**
   Generate a QR code for the URL "https://www.python.org" and save it as python_qr.png.

2. **Custom Colors:**
   Create a QR code for the text "Welcome to QR Codes!" with orange fill color and light blue background. Save the image as colored_qr.png.

Custom Size and Border:
Use qrcode.QRCode() to generate a QR code for "https://www.example.com", set box_size to 20 and border to 6, and save it as large_qr.png.

Yagmail

Yagmail is a powerful and easy-to-use Python library for sending emails. It simplifies the process of composing and delivering emails by wrapping around Python's built-in smtplib, making it ideal for developers who want to send text, HTML content, or files like PDFs and images without dealing with low-level configurations.

Installation

Yagmail can be installed using pip, just like most other Python libraries.

```
pip install yagmail
```

Key Features of Yagmail

- **Easy Email Sending**
  Send emails with a few lines of Python code.
- **Rich Content Support**
  Supports plain text, HTML, and mixed content emails.
- **File Attachments**
  Easily attach files like PDFs, images, or documents.
- **Multiple Recipients**
  Send emails to one or multiple recipients at once.
- **Secure Authentication**
  Uses keyring for secure credential storage or supports login per session.
- **Inline Images**
  Embed images directly in the email body.
- **Readable Syntax**
  Clean, Pythonic syntax that's beginner-friendly.
- **SMTP Configuration**
  Easily connect to Gmail, Outlook, or any custom SMTP server.
- **Auto-Signature Support**
  Supports default signatures and reusable templates.

Yagmail Methods

Method	Definition
yagmail.SMTP	The main class for initializing an email session and sending messages. It wraps around the standard SMTP protocol with added convenience.
yagmail.compat	Handles compatibility between different Python versions to ensure smooth operation.
yagmail.dkim	(DomainKeys Identified Mail) Handles cryptographic email verification for enhanced email authentication.
yagmail.error	Contains custom exceptions and error handling specific to Yagmail operations.
yagmail.headers	Manages and formats email headers such as Subject, From, To, etc.
yagmail.inline	Allows embedding images or other media within the body of the email (inline attachments).
yagmail.logging	Internal logging module used for debugging and tracking email sending activity.
yagmail.message	Constructs the email content including body, subject, attachments, etc.
yagmail.oauth2	Provides OAuth2-based authentication support (especially for Gmail or Google Apps users).
yagmail.password	Manages and retrieves stored passwords securely from the system's keyring or other sources.
yagmail.raw	Sends raw email content directly, used for more customized or low-level email structures.
yagmail.register	Used to register user credentials with Yagmail (especially to use stored credentials via keyring).
yagmail.sender	Handles sending logic for messages, used internally by the SMTP object.
yagmail.utils	Utility functions that support parsing, formatting, and general tasks.
yagmail.validate	Validates email addresses, parameters, and content before sending.

Table 9.8

Note

Gmail and other email providers often require enhanced security when accessing email through third-party apps or programs. Instead of using your actual email password, you should enable Two-Factor Authentication (2FA) and generate an App Password specifically for the application.

For Gmail users, you can generate an App Password by visiting: https://myaccount.google.com/apppasswords

Use this App Password when registering your email with Yagmail instead of your regular email password.

Sending Messages with Yagmail

SMTP()

To send emails using Yagmail, you start by creating an instance of the SMTP class:

Parameters

user	The email address you want to send from. This can also be an alias registered with Yagmail via yagmail.register().
password	(Optional) The password for the email account. If not provided, Yagmail will try to fetch it securely from the system keyring.
host	(Optional) The SMTP server host (e.g., smtp.gmail.com). If not specified, Yagmail auto-detects based on the email domain.
port	(Optional) The SMTP port number. Default is 587 for TLS, or 465 for SSL.
smtp_starttls	(Optional) Set to True or False to enable or disable STARTTLS encryption.
smtp_ssl	(Optional) Set to True to connect via SSL. Typically used when port 465 is set.
smtp_set_debuglevel	(Optional) Sets debug output level. 0 = silent, 1 = verbose logging.
encoding	(Optional) Sets the character encoding. Default is 'utf-8', which supports international characters.
smtp_skip_login	(Optional) If True, skips the SMTP login step. Useful if authentication is not required.

Table 9.9

Basic Email Sending

Syntax

```
yag = yagmail.SMTP("username@mail.com", "app_password")

yag.send(
    to = "recipient@mail.com",
    subject = "email subject",
    contents = "your message"
)
```

Other Parameters of the send() Method

In addition to the required fields like **to**, **subject**, and **contents**, the send method in Yagmail supports several optional parameters to enhance functionality:

- **attachments**: Any – Files to be attached to the email.

- **cc**: Any – Carbon copy recipients.
- **bcc**: Any – Blind carbon copy recipients.
- **preview_only**: bool – If set to True, the email will be printed to the console instead of being sent.
- **headers**: Any – Additional custom headers for the email.
- **prettify_html**: bool – If True, formats HTML content for better readability.
- **message_id**: Any – Custom message ID for the email.
- **group_messages**: bool – Allows grouping of similar messages to reduce duplication.

Example 1,

Python
```
import yagmail

yag  = yagmail.SMTP("alice@gmail.com", "ali_xyz")

yag.send(
    to = "john@gmail.com",
    subject = "Greetings",
    contents = "Hello John, how is your morning?"
)
```

Example 2,

Python
```
import yagmail

email = "oliviabridge@gmail.com"
password = "password_from_google"
message = '''
        Hello Irene,
        I just wanted to check up on you.
        Have a blessed day.

        Best regards,
        Olivia Bridge.
        '''
yag  = yagmail.SMTP( email,  password)
```

```
yag.send(
    to = "irene@outlook.com",
    subject = "Friends Duty",
    contents = message
)
```

Sending Email With Attachments

Example 1- Sending a single file,

```
Python
import yagmail

yag  = yagmail.SMTP("bob@gmail.com",  "my_gen_app_pass_google")

image = "pictures/birthday_image.png"
yag.send(
    to = "gloria@gmail.com",
    subject = "Birthday Wishes",
    contents = "Happy Birthday Buddy.!",
    attachments = image
)
```

Example 2 - Sending multiple files,

```
Python
import yagmail

yag  = yagmail.SMTP("steve@gmail.com",  "pass_google_app_pass")

attach = ["pictures/site.png", "project.pdf", "credentials.docx"]
yag.send(
    to = "director@gmail.com",
    subject = "Agenda",
    contents = "Attached are copies of received documents.",
    attachments = attach
)
```

Sending Email With HTML Content

Example,

```python
import yagmail

yag  = yagmail.SMTP("marrie@gmail.com",  "mar_@_r")

html_content = "<h1>Hello</h1><p>This is a <b>HTML</b> email</p>"
yag.send(
    to = "buddy@gmail.com",
    subject = "HTML Message",
    contents = html_content
)
```

Sending Email With Inline Image

Example,

```python
import yagmail

yag  = yagmail.SMTP("steve25@gmail.com",  "gen_google_app_pass")

yag.send(
    to = "director@gmail.com",
    subject = "Agenda",
    contents = [
        "Hi Boss, check out this image: ",
        yagmail.inline("doc/site_plan.jpg"),
    ]
)
```

Key Terms

SMTP
App Password
inline
attachments
prettify_html

Review Questions

1. Which Python library is designed for easy email sending with attachments and HTML support?
   a) smtplib
   b) pyttsx3
   c) yagmail
   d) email
   Answer: c

2. Which parameter of yagmail.SMTP can store login credentials securely?
   a) password
   b) keyring
   c) host
   d) attachments
   Answer: b

3. How do you send an email with an inline image using Yagmail?
   a) contents = "image.png"
   b) contents = yagmail.inline("image.png")
   c) attachments = ["image.png"]
   d) save_to_file("image.png")
   Answer: b

4. What must Gmail users enable before using an App Password with Yagmail?
   a) SSL only
   b) 2FA (Two-Factor Authentication)
   c) HTML support
   d) SMTP logging
   Answer: b

5. Which method allows sending emails to multiple recipients in one call?
   a) yagmail.SMTP.send()
   b) yagmail.register()
   c) yagmail.inline()
   d) yagmail.validate()
   Answer: a

Review Exercises

1. **Basic Email Sending**
   Use Yagmail to send a simple email from your Gmail account to another email address. Include a subject and plain text content. Ensure you use an App Password securely.

2. **Send Email with Attachments**
   Send an email with at least two file attachments (e.g., PDF and image). Include a descriptive subject and message.

3. **Send HTML Email with Inline Image**
   Create an HTML email with headings, paragraphs, and bold text. Embed an inline image using yagmail.inline() and send it to a recipient.

Faker - Generating Fake Data

The **Faker** library in Python is a powerful tool for generating **synthetic** or **mock** data for testing, prototyping, and development. It provides a wide range of fake data generators (known as *providers*) that can produce realistic values such as names, email addresses, phone numbers, locations, dates, company names, and more.

Faker supports multiple **locales**, allowing you to generate data specific to different countries or regions (e.g. U.S., Germany, France). This makes it especially useful for building and testing applications that rely on user, business or location data without exposing real information.

It is especially useful for:

- Testing databases
- Creating mock APIs
- Prototyping applications
- Populating UI elements with realistic-looking data

Installation

To install **Faker**, use the following command:

```
pip install faker
```

Why Use Faker?

Using **Faker** offers several advantages during development, testing, and prototyping. Here are some key reasons to use it:

📌 **Eases Data Guesswork**
No need to manually guess or create fake data — Faker generates it instantly.

📌 **Provides Templated Data**
Faker follows consistent templates for generating realistic data, such as emails, phone numbers, names, etc.

📌 **Speeds Up Development**
Quickly populate your app or database with mock data to test logic and UI.

📌 **Serves as Placeholders**
Use generated data as temporary placeholders until real data is available.

Faker Methods

Method	Definition
Faker	Main class used to generate fake data. You typically instantiate this class (Faker()) to access all fake data methods (like .name(), .email())
Factory	Internal utility used to create and manage Faker instances. It handles locale settings and initializes the Faker environment.
Generator	The core engine behind data generation. It manages the actual logic and calls to data providers. Developers rarely use this directly.
config	Contains configuration settings for Faker, such as default locales or seeding options.
decode	Handles decoding operations (e.g., Unicode or encoded content). Typically used internally.
exceptions	Manages all exception classes used in Faker, such as UnsupportedLocaleError.
factory	Similar to Factory, this module assists in creating Faker instances, usually invoked behind the scenes.
generator	The module containing the Generator class. Handles the actual mechanics of how data is randomly selected from providers.
providers	This is where all the fake data providers live — name, address, email, job, etc. You can even add custom providers here.
proxy	Used for dynamic attribute access. Supports lazy loading of certain components.
typing	Contains type hints and annotations to help with static type checking (introduced for better code clarity and IDE support)
utils	A helper module with utility functions like string formatting, randomizers, and helper tools used by providers and core components.

Table 10.0

Generating Faker Data

The faker module offers a wide range of pre-defined methods through the **Faker** class that can be used to generate various types of fake data — such as names, addresses, emails, jobs, and more. These methods are extremely useful for testing, prototyping, or populating databases with placeholder data.

Some of these methods accept optional parameters to customize the output (e.g., locale, gender, or formatting), while others work perfectly without any arguments.

Below is a list of some commonly used methods available in the **Faker** class:

binary	add_provider	administrative_unit	building_number
boolean	date_between	date_time_between_dates	ascii_email
bothify	date_this_century	rgb_color	ascii_free_email
ssn	date_this_decade	domain_word	ascii_safe_email
csv	date_this_month	android_platform_token	bank_country
currency	date_this_year	ascii_company_email	country_code
address	future_datetime	image	company_suffix
century	generator_attrs	image_url	credit_card_full

chrome	get_arguments	year	company_email
city	get_formatter	zip	color_rgb_float
city_prefix	get_providers	basic_phone_number	cache_pattern
city_suffix	get_words_list	domain_name	catch_phrase
color	ipv4	country_calling_code	currency_code
color_hsl	suffix	postcode_in_state	currency_name
color_hsv	ipv4_private	credit_card_expire	currency_symbol
color_name	ipv4_public	texts	current_country
color_rgb	ipv6	credit_card_number	date_time_between
file_path	isbn10	credit_card_provider	ipv4_network_class
company	isbn13	credit_card_security_code	date_time_this_century
coordinate	profile	cryptocurrency	date_time_this_decade
country	provider	cryptocurrency_code	date_time_this_month
am_pm	providers	cryptocurrency_name	date_time_this_year
bban	psv	current_country_code	passport_full
date	pybool	random_digit_above_two	passport_gender
dsv	pydecimal	random_digit_not_null	passport_number
ean	pydict	mac_address	passport_owner
ean13	pyfloat	random_digit_or_empty	password
ean8	pyint	random_element	past_date
ein	pyiterable	random_elements	past_datetime
email	pylist	free_email	phone_number
emoji	pyobject	free_email_domain	port_number
enum	pyset	future_date	postalcode
factories	state	hex_color	state_abbr
day_of_week	state_abbr	hexify	street_address
del_arguments	street_address	random_elements	street_name
items	street_name	random_digit_above_two	street_suffix
itin	street_suffix	first_name	paragraphs
job	suffix	first_name_female	suffix_female
job_female	suffix_female	first_name_male	suffix_male
job_male	suffix_male	first_name_nonbinary	suffix_nonbinary
json	suffix_nonbinary	month_name	file_extension
language_code	name	sentence	text
language_name	name_female	sentences	time
last_name	name_male	state	passport_dates
last_name_female	license_plate	swift	passport_dob

Insight

You can explore even more by running:

```
>>> from faker import Faker
>>> fake = Faker()
>>> print( dir(fake) )     # List all available methods
...... [...........]
```

Locales

By default, Faker generates data such as names, addresses, emails and company information based on the **U.S. locale** (en_US). However, Faker supports multiple locales that allow you to create data specific to other countries or regions.
You can specify a locale when creating a Faker instance using the Faker(locale) parameter.

For example,

```python
from faker import Faker

fake_fr = Faker('fr_FR')   # French locale
fake_de = Faker('de_DE')   # German locale
fake_jp = Faker('ja_JP')   # Japan locale

print(fake_fr.name())  # Generates a French-style name
print(fake_de.city())  # Generates a German-style city
print(fake_jp.male_name())  # Generates a Japan-style male name
```

```
#Output
Michelle de Rousseau
Hainichen
林 洋介
```

Locales are defined using **language and country codes** (e.g., "en_US", "fr_FR", "de_DE"), following the ISO 639−1 and ISO 3166−1 standards.

- en_US → English (United States)
- fr_FR → French (France)
- de_DE → German (Germany)

Common Faker Locales

Locale Code	Language / Region	Description
en_US	English (United States)	Default locale; U.S. names and addresses
en_GB	English (United Kingdom)	UK-style names, postcodes, and phones
fr_FR	French (France)	French names and addresses
de_DE	German (Germany)	German names, streets, and cities
es_ES	Spanish (Spain)	Spain-specific formatting
it_IT	Italian (Italy)	Italian names and companies
pt_BR	Portuguese (Brazil)	Brazilian data (CPF, CNPJ, etc.)
ja_JP	Japanese (Japan)	Japanese-style names and cities
zh_CN	Chinese (China)	Chinese names and addresses

ru_RU	Russian (Russia)	Cyrillic-based names and cities
en_IN	English (India)	Indian-style names and phone numbers

Table 10.1

Note

You can also generate **multiple locales** by passing a list of locales to Faker. In that case, Faker will randomly select one for each data generation call:

```
>>> fake_multi = Faker(['en_US', 'fr_FR', 'de_DE'])
>>> print(fake_multi.name())  # Randomly from one of the three locales
```

Generating Fake Identity

Example 1- Generating single identity,

```python
from faker import Faker
fake = Faker()

print(f"Full Name -> {fake.name()}")
print(f"First Male Name -> {fake.first_name_male()}")
print(f"Last Female Name -> {fake.last_name_female()}")
print(f"Email -> {fake.email()}")
print(f"Email (gmail) -> {fake.email(domain='gmail.com')}")
print(f"Phone -> {fake.phone_number()}")
print(f"SSN -> {fake.ssn()}")
print(f"Password -> {fake.password()}")
print(f"User Name -> {fake.user_name()}")
print(f"Credit Card -> {fake.credit_card_full()}")
print(f"Passport -> {fake.passport_full()}")
```

```
#Output
Full Name -> Paul Jordan
First Male Name -> Tony
Last Female Name -> Washington
```

```
Email -> wrightjason@example.com
Email (gmail) -> diazmackenzie@gmail.com
Phone -> 001-209-372-6781x138
SSN -> 308-04-3965
Password -> a6ZXPC_m&k
User Name -> jenniferhernandez
Credit Card -> Diners Club / Carte Blanche
               Kimberly Jordan
               30280910725441 03/35
               CVC: 193

Passport -> Anthony
            Henderson
            M
            18 Jan 1935
            01 Jul 2024
            01 Jul 2034
            X28445130
```

Example 2 - Generating Full identity,

```python
from faker import Faker
fake = Faker()

profile = fake.profile()
for identity, value in profile.items():
    print(f"{identity} -> {value}")
```

```
#Output
job -> Illustrator
company -> Maldonado Group
ssn -> 706-27-0623
residence -> Unit 5019 Box 5517
DPO AE 48178
current_location -> (Decimal('-84.607321'), Decimal('-88.548296'))
blood_group -> AB-
website -> ['http://robinson.com/', 'http://knapp.net/',
'https://cochran.org/', 'https://www.hernandez-krueger.net/']
username -> kim35
name -> Alexandra Medina
```

```
sex -> F
address -> 4046 Amy Estate
Torreschester, NC 21613
mail -> xhall@yahoo.com
birthdate -> 2003-01-16
```

Generating Fake Addresses

```python
from faker import Faker
fake = Faker()

print(f"Country -> {fake.country()}")
print(f"State -> {fake.state()}")
print(f"City -> {fake.city()}")
print(f"Address -> {fake.address()}")
print(f"Zip code -> {fake.zipcode()}")
print(f"IP address -> {fake.ipv4()}")
print(f"Street name-> {fake.street_name()}")
print(f"Street address -> {fake.street_address()}")
print(f"Postal code -> {fake.postalcode()}")
print(f"Currency -> {fake.currency()}")
print(f"Currency symbol -> {fake.currency_symbol()}")
print(f"Latitude -> {fake.latitude()}")
```

```
#Output
Country -> Saint Pierre and Miquelon
State -> South Carolina
City -> Brooketon
Address -> 862 Annette Lakes
Port Daniel, MO 09310
Zip code -> 88064
IP address -> 195.184.110.57
Street name-> Amanda Throughway
Street address -> 19278 Vanessa Points Suite 013
Postal code -> 19034
Currency -> ('SGD', 'Singapore dollar')
Currency symbol -> Fr
Latitude -> 27.9287505
```

Generating Fake System Information

```python
from faker import Faker
fake = Faker()

print(f"Time -> {fake.time()}")
print(f"Date -> {fake.date()}")
print(f"Timezone -> {fake.timezone()}")
print(f"Color -> {fake.color()}")
print(f"Color name -> {fake.color_name()}")
print(f"Sentence -> {fake.sentence()}")
print(f"Paragraph -> {fake.paragraph()}")
print(f"Text -> {fake.text()}")
```

```
#Output
Time -> 06:04:41
Date -> 1990-09-02
Timezone -> Africa/Dar_es_Salaam
Color -> #a1a3ed
Color name -> SlateBlue
Sentence -> Whether return field kitchen resource war front fact.
Paragraph -> Chance appear local class. Respond amount trouble.
             Usually will camera any.
Text -> Edge her movement too energy. Red account pass account up
        head.
        Hear size top general.
        Hope place throughout half. Third adult structure strategy
        tax go.
```

Generating Fake Graphics and Tables

Example 1 – Generating emojis (**fake.emoji()**)

```python
from faker import Faker
fake = Faker()

for i in range(0, 100):
    print(fake.emoji(), end=" ")
    if i%10 == 0:
        print()
```

```
#Output
```

Example 2 – Generating images

```python
from pathlib import Path
from faker import Faker

fake = Faker()
image = fake.image()
Path("faker_image.png").write_bytes(image)
```

Example 3 – Generating CSV data,

```python
from faker import Faker

fake = Faker()

data = fake.csv()
print(data)
```

```
#Output
"Abigail Caldwell","78698 Christina Ways
Diazstad, CO 74123"
"Gina Smith","7317 Linda Light
South David, PA 45750"
......
```

Example 4 – Generating customized CSV data,

```python
from faker import Faker

fake = Faker()

data1=fake.csv(
    header=["name", "country", "email"],
    data_columns=[fake.name(), fake.country(), fake.email()],
    num_rows=1
)

data2=fake.csv(
    header=["name", "country", "email"],
    data_columns=[fake.name(), fake.country(), fake.email()],
    num_rows=1
)

print(data1)
print(data2)
```

```
#Output
"name","country","email"
"Nancy Fields","Mauritius","rhonda544example.net"

"name","country","email"
"Alison Avila","Netherlands","ronniegeorge6example.org"
```

Key Terms

Faker
Provider
Locale
profile
CSV

Review Questions

1. Which Faker method generates a full fake identity including name, birthdate, and address?
   a) fake.address()
   b) fake.profile()
   c) fake.first_name()
   d) fake.user_name()
   Answer: b

2. How do you generate data specific to a French locale?
   a) Faker('fr')
   b) Faker('fr_FR')
   c) Faker('FR')
   d) Faker(locale='fr')
   Answer: b

3. Which method generates fake email addresses?
   a) fake.email()
   b) fake.user_name()
   c) fake.domain_name()
   d) fake.company_email()
   Answer: a

4. What type of data does fake.csv() generate?
   a) JSON data
   b) Comma-Separated Values (CSV)
   c) HTML table
   d) Plain text only
   Answer: b

5. Which Faker provider is used to generate fake colors?
   a) fake.color_name()
   b) fake.timezone()
   c) fake.country()
   d) fake.company_suffix()
   Answer: a

Review Exercises

1. **Basic Fake Identity**
   Generate a fake full name, first name (male), last name (female), email, phone number, and password.

2. **Locale-Based Data**
   Create Faker instances for French, German, and Japanese locales. Generate a name and city for each locale.

3. **CSV Data Generation**
   Generate a CSV file with headers name, country, email and populate it with 5 rows of fake data.

4. **Profile Dictionary**
   Use fake.profile() to generate a full fake profile, and print each key-value pair in a readable format.

5. **Fake Graphics / Emoji**
   Generate 50 random emojis using fake.emoji() and print them in a grid format (e.g., 10 per row).

TextBlob

TextBlob is a Python library that provides a simple and convenient interface for performing common **Natural Language Processing (NLP)** tasks. NLP is a branch of computing concerned with enabling computers to process, analyze, and work with human language.

Working directly with natural-language data can involve complex operations such as tokenization, grammatical analysis, spelling correction, sentiment analysis, and linguistic classification. TextBlob simplifies many of these operations by providing an easy-to-use API that allows developers to perform common text-processing tasks with relatively little code.

TextBlob is particularly useful for learning NLP concepts and for developing applications that need to analyze or manipulate human-readable text.

Key Features of TextBlob

TextBlob provides several features for working with natural-language data. Some of its commonly used capabilities include:

1. **Word definitions** — Retrieve definitions of words through WordNet integration.
2. **Sentiment analysis** — Analyze text and obtain values representing polarity and subjectivity.
3. **Tokenization** — Divide text into individual words or sentences.
4. **Part-of-speech (POS) tagging** — Identify grammatical categories such as nouns, verbs, adjectives, and adverbs.
5. **Word inflection** — Convert words between singular and plural forms.
6. **Lemmatization** — Reduce words to their base or dictionary forms.
7. **Spelling correction** — Suggest possible corrections for misspelled words and attempt to correct text.
8. **Noun phrase extraction** — Identify noun phrases within a body of text.
9. **Language-related processing** — Provide functionality for working with language information where supported by the installed TextBlob components and configuration.
10. **Text parsing** — Analyze the grammatical structure of text.
11. **Word frequency analysis** — Examine how frequently particular words or noun phrases occur.

12. **Text manipulation** — Work with words and sentences using TextBlob's convenient object-oriented interface.

Installation

TextBlob is not included in the Python standard library. It must be installed separately from the Python Package Index (PyPI).

```
pip install textblob
```

> 📖 **Note**
>
> Depending on the features being used, additional linguistic data or dependencies may need to be installed or downloaded. For example, WordNet-based functionality requires the relevant NLTK WordNet data to be available.

1. Word Definition

One useful feature of TextBlob is its integration with **WordNet**, a lexical database of English words. WordNet organizes words into groups of related meanings called **synsets**. TextBlob provides access to WordNet information through the **Word** class.

Example 1,

```python
from textblob import Word

word = Word("wolf")
results = word.define()  #Returns list of definitions

for value in results:
    print(f"-> {value}")
```

```
#Output
-> any of various predatory carnivorous canine mammals of North America
and Eurasia that usually hunt in packs
-> Austrian composer (1860-1903)
-> German classical scholar who claimed that the Iliad and Odyssey were
composed by several authors (1759-1824)
-> a man who is aggressive in making amorous advances to women
-> a cruelly rapacious person
-> eat hastily
```

Example 2,

```python
from textblob import Word

word = Word("usa")
results = word.definitions
print(results)
```

```
#Output
['North American republic containing 50 states - 48 conterminous states in North America plus Alaska in northwest North America and the Hawaiian Islands in the Pacific Ocean; achieved independence in 1776', 'the army of the United States of America; the agency that organizes and trains soldiers for land warfare']
```

2. Spelling Suggestion

TextBlob can also be used to **suggest corrections for misspelled words**. This can be useful when processing user-generated text, building simple text-cleaning applications, or demonstrating basic NLP concepts.

The Word class provides the **spellcheck()** method, which returns a list of possible spelling corrections together with confidence scores. The returned value consists of tuples containing (candidate_word, confidence).

The **candidate word** represents a possible correction, while the **confidence value** indicates the relative confidence associated with that suggestion.

Example 1,

```python
from textblob import Word

word = Word("fother")
results = word.spellcheck()

for value, prob in results:
    print(f"value-> {value} - Probability-> {prob}")
```

```
#Output
value-> other - Probability-> 0.6388770735857082
value-> father - Probability-> 0.22671203743088048
value-> mother - Probability-> 0.13270948532539345
value-> bother - Probability-> 0.0017014036580178648
```

Example 2,

```python
from textblob import Word

word = Word("lave")
results = word.spellcheck()

for item, score in results:
    value = round((score),3)
    print(f"Word-> {item} - Scores-> {(value/1)*100} %")
```

```
#Output
Word-> have - Scores-> 65.9 %
Word-> love - Scores-> 9.1 %
Word-> gave - Scores-> 8.3 %
Word-> leave - Scores-> 5.7 %
Word-> late - Scores-> 3.1 %
Word-> live - Scores-> 2.4 %
Word-> save - Scores-> 2.1 %
Word-> slave - Scores-> 1.5 %
Word-> lane - Scores-> 0.5 %
Word-> lake - Scores-> 0.5 %
Word-> wave - Scores-> 0.5 %
Word-> lace - Scores-> 0.2 %
Word-> lame - Scores-> 0.1 %
Word-> cave - Scores-> 0.1 %
Word-> lava - Scores-> 0.0 %
Word-> dave - Scores-> 0.0 %
Word-> ave - Scores-> 0.0 %
```

Note

It is important to understand that spelling correction is an **attempt**, not a guarantee of correctness. The highest-confidence suggestion is not necessarily correct in every context.

3. Spelling Correction

In addition to suggesting possible corrections for individual misspelled words, TextBlob can attempt to correct spelling throughout an entire piece of text. The **correct()** method analyzes the words in a TextBlob and returns a new text with suggested spelling corrections.

Example:

```python
from textblob import TextBlob

text1 = TextBlob("l hove a goood camputer")
text2 = TextBlob("Can I habe some koffee?")

print(f"{text1} -> {text1.correct()}")
print(f"{text2} -> {text2.correct()}")
```

```
#Output
l hove a goood camputer -> l have a good computer
Can I habe some koffee? -> Can I have some coffee?
```

The **correct()** method is particularly useful when working with user-generated text, comments, messages, or other content that may contain common spelling errors.

> **Note**
>
> It is important to remember that TextBlob's spelling correction is probabilistic. Therefore, the returned result should be considered a suggestion rather than a guaranteed correction. Uncommon words, names, technical terms, and words whose meaning depends on context may not always be corrected as expected.

4. Singularization and Pluralization

Singularization and pluralization are operations used to change the grammatical number of a word.

Singularization converts a plural word into its singular form. For example: cars → car

Pluralization performs the opposite operation, converting a singular word into its plural form: book → books

TextBlob provides these operations through the **Word** class. The **singularize()** method attempts to convert a plural word to its singular form, while **pluralize()** attempts to convert a singular word to its plural form.

Example 1 - Pluralization

```
●●● Python
from textblob import Word

dog = Word("dog").pluralize()
table = Word("table").pluralize()
wife = Word("wife").pluralize()

print(f"dog -> {dog}")
print(f"table -> {table}")
print(f"wife -> {wife}")
```

```
#Output
dog -> dogs
table -> tables
wife -> wives
```

Example 2 - Singularization

```
●●● Python
from textblob import Word

computers = Word("computers").singularize()
mice = Word("mice").singularize()
women = Word("women").singularize()
knives = Word("knives").singularize()

print(f"computers -> {computers}")
print(f"mice -> {mice}")
print(f"women -> {women}")
print(f"knives -> {knives}")
```

```
#Output
computers -> computer
mice -> mouse
women -> woman
knives -> knife
```

5. Stemming and Lemmatization

Words can appear in different grammatical forms while representing the same underlying concept. For example:

There are two related concepts that are important in text processing: stemming and lemmatization.

Stemming attempts to reduce a word to a shorter stem by removing or modifying word endings. The resulting stem is not necessarily a complete dictionary word. The **stem()** method uses a stemming algorithm to reduce a word to its stem.

Lemmatization, on the other hand, attempts to reduce a word to its lemma, or dictionary/base form, using linguistic information. The **lemmatize()** method attempts to return the dictionary form of a word.

Example 1 - Stemming

```
Python
from textblob import Word

running = Word("running").stem()
programming = Word("programming").stem()
played = Word("played").stem()

print(f"running -> {running}")
print(f"programming -> {programming}")
print(f"played -> {played}")
```

```
#Output
running -> run
programming -> program
played -> play
```

Example 2 - Lemmatization

```
Python
from textblob import Word, wordnet

#Example 1 - Noun
tomatoes = Word("tomatoes").lemmatize()
print(f"Example 1 - tomatoes -> {tomatoes}")
```

```
#Example 2 - Verb
eaten = Word("eaten").lemmatize()      #Part OF Speech is Noun (default)
eaten_verb = Word("eaten").lemmatize(wordnet.VERB)  #POS is Verb
print(f"Example 2 - {eaten} -> {eaten_verb}")

#Example 3 - Adjective
fastest = Word("fastest").lemmatize()
fastest_adj = Word("fastest").lemmatize(wordnet.ADJ)  #POS is Adjectives
print(f"Example 3 - {fastest} -> {fastest_adj}")
```

```
#Output
Example 1 - tomatoes -> tomato
Example 2 - eaten -> eat
Example 3 - fastest -> fast
```

6. Tokenization

Tokenization is the process of dividing text into smaller units called tokens. Depending on the task, tokens may be individual words, sentences, or other meaningful units of text.

TextBlob provides convenient properties for accessing both word tokens and sentence tokens.

```
Python
from textblob import TextBlob

text = TextBlob("Python is great!. I love it")

#Example 1 - Accessing Individual Tokens
token = text.tokens  #Alternative: text.tokenizer()
print(f"Tokens -> {token}")

#Example 2 - Splitting Text into Words
words = text.words
print(f"Words -> {words}")

#Example 3 - Splitting Text into Sentences
sentence = text.sentences
for value in sentence:
    print(f"Sentence -> {value}")
```

```
#Output
Tokens -> ['Python', 'is', 'great', '!', '.', 'I', 'love', 'it']
Words -> ['Python', 'is', 'great', 'I', 'love', 'it']
Sentence -> Python is great!.
Sentence -> I love it
```

7. Noun Phrase Extraction

A noun phrase is a group of words centered around a noun. It can represent a person, place, object, organization, concept, or other entity. Noun phrase extraction can be useful when identifying important concepts or subjects within a larger body of text.

TextBlob can extract noun phrases from a text using the **noun_phrases** property.

```
Python
from textblob import TextBlob

text = "Gloria works at Microsoft as deputy CEO alongside Jackson."
tb = TextBlob(text)
nouns = tb.noun_phrases

for names in nouns:
    value = str(names).capitalize()
    print(value)
```

```
#Output
Gloria
Microsoft
Ceo
Jackson
```

8. Part-of-Speech (POS) Tagging

Part-of-speech (POS) tagging is the process of assigning a grammatical category to each word in a sentence. POS tagging is useful in applications that need to analyze sentence structure, identify particular types of words or perform more advanced natural-language processing. For example, a program could use POS tags to identify all nouns in a paragraph:

TextBlob provides POS tagging through the **tags** or **pos_tags** property to return a tuple – (word, tag).

The first item in each pair is the word, while the second item is its POS tag.

Common POS Tags

Tag	Meaning	Tag	Meaning
NN	Noun, singular	VBP	Verb, non-3rd-person singular present
NNS	Noun, plural	VBZ	Verb, 3rd-person singular present
NNP	Proper noun, singular	JJ	Adjective
VB	Verb, base form	RB	Adverb
VBD	Verb, past tense	DT	Determiner
VBG	Verb, gerund or present participle	PRP	Personal pronoun
VBN	Verb, past participle	IN	Preposition

Table 10.2

Example

Python
```
from textblob import TextBlob

text= "The black cat jumps over the white dog, which sleeps on the couch."
tb = TextBlob(text)
tags = tb.tags  #Alternative : tb.pos_tags

for word, tag  in tags:
    print(f"{word} -> {tag}")
```

```
#Output
The -> DT
black -> JJ
cat -> NN
jumps -> VBZ
over -> IN
the -> DT
white -> JJ
dog -> NN
which -> WDT
sleeps -> VBZ
on -> IN
the -> DT
couch -> NN
```

9. n-Grams

An n-gram is a sequence of n consecutive items extracted from a body of text. In many NLP applications, the items are words. The value of ***n*** determines the number of consecutive items included in each sequence. TextBlob provides the **ngrams()** method for generating n-grams.

Generating Bigrams

```
Python
from textblob import TextBlob

text = "Roses are red, grapes are always purple."
tblob = TextBlob(text)
bigrams = tblob.ngrams(n=2)

for item in bigrams:
    print(item)
```

```
#Output
['Roses', 'are']
['are', 'red']
['red', 'grapes']
['grapes', 'are']
['are', 'always']
['always', 'purple']
```

Generating Trigrams

```
Python
from textblob import TextBlob

text = "To every long road, there is an end."
tblob = TextBlob(text)
trigrams = tblob.ngrams(n=3)

for item in trigrams:
    print(item)
```

```
#Output
['To', 'every', 'long']
['every', 'long', 'road']
['long', 'road', 'there']
['road', 'there', 'is']
['there', 'is', 'an']
['is', 'an', 'end']
```

Key Terms

Bigram
Trigram
Part Of Speech
Tokenizer
Noun phrase
Stem
Definitions
Tags
Tokens

Review Questions

1. What is the primary purpose of TextBlob?
A. Database management
B. Natural Language Processing
C. Image manipulation
D. Network programming
Answer: B
2. Which technology provides lexical information used by TextBlob for word definitions?
A. SQLite
B. WordNet
C. Pillow
D. PyAutoGUI
Answer: B
3. Which TextBlob property can be used to obtain the definitions of a Word object?
A. meaning
B. definitions
C. dictionary
D. description
Answer: B
4. Which method attempts to correct the spelling of an entire TextBlob?
A. spellcheck()
B. correct()
C. fix()
D. correct_text()
Answer: B
5. What does the spellcheck() method return?
A. Only the corrected word
B. A list of possible corrections with confidence scores
C. A list of sentences
D. A Boolean value
Answer: B
6. Which method converts a plural word into its singular form?
A. pluralize()
B. singularize()
C. lemmatize()
D. normalize()
Answer: B
7. Which method of the Word class performs stemming?
A. stem()
B. lemmatize()
C. root()
D. base()
Answer: A
8. Which TextBlob property can be used to obtain the words in a text?
A. tokens
B. words
C. word_list
D. vocabulary
Answer: B
9. Which property can be used to obtain the sentences in a TextBlob?
A. sentences
B. paragraphs
C. sentence_list
D. lines
Answer: A
10. Which property is used to extract noun phrases from a TextBlob?
A. nouns
B. noun_phrases
C. phrases
D. noun_words
Answer: B
11. Which property is used to obtain POS tags from a TextBlob?
A. tags
B. pos
C. part_of_speech
D. grammar
Answer: A

12. What does the POS tag NN generally represent?
A. Adjective
B. Adverb
C. Singular noun
D. Verb
Answer: C
13. Which method generates n-grams from a TextBlob?
A. generate()
B. ngrams()
C. tokens()
D. sequence()
Answer: B
14. Which of the following creates a TextBlob object correctly?
A. blob = TextBlob("Python is powerful.")
B. blob = Text("Python is powerful.")
C. blob = NLP("Python is powerful.")
D. blob = TextBlob.create("Python is powerful.")
Answer: A

Review Exercises

1. Word Definition Practice
Create a Python program that asks the user to enter a word and uses TextBlob's Word class to display its available definitions. Test the program with at least five different words.

2. Spelling Correction Practice
Create a program containing a paragraph with several intentionally misspelled words. Use TextBlob to produce a corrected version of the paragraph. Compare the original and corrected versions.

3. Singularization and Pluralization Practice
Create a program that contains at least ten singular and plural words. Use singularize() and pluralize() to convert the words and display the results.

4. Stemming and Lemmatization Practice
Create a list containing words such as running, studies, studying, connected, and cars. Use both stem() and lemmatize() to process the words and compare the results.

5. Tokenization Practice
Write a program that accepts a paragraph from the user and displays all the individual words contained in the paragraph. Modify the program to display the sentences separately.

6. Noun Phrase Extraction Practice
Create a paragraph describing a technology company, its products, and its software developers. Use TextBlob to extract and display the noun phrases found in the paragraph.

7. POS Tagging Practice
Write a program that accepts a sentence and displays every word together with its POS tag. Modify the program so that it displays only the nouns and adjectives.

8. n-Gram Practice
Create a TextBlob containing a paragraph of at least 20 words. Generate and display its unigrams, bigrams, and trigrams. Observe how the number and structure of the resulting sequences differ.

9. Text Analysis Practice
Create a program that accepts a paragraph from the user and displays:

- The number of words
- The number of sentences
- The noun phrases
- The POS tags
- The bigrams

10. Mini NLP Project
Build a simple **Text Analyzer** using TextBlob. The program should accept text from the user and provide a report containing the words, sentences, noun phrases, POS tags, spelling-corrected text, and selected n-grams.

Emoji

Human communication is multifaceted, encompassing text, speech, visuals, gestures, images, symbols, and more. While visual communication—such as images—can often convey meaning more effectively than plain text, it's not always practical. For example, when dealing with small-sized messages or limited **bandwidth**, sending full images becomes less feasible.

This is where emojis come in. Emojis are compact, expressive text-based visuals formed using **Unicode** characters. They allow users to convey emotion, context, or tone quickly and efficiently—without needing large files or complex graphics.

In Python, the emoji module provides functionality for:

- Converting text or keywords into emojis
- Converting emojis back to their names
- Handling Unicode emoji characters programmatically

Installation

You can install the emoji module using pip:

```
pip install emoji
```

Why the Need for Emojis in Programming?

Emojis aren't just for fun—they serve practical purposes in programming as well:

📌 **Enhance User Interface**
Emojis can make UIs (especially chat apps, dashboards, and notifications) more expressive and engaging.

📌 **Convey Emotions & Context**
Emojis help convey the tone of a message without extra text.

📌 **Reduce Text Length**
A single emoji can replace several words (e.g., 👍 instead of "I agree").

📌 **Improve Readability**
They break monotony in long texts or logs and highlight key points.

📌 **Placeholders in Testing**
Useful in testing emoji-related features or generating placeholder text.

📌 **Cross-Platform Consistency**
Unicode-based emojis look similar across systems and devices.

Emoji Methods

Method	Definition
emojize(text)	Converts emoji names (e.g., :smile:) to actual emojis.
demojize(text)	Converts emojis in the given text to their descriptive names (e.g., '😊' → ':smile:').
config	Contains configuration settings for the emoji module.
core	Core internal functions used by the module (not often used directly).
distinct_emoji_list(text)	Returns a list of unique emojis found in the text.
emoji_count(text)	Returns the number of emojis in a given string.
emoji_list(text)	Returns a list of all emojis found in the text along with their positions.
get_emoji_by_name(name)	Returns the emoji corresponding to a name like 'thumbs_up'.
is_emoji(text)	Returns True if the character is a valid emoji.
load_from_json(file)	Loads custom emoji data from a JSON file.
purely_emoji(text)	Checks whether a string consists only of emojis.
replace_emoji(text, replace)	Replaces all emojis in the text with the given replacement.
tokenizer(text)	Tokenizes the text into emojis and words for analysis.
unicode_codes	Contains mappings between emoji names and Unicode points.
version	Returns the version of the emoji module being used.

Table 10.3

Emoji Names

Each emoji can be referenced either by its **Unicode** character or by a descriptive name wrapped in colons (e.g., :smile:). Using Unicode directly works in many environments, but using the **emoji name** is more readable and maintainable—especially in dynamic or multilingual applications.

Python's emoji module provides a powerful function called **emojize()** that converts emoji names into actual emojis.

emoji.emojize()

The emojize() function takes in a string containing emoji names in a specific format and returns a string with the corresponding emojis.

Basic Usage

```python
import emoji
print(emoji.emojize("Clown Face -> :clown_face:"))
print(emoji.emojize("Kiss and love -> :kiss_mark::red_heart:"))
```

```
#Output
Clown Face -> 🤡
Kiss and love -> 💋❤️
```

Using custom delimiter, like curly braces

```python
import emoji
print(emoji.emojize("Sports ->{basketball}", delimiters=("{","}")))
```

```
#Output
Sports -> 🏀
```

Using alias names

```python
import emoji
print(emoji.emojize("It's ok :thumbs_up:"))
print(emoji.emojize("I'm great :thumbsup:",  language='alias'))
```

```
#Output
It's ok 👍
I'm great 👍
```

Specifying variants

```python
import emoji
# text-based variant
print(emoji.emojize("Love leads :red_heart:",variant="text_type"))
# emoji-style variant
print(emoji.emojize("Love leads :red_heart:",variant="emoji_type"))
```

```
#Output
Love leads ❤︎
Love leads ❤️
```

Key Points

- 📌 Default delimiters are : for both sides (e.g., :rocket:).
- 📌 language='alias' allows common names like :thumbsup:, :smile:, etc.
- 📌 variant='text_type' may return text-style emojis, depending on the emoji and platform.
- 📌 Custom delimiters let you use any other character (e.g., {}) if : conflicts with your data.

Available Emoji Names and Their Unicode Characters

Emojis are standardized by the Unicode Consortium, each assigned a unique name and Unicode character. Below is a selection of commonly used emojis with their names and Unicode representations:

Emoji	Name	Unicode	Emoji	Name	Unicode
😀	grinning_face	U+1F600	🖐	hand with fingers splayed	U+1F590
😃	grinning_face_with_big_eyes	U+1F603	🤙	call me hand	U+1F919
😄	grinning_face_with_smiling_eyes	U+1F604	✍	writing hand	U+270D
😁	beaming_face_with_smiling_eyes	U+1F601	🧠	brain	U+1F9E0
😆	grinning_squinting_face	U+1F606	🫀	anatomical heart	U+1FAC0
🤣	rolling_on_the_floor_laughing	U+1F923	🧑	person	U+1F9D1
😂	face_with_tears_of_joy	U+1F602	👴	old man	U+1F474
😉	winking face	U+1F609	🙆	person gesturing OK	U+1F646
🤩	star-struck	U+1F929	🤷	person shrugging	U+1F937
🤑	money-mouth face	U+1F911	🧑‍⚕️	health worker	U+1F9D1
🥸	disguised face	U+1F978	👩‍⚖️	woman judge	U+1F469
🤠	cowboy hat face	U+1F920	🧑‍✈️	pilot	U+1F9D1
🤡	clown face	U+1F921	🧑‍🚀	astronaut	U+1F9D1
👹	ogre	U+1F479	🎅	Santa Claus	U+1F385
😺	grinning cat	U+1F63A	🤶	Mrs. Claus	U+1F936
😹	cat with tears of joy	U+1F639	🧛	vampire	U+1F9DB
🙈	see-no-evil monkey	U+1F648	🐶	dog face	U+1F436

🙉	hear-no-evil monkey	U+1F649	🐺	wolf	U+1F43A
💘	heart with arrow	U+1F498	🐭	mouse face	U+1F42D
💞	revolving hearts	U+1F49E	🐼	panda	U+1F43C
💔	broken heart	U+1F494	🐻	bear	U+1F43B
💋	kiss mark	U+1F48B	🐧	penguin	U+1F427
💯	hundred points	U+1F4AF	🏵	rosette	U+1F3F5
💥	collision	U+1F4A5	🍁	maple leaf	U+1F341
💫	dizzy	U+1F4AB	🍓	strawberry	U+1F353
👋	waving hand	U+1F44B	🥕	carrot	U+1F955
🍔	hamburger	U+1F354	🏠	house	U+1F3E0
🍕	pizza	U+1F355	🚑	ambulance	U+1F691
🍲	pot of food	U+1F372	🚁	helicopter	U+1F681
🍩	doughnut	U+1F369	🚀	rocket	U+1F680
🌍	globe showing Europe-Africa	U+1F30D	🌤	sun behind small cloud	U+1F324
🏈	american football	U+1F3C8	🎓	graduation cap	U+1F393
🎲	game die	U+1F3B2	📢	loudspeaker	U+1F4E2

Table 10.4

Note

This is a partial list. For a complete and up-to-date list of all emojis, please refer to the Unicode Full Emoji List

Generating Emojis Using Unicode

In Python, emojis are represented using **Unicode code points**, which are unique identifiers assigned to characters and symbols across languages and scripts. Each emoji can be displayed by inserting its Unicode value into a string using a **Unicode escape sequence**.

Python supports two escape prefixes for Unicode characters:

- \u – for 4-digit Unicode codes
- \U – for 8-digit Unicode codes (used for emojis and extended characters)

Example 1,

Python
```
print("Hahaha \U0001F600")
print("Hihihi, really \U0001F602")
print("Alright Sir \U0001F44D")
print("Congratulations \U0001F389")
```

```
#Output
Hahaha 😀
Hihihi, really 😂
Alright Sir 👍
Congratulations 🎉
```

Explanation

Each emoji has a Unicode identifier such as U+1F600.

In Python, this is written as \U0001F600 (uppercase "U" followed by eight hexadecimal digits).

Example 2,

```python
print("I love you \u2764")
print("Flower \u2740")
```

```
#Output
I love you ❤
Project ❀
```

Converting Emojis to Unicode Names

The Python emoji module provides a convenient method called **demojize()** that converts emojis into their respective Unicode names. This is particularly useful when you need to process or analyze text containing emojis. The **demojize()** function replaces each emoji in the text with its corresponding Unicode name, enclosed in colons.

Example,

```python
import emoji
text = 'I love Python! 😍🐍'
converted_emoji = emoji.demojize( text )
print(converted_emoji )
```

```
#Output
I love Python! :smiling_face_with_heart-eyes::snake:
```

Key Terms

emojize()
demojize()
Unicode
Variant
bandwidth
delimiters

Review Questions

1. Which emoji method converts emoji names to actual emojis?
   a) emojize()
   b) demojize()
   c) unicode_codes()
   d) replace_emoji()
   Answer: a

2. Which prefix is used for 8-digit Unicode escape sequences in Python?
   a) \u
   b) \U
   c) \x
   d) \e
   Answer: b

3. What does the demojize() function do?
   a) Converts emoji names to Unicode
   b) Converts emojis into their descriptive names
   c) Counts emojis in a string
   d) Removes all emojis from text
   Answer: b

4. How can you use a custom delimiter in emojize()?
   a) delimiters=("[", "]")
   b) variant='emoji_type'
   c) language='alias'
   d) replace_emoji=":"
   Answer: a

5. Which Python module is primarily used for handling emojis programmatically?
   a) unicodedata
   b) emoji
   c) smtplib
   d) qrcode
   Answer: b

Review Exercises

1. **Basic Emoji Conversion**
   Use emoji.emojize() to convert the following emoji names into emojis: :rocket:, :birthday:, :smile:. Print the result.

2. **Demojize Text**
   Take a string containing emojis like "I love coding 😍 💻 🚀 " and use emoji.demojize() to convert it into readable names.

3. **Unicode Escape Usage**
   Write a Python program that prints five different emojis using Unicode escape sequences (\U or \u). Include both text-style and emoji-style variants where possible.

PyAutoGUI

PyAutoGUI is a powerful cross-platform Python module that automates interactions with the computer's graphical user interface (GUI). It allows developers to control the mouse and keyboard, simulate clicks, type text, take screenshots, and even locate on-screen images.

It is particularly useful for automating repetitive tasks, testing GUI applications, and creating custom desktop bots.

Installation
PyAutoGUI is not part of the Python standard library. It must be installed separately from the Python Package Index (PyPI) using:

```
pip install pyautogui
```

Core Concept

PyAutoGUI works by simulating human interaction with the computer screen. It can:

- Move and click the mouse programmatically.
- Type characters and key combinations.
- Scroll, drag, and drop items.
- Capture screenshots and locate images on the screen.

All coordinates and screen positions are handled in **pixels (x, y)** where (0, 0) represents the top-left corner of the screen.

Pyautogui Methods

absolute_import	division	move	failSafeCheck
alert	doubleClick	moveRel	functools
center	drag	moveTo	getActiveWindow
click	dragRel	onScreen	getActiveWindowTitle
collections	dragTo	os	getAllTitles
confirm	easeInBack	password	getAllWindows
contextmanager	easeInBounce	pixel	getInfo
countdown	easeInCirc	pixelMatchesColor	getPointOnLine
datetime	easeInCubic	platform	getWindowsAt
displayMousePosition	easeInElastic	platformModule	getWindowsWithTitle
hold	locateAll	vscroll	position

hotkey	locateAllOnScreen	write	press
hscroll	locateCenterOnScreen	sys	printInfo
isShiftCharacter	locateOnScreen	time	print_function
isValidKey	locateOnWindow	tripleClick	prompt
keyDown	middleClick	typewrite	pyscreeze
keyUp	mouseDown	screenshot	run
leftClick	mouseInfo	scroll	re
linear	mouseUp	shortcut	resolution
locate	mouseinfo	size	rightClick
run	sleep		

Table 10.5

position()

Returns the current coordinates of the mouse cursor.

```
Python
import pyautogui
pyautogui.sleep(2)  #Delay execution by 2 seconds
print(pyautogui.position())
```

```
#Output
Point(x=717, y=229)
```

moveTo(x, y, duration=0)

Moves the mouse pointer to the specified screen position.

```
Python
import pyautogui
pyautogui.moveTo(200, 300, duration=1)
```

moveRel(x, y, duration=0)

Moves the mouse relative to its current position.

```
Python
import pyautogui
pyautogui.moveRel(100, 0, duration=0.5) #move right by 100 pixels
```

click(x=None, y=None, button='left')

Performs a mouse click. You can specify coordinates and which button to use.

```python
import pyautogui
pyautogui.click(400, 400)  # Left-click at coordinates (400,400)
```

doubleClick() , tripleClick() , rightClick() , middleClick()

Perform multiple or specific types of clicks.

```python
import pyautogui
pyautogui.doubleClick(500, 500)
pyautogui.rightClick()
```

dragTo(x,y, duration=1)

Drags the mouse from its current position to another.

```python
import pyautogui
pyautogui.dragTo(800, 400, duration=2)
```

scroll(amount) , hscroll(amount) , vscroll(amount)

Scrolls the mouse wheel vertically or horizontally.

```python
import pyautogui

pyautogui.scroll(-300)   # Scroll down
pyautogui.scroll(300)    # Scroll up
```

write(text, interval) , typewrite(text, interval)

Simulates typing of text character by character.

●●● Python

```python
import pyautogui
pyautogui.write("Hello, this is automated typing!", interval=0.05)
pyautogui.typewrite("Hi! fellow Pythonist!")
```

press() , keyDown() , keyUp() , hotkey()

Simulates keyboard presses or combinations.

●●● Python

```python
import pyautogui
pyautogui.press('enter')
pyautogui.hotkey('ctrl', 'a')  # Select All shortcut
pyautogui.keyDown('A')
pyautogui.keyUp('A')
```

screenshot(filename = None)

Takes a screenshot of the screen or specific region.

●●● Python

```python
import pyautogui
screenshot_1 = pyautogui.screenshot("capture.png")
screenshot_2 = pyautogui.screenshot("image.jpg", (400,400,400,400))

screenshot_1.show()
screenshot_2.show(title="Captured Screen")
```

Methods of the screenshot() Object

alpha_composite	effect_spread	save	paste
apply_transparency	encoderconfig	seek	point
close	encoderinfo	show	putalpha
convert	entropy	size	putdata
copy	filter	split	putpalette
crop	format	tell	putpixel
draft	format_description	thumbnail	pyaccess
getpalette	frombytes	tobitmap	quantize
getpixel	transpose	tobytes	readonly
getprojection	verify	toqimage	reduce

getxmp	width	toqpixmap	paste
get_child_images	getbbox	getcolors	getexif
getbands	getchannel	getdata	getextrema

Table 10.6

Example,

```python
import pyautogui
screenshot = pyautogui.screenshot()
screenshot.putalpha(100) #Make image transparent
screenshot.show()

screenshot.save("myshot.png") #Save image
```

Note

- When a file name is provided in **screenshot(*filename*)**, the captured image is automatically saved with that name. Alternatively, you can store the image in a variable and save it later using the **save(*filename*)** method.
- The **screenshot()** function is implemented using the **Pillow (PIL)** library, which provides additional features for image processing and editing. The **Pillow** module will be covered in the next chapter.

locateOnScreen(image) , locateCenterOnScreen(image)

Searches for an image on the screen and returns its position.

```python
import pyautogui
button = pyautogui.locateCenterOnScreen('button.jpg')
pyautogui.click(button)
```

getActiveWindow() , getActiveWindowTitle()

Retrieves information about the currently active window.

```python
import pyautogui
window = pyautogui.getActiveWindow()
```

```
print(f"title -> {window.title}")
print(f"width -> {window.width}")
print(f"height -> {window.height}")
```

```
#Output
title -> file.py - Main - Visual Studio Code
width -> 1382
height -> 736
```

Methods of the getActiveWindow() Object

activate	height	midtop	show
area	hide	minimize	size
bottom	isActive	move	title
bottomleft	isMaximized	moveRel	top
bottomright	isMinimized	moveTo	topleft
box	left	resize	topright
center	maximize	resizeRel	visible
centerx	midbottom	resizeTo	

Table 10.7

Example,

```
Python
import pyautogui

window = pyautogui.getActiveWindow()
window.minimize()
window.maximize()
pyautogui.sleep(2)
window.close()
```

alert() , confirm() , prompt()

Displays simple GUI dialogs for interaction.

Example 1 – alert()

```python
import pyautogui

pyautogui.alert("Operation completed successfully!")
```

#Output

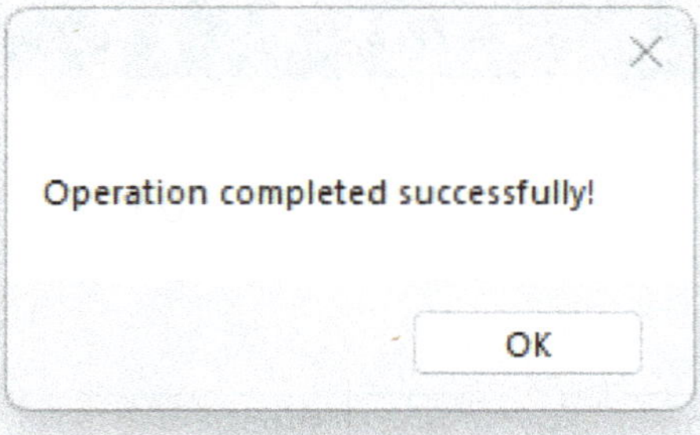

Example 2 – confirm()

```python
import pyautogui

choice = pyautogui.confirm(
    "Do you want to continue?",
    buttons=['Yes', 'No']
)

print(choice)
```

#Output

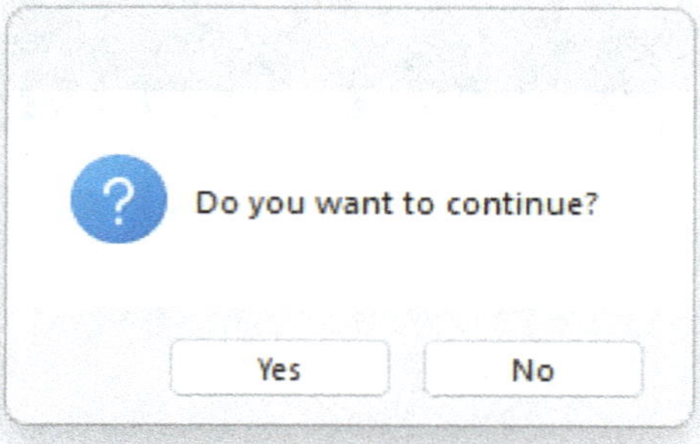

Example 3 – prompt()

```
●●● Python
import pyautogui

password = pyautogui.prompt("Enter Password")
print(password)
```

#Output

countdown()

Displays a visible countdown in the terminal.

```
●●● Python
import pyautogui
count = pyautogui.countdown(10)
print(count)
```

```
#Output
10 9 8 7 6 5 4 3 2 1
```

displayMousePosition()

Continuously displays the current mouse position in the console until stopped.

```
●●● Python
import pyautogui
count = pyautogui.displayMousePosition()
print(count)
```

```
#Output
Press Ctrl-C to quit.
X:   326 Y:   669 RGB: ( 38,   79, 120)
```

Easing Functions (for smooth movement)

These functions define how the mouse moves from one position to another. For example, easeInQuad, easeOutBounce, easeInOutCubic, etc.

Example:

```python
import pyautogui

pyautogui.moveTo(
    1000,
    500,
    duration=2,
    tween=pyautogui.easeInOutBounce
)
```

📌 This makes the mouse movement appear natural and animated.

easeInBack	easeInOutBack	easeInOutQuad	easeInQuint
easeInBounce	easeInOutBounce	easeInOutQuart	easeInSine
easeInCirc	easeInOutCirc	easeInOutQuint	easeOutBack
easeInCubic	easeInOutCubic	easeInOutSine	easeOutBounce
easeInElastic	easeInOutElastic	easeInQuad	easeOutCirc
easeInExpo	easeInOutExpo	easeInQuart	easeOutCubic

Table 10.8

Key Terms

PyAutoGUI
Coordinates (x, y)
Screenshot
Easing Functions
locateOnScreen()

Review Questions

1. Which PyAutoGUI function moves the mouse to a specific screen position?
   a) moveTo()
   b) moveRel()
   c) dragTo()
   d) click()
   Answer: a

2. How do you simulate typing a string character by character in PyAutoGUI?
   a) press()
   b) typewrite()
   c) keyDown()
   d) write()
   Answer: b

3. Which method captures the current screen and saves it to a file?
   a) screenshot()
   b) displayMousePosition()
   c) locateOnScreen()
   d) alert()
   Answer: a

4. What does pyautogui.locateCenterOnScreen('image.png') return?
   a) The pixel color of the image
   b) The center coordinates of the found image
   c) A screenshot of the screen
   d) Boolean indicating if image exists
   Answer: b

5. What is the purpose of easing functions in PyAutoGUI?
   a) Change text color
   b) Create smooth mouse movement
   c) Click multiple times
   d) Take screenshots
   Answer: b

Review Exercises

1. **Mouse Automation**
   Use PyAutoGUI to move the mouse in a square pattern (100 px per side) and click at each corner.

2. **Screenshot Automation**
   Write a script that takes a screenshot of a 500x500 pixel region at coordinates (200, 200) and saves it as "region.png".

3. **Keyboard Automation**
   Automate typing the sentence "Python is fun!" with a 0.1-second interval between characters, then press Enter.

4. **Image Recognition**
   Place an image (button.png) on your screen and write a script to locate it using locateCenterOnScreen() and perform a click. Handle the case if the image is not found.

Turtle

The Python Turtle module is a powerful tool for drawing geometric shapes, animations, and patterns by moving the turtle (cursor) in different directions on the screen. The turtle follows a set of programmed instructions, allowing users to create intricate designs. This module is pre-packaged in Python and can be imported using the **import turtle** statement.

Turtle graphics are widely used in educational environments to introduce programming concepts in a fun and interactive way. It helps beginners understand loops, functions, and event-driven programming by visually representing code execution.

Features of Python Turtle

- Cursor as a Drawing Tool
  The turtle acts as a pen or cursor controlled by user-defined commands. It draws shapes or patterns as it moves on the screen.

- Directional Movement
  The turtle can move forward, backward, left, and right, each defined with a specific length or angle.

- Customizable Appearance
  Users can change the turtle's color, shape, and size. Some predefined shapes include arrow, classic, square, triangle, and circle.

- Drawing Geometric Shapes
  By combining movement commands and loops, users can create polygons, fractals, spirals, and stars, among other complex patterns.

- Animation Capabilities
  Animations can be created by adjusting the speed, timing, and using loops to control the turtle's motion.

Methods

done	goto	home	penup
mainloop	setx	undo	pendown
forward	sety	pencolor	teleport
fd	setheading	color	getshapes
backwards	seth	bgcolor	shape
bk	setpos	fillcolor	shapesize
right	setposition	begin_fill	hideturtle
rt	position	end_fill	hd

left	pos	pensize	showturtle
lt	clone	width	st
bye	write	stamp	speed
clear	reset	begin_poly	delay
clearscreen	resetscreen	end_poly	circle
title	exitonclick	bgpic	dots
tracer	clearstamp	pu	isdown
textinput	clearstamps	pd	isinvisible
back	numinput	up	turtlesize
distance	addshape	update	towards

Table 10.9

Insight

To discover additional methods and attributes in the turtle module, use the dir() function

```
>>> import turtle
>>> tut = turtle.Turtle()
>>> dir(turtle)
```

Basic Turtle Operations

done() and mainloop()

After drawing a shape, the screen normally closes immediately. The following methods prevent the screen from closing automatically after the drawing is completed:

- *turtle.done()*: Keeps the window open until manually closed.
- *turtle.mainloop()*: Similar to turtle.done(), keeps the turtle graphics window active.

bgcolor(color):

bgcolor() defines the background color of the turtle graphics window.
Colors can be specified in two formats:

- Named colors such as **"red"**, **"blue"**, **"purple"**, etc.
- Hexadecimal format **"#rrggbb"**, where **r**, **g**, and **b** are values from 0-9 or A-F.

Python
```python
import turtle

turtle.bgcolor("red")
turtle.mainloop()
```

#Output

Movement and Positioning

forward(float) , fd(float)

Moves the turtle forward by the specified distance.

```
Python
import turtle

turtle.forward( 250 )
turtle.mainloop()
```

#Output

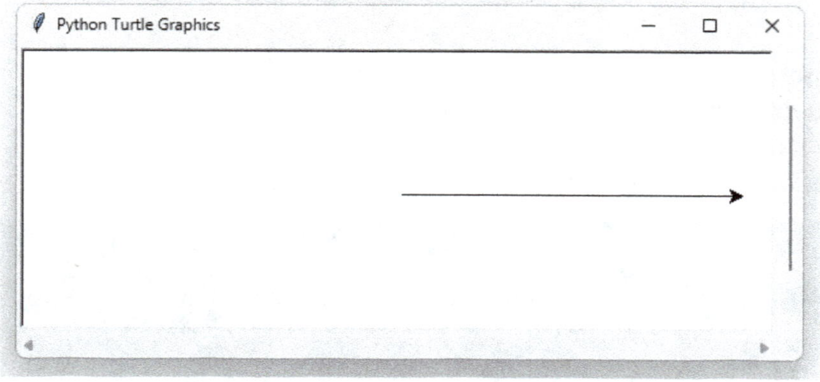

backward(float) , bk(float)

Moves the turtle backward by the specified distance.

```
••• Python
import turtle
turtle.bk( 100 )
turtle.mainloop()
```

right(angle) , rt(angle)

Rotates the turtle clockwise by the specified angle.

```
••• Python
import turtle
turtle.fd( 200 )      #moves forward by 200
turtle.right( 90 )    #turns to 90 degrees clockwise
turtle.fd( 100 )      #continue moving forward by 100
turtle.mainloop()
```

#Output

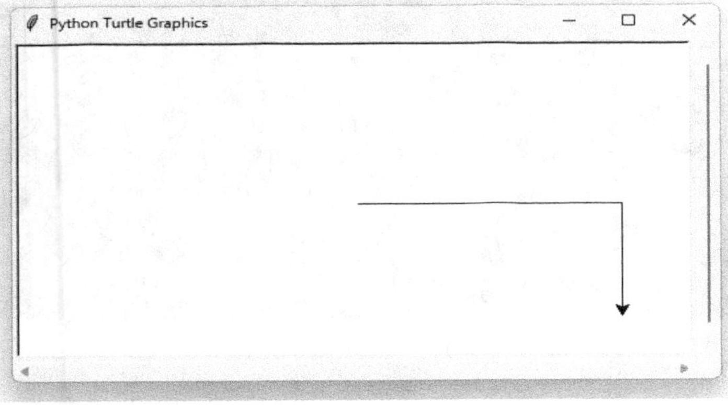

left(angle) and lt(angle)

Rotates the turtle counterclockwise by the specified angle.

```
••• Python
import turtle
turtle.forward( 200 )   #move forward by 200
turtle.left( 120 )      #turn 120 anticlockwise
```

```
turtle.forward(200)    #move forward by 200
turtle.left( 120 )     #turn 120 anticlockwise
turtle.forward(200)    #move forward by 200
```

#Output

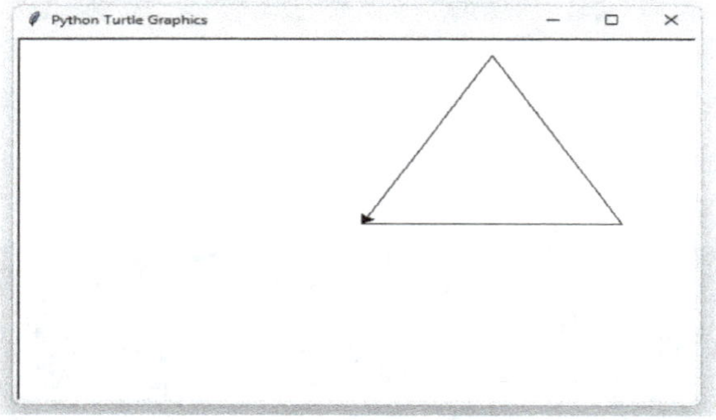

goto(x, y)

Moves the turtle to the specified (x, y) coordinates.

```
Python
import turtle
turtle.goto(-100, 0)
turtle.goto(100, 0)
turtle.goto(100, 100)
turtle.goto(-100, 100)
turtle.goto(-100, 0)

turtle.done()
```

#Output

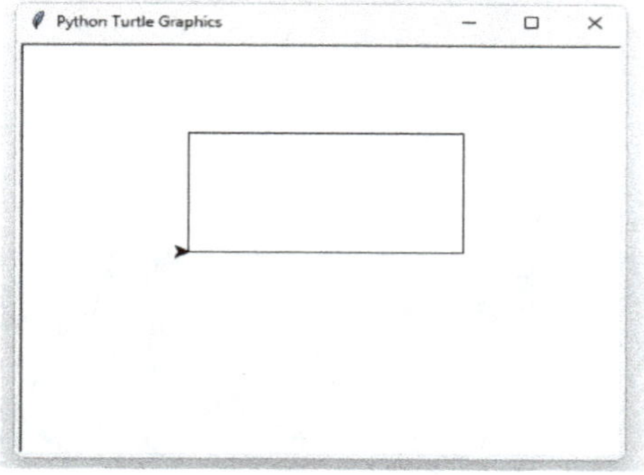

setx(x) , sety(y)

setx(x): Moves the turtle to a specific x-coordinate while keeping the y-coordinate constant.
sety(y): Moves the turtle to a specific y-coordinate while keeping the x-coordinate constant.

```
●●● Python
import turtle
turtle.setx(-100)
turtle.sety(-100)
turtle.setx(150)
turtle.sety(50)
turtle.setx(-150)
turtle.sety(-100)
turtle.done()
```

#Output

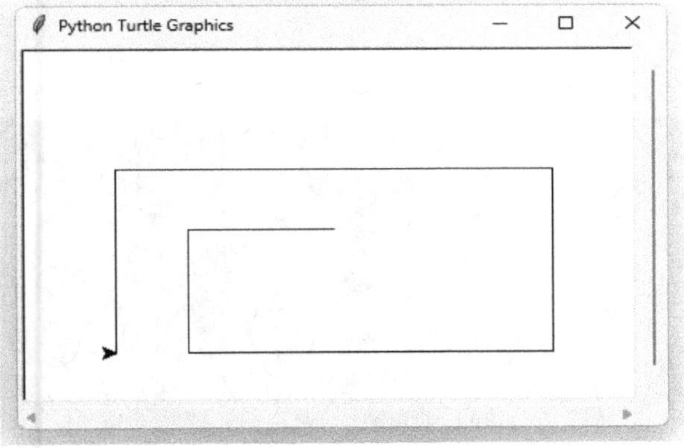

setheading(angle) , seth(angle)

Sets the turtle's heading to the specified angle.

```
●●● Python
import turtle
turtle.seth(90)
turtle.fd(100)
turtle.seth(125)
turtle.fd(100)
turtle.seth(235)
turtle.fd(100)
turtle.seth(270)
turtle.fd(100)
turtle.seth(0)
turtle.fd(120)
turtle.mainloop()
```

#Output

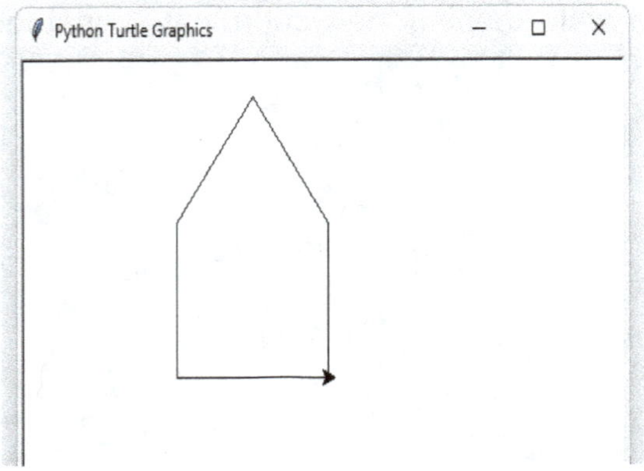

setposition(x, y) , setpos(x, y)

Moves the turtle to the specified (x, y) coordinates and begins drawing from that point.

```
Python
import turtle

turtle.setpos(10, 50)
turtle.backward(100)
turtle.done()
```

position( ) , pos( )

Returns the current (x, y) coordinates of the turtle.

```
Python
import turtle

turtle.setposition(400, 100)
pos = turtle.pos()
print(pos)
turtle.done()
```

```
#Output
(400.00,100.00)
```

Insight

- **clone()**: Creates a duplicate instance of the turtle at the current position.
- **home()**: Moves the turtle to the origin (0,0) and resets the heading to 0 degrees.
- **undo()**: Removes the last action performed by the turtle, such as a drawn line.

Insight

After drawing shapes with Turtle, you can save everything on the screen as an *.eps* file using **getcanvas()** and **postscript(file)**. This *.eps* file can later be converted to an image. For example:

```
>>> from PIL import Image
>>> import turtle
>>> turtle.circle(100)
>>> screen = turtle.getscreen()
>>> screen.getcanvas().postscript(file = "shape.eps")

#opening and saving image
>>> img = Image.open("shape.eps")
>>> img.save("mydrawing.png")
```

Pen Control

pencolor(color) , color(color)

These set the line color for drawing. It accepts:

- Named colors: **"red"**, **"green"**, **"blue"**, etc.
- Hexadecimal format **"#rrggbb"**, where **r**, **g**, and **b** are values from 0-9 or A-F.

Python

```
import turtle
turtle.color("orange")    #line color is set to red

for width in [200, 100, 200, 100]:
      turtle.bk( width )
      turtle.right( 90 )
turtle.done()
```

#Output

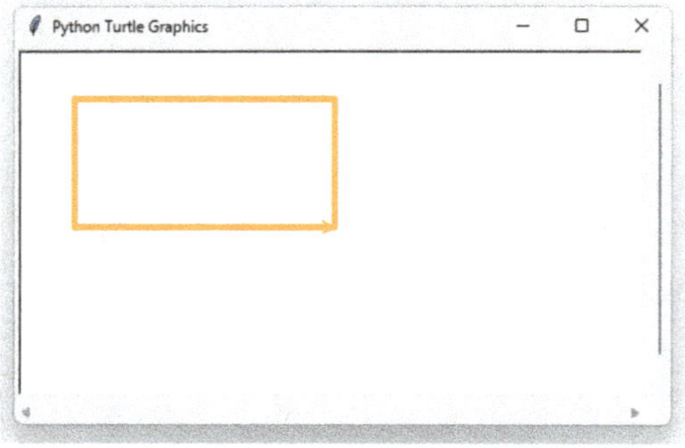

fillcolor(color) , begin_fill( ) , end_fill( )

fillcolor: defines the fill color for closed shapes.
begin_fill(): Marks the start of filling.
end_fill(): Completes and fills the drawn shape.

```
Python
import turtle
turtle.fillcolor("#ac92ec")
turtle.begin_fill()
turtle.circle(radius=100)
turtle.end_fill()
turtle.done()
```

#Output

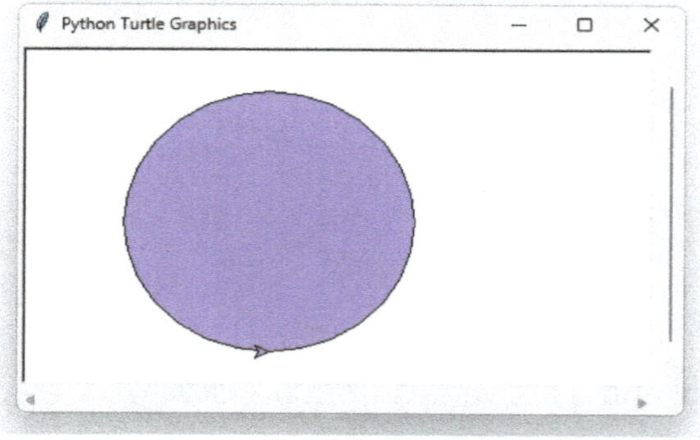

pensize(float) and width(float)

turtle.pensize(): Defines the thickness of the drawing line.
turtle.width(): Functions the same as pensize(), adjusting the pen thickness.

```python
import turtle
turtle.pensize(5)
turtle.done()
```

penup( ) , pu( ) , pendown( ) , pd( )

turtle.penup() or *turtle.pu()* lifts the pen so the turtle moves without drawing.
turtle.pendown() or *turtle.pd()* lowers the pen so the turtle resumes drawing.

```python
import turtle

turtle.goto( 50, 100 )
turtle.goto( 100, 0 )
turtle.goto( 0, 0 )

turtle.penup( )
turtle.goto( -200, 0 )
turtle.pendown( )

for i in range( 4 ):
    turtle.forward( 100 )
    turtle.right( 90 )

turtle.done()
```

#Output

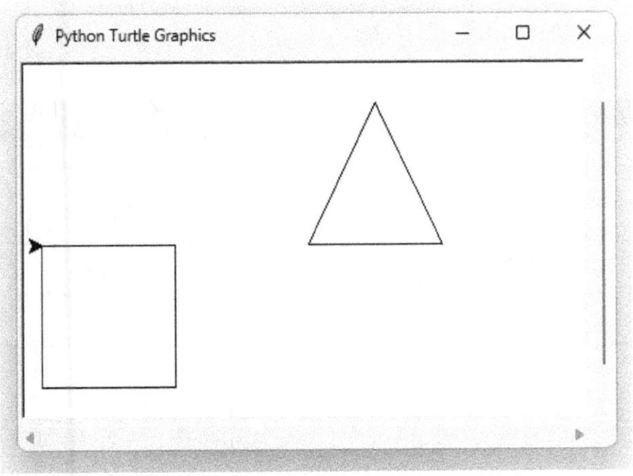

📖 **Note**

turtle.teleport(x, y):
Moves the turtle to a new position without drawing, similar to **penup()** and **pendown()** but with specified coordinates.

Appearance and Shape Control

hideturtle( ) , ht( ) , showturtle( ) , st( )

hideturtle() or ht(): hides the turtle cursor from the screen.
showturtle() or st(): makes the turtle visible after hiding.

```python
import turtle

turtle.showturtle()
turtle.hideturtle()
turtle.done()
```

shape(shape) , shapesize(stretch_wid, stretch_len, outline), getshapes( )

The *shape()* sets the shape of the turtle cursor.
The *shapesize()* modifies the shape's width, length, and outline thickness.
The *getshapes()* returns a list of all available shapes. The following are available shapes.
"arrow", "blank", "circle", "classic", "square", "triangle", "turtle"

Shape	Icon	Shape	Icon
arrow		triangle	
square		turtle	
circle		blank	
classic			

Table 11.0

```python
import turtle

turtle.shape("turtle" )
turtle.shapesize(stretch_wid= 10,stretch_len=20,outline=2)

#Getting shapes
shapes = turtle.getshapes()
print(shapes)
turtle.done()
```

```
#Output
['arrow', 'blank', 'circle', 'classic', 'square', 'triangle', 'turtle']
```

speed(int) , delay(number)

The *speed()* sets the drawing speed from 0 (slowest) to 10 (fastest). Accepts strings: **"slow"**, **"normal"**, **"fast"**.

The *delay()* defines the time delay between turtle movements.

```python
import turtle
turtle.speed(5)
turtle.delay(3.5)
turtle.done()
```

Drawing Shapes

circle(radius, extent=None, steps=None)

The *circle()* method allows the turtle to draw a circle with the specified radius.

- **extent** → (float) [Optional]: Defines the length of the circumference to be drawn.
- **steps** → (int) [Optional]: Specifies the number of points to form an enclosed polygon. Using steps, you can draw different polygons instead of a perfect circle.

Example 1,

```python
import turtle
turtle.shape('turtle')
turtle.pencolor("red"),
turtle.pensize(2)

turtle.circle(radius= 50)
turtle.done()
```

#Output

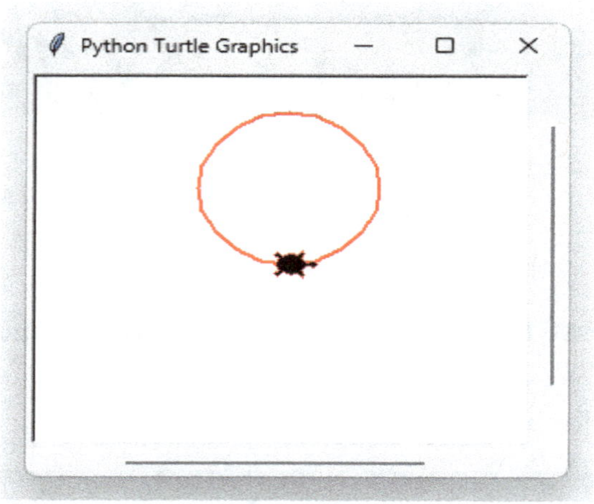

Example 2,

```python
import turtle
turtle.circle(radius=100, steps=5)
turtle.done()
```

#Output

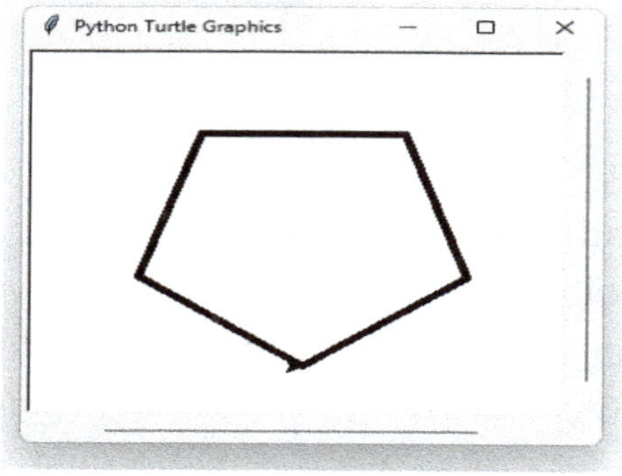

Example 3,

```
●●● Python
import turtle
turtle.fillcolor('#4fc1e9')
turtle.begin_fill()
turtle.circle(radius=100, steps=8)
turtle.end_fill()
turtle.done()
```

#Output

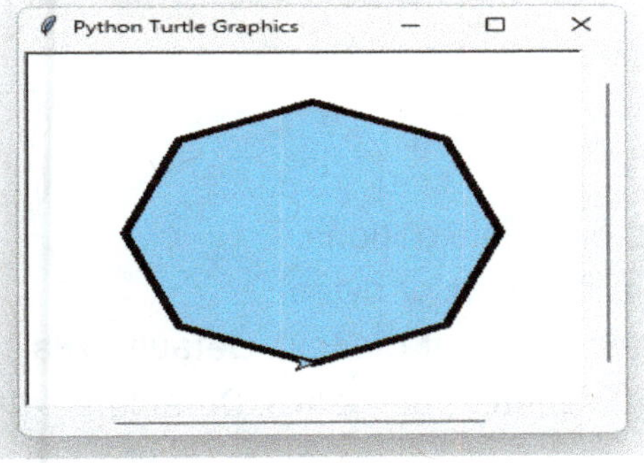

dot(size)

The *dot()* method creates dots on the screen with a specified size (integer).

```
●●● Python
import turtle
import random

colors = ["red", "orange", "green", "purple", "blue"]
for i in range(1, 500):
    turtle.pencolor(colors[random.randint(0,len(colors) -1)])
    turtle.dot(size=10)
    turtle.teleport(x=random.randint(-i,i),y=random.randint(-i,i))

turtle.mainloop()
```

#Output

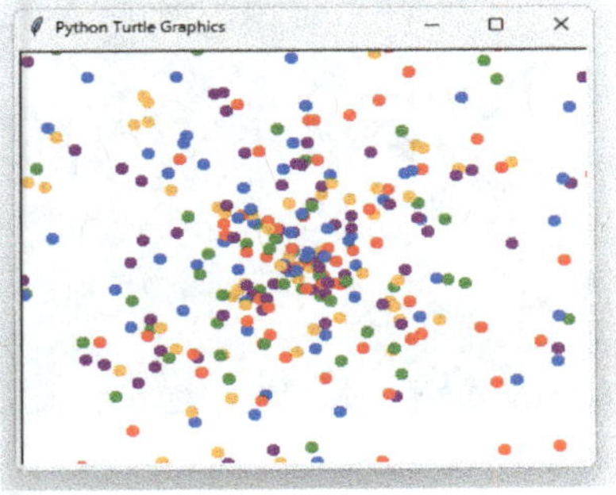

begin_poly( ) , end_poly( )

The *begin_poly()* marks the start of a polygon, allowing you to define custom shapes.
The *end_poly()* marks the completion of the polygon.

```python
import turtle

turtle.begin_poly()
turtle.end_poly()
turtle.mainloop()
```

write(arg, move, align, font)

The *write()* method prints text onto the screen with customizable options.

arg → Can be a string, number, list, dictionary, set, tuple, boolean, or bytes.

move → (bool) [Optional]: If True, the turtle moves by the length of the text. Default is False.

align → (string) [Optional]: Defines text alignment ("left", "center", or "right"). Default is "left".

font → (tuple) [Optional]: Defines the text appearance:

- Font Family (str) – Example: "Arial", "Consolas", "Times New Roman", "Tahoma", "Georgia".
- Font Size (int) – Defines the text size.
- Font Style (str) – "normal", "bold", "italic", or "underline"

```python
import turtle

turtle.bgcolor("#5D9CEC")
turtle.color("white")
turtle.teleport(x=-180, y=50)
turtle.write(arg="Hello Pythonista!", font=("tahoma", 25, "bold"))
turtle.teleport(x=-200, y=0)
turtle.write(arg="Hello Pythonista!", font=("Georgia", 30))
turtle.teleport(x=-30, y=-50)
turtle.write(
     arg="Hello Pythonista!",
     align="center",
     font=("Georgia", 25, "italic")
  )

turtle.done()
```

```
#Output
```

Insight

The **stamp()** method leaves an impression of the turtle's shape at its current position on the screen.

Screen and Window Control

bye( ) , reset( ) , clearscreen( ), clear( )

The *bye()* closes the turtle window immediately.
The *reset()* resets the screen and clears all drawings.
The *clearscreen()* clears all shapes drawn by the turtle.
The *clear()* clears only the currently drawn object.

```python
import turtle

turtle.bye()
turtle.reset()
turtle.clearscreen()
turtle.clear()
turtle.mainloop()
```

title(title) , exitonclick()

The *title()* sets the window title.

The *exitonclick()* closes the window when clicked.

```python
import turtle

turtle.title( "My Title" )
turtle.exitonclick()
turtle.mainloop()
```

Shapes Created Using Turtle

Example 1 – Program to draw a simple flower,

```python
import turtle

turtle.pencolor("#ED5565")
turtle.pensize(5)
for angle in range(0, 360, 30):
    turtle.seth(angle)
    turtle.circle(100)

turtle.mainloop()
```

#Output

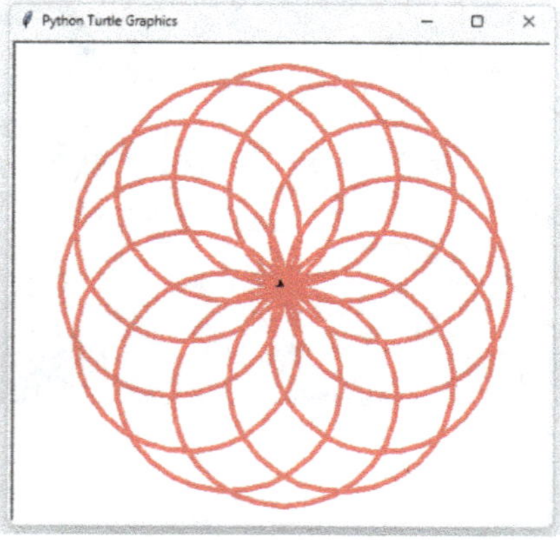

Example 2 – Program to draw flower with Spiral Petals,

```
••• Python
import turtle
import math

turtle.speed(0)

# Function to draw a spiral flower
def flower(petals, angle_step, size_factor):
    for i in range(petals):
        turtle.forward(math.sqrt(i) * size_factor)
        turtle.left(angle_step)

# Draw the flower
flower(360, 65, 10)

turtle.done()
```

#Output

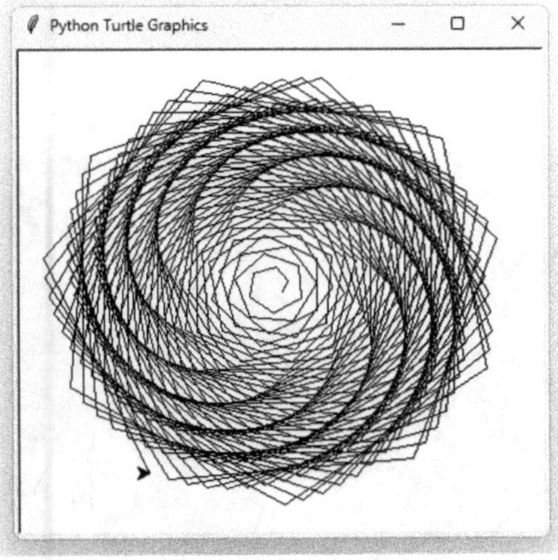

Example 3 – Program to draw sun flower

```
••• Python
import turtle
import math

turtle.speed(0)
turtle.pensize(1)
# Function to draw a spiral flower
def flower(petals, angle_step, size_factor):
    for i in range(petals):
        turtle.forward(math.sqrt(i) * size_factor)
        turtle.left(angle_step)
```

```
# Draw the flower
flower(360, 100, 20)

turtle.done()
```

#Output

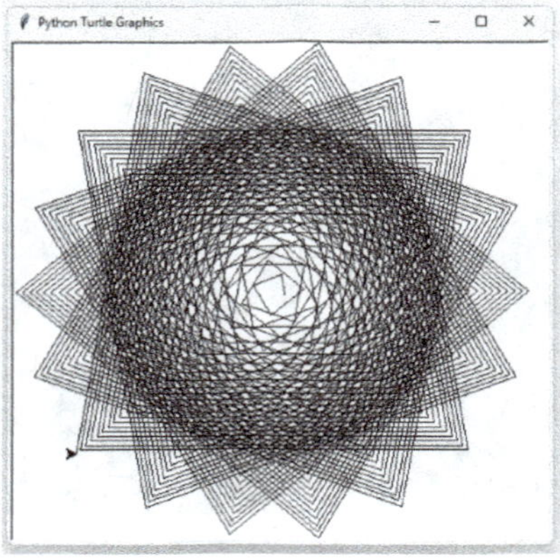

Example 4 – Program to draw colorful square flower

```
Python
import turtle
import random

turtle.speed(0)
turtle.bgcolor("#14171A")
colors = ["red","yellow","green","blue","orange","purple"]

def create_square(size):
    for i in range(4):
        turtle.forward( size )
        turtle.right(90)

def flower(repeat, size, angle):
    for i in range(repeat):
        turtle.pencolor(random.choice(colors))
        create_square(size )
        turtle.right(angle)

flower(72, 100, 10)
turtle.done()
```

#Output

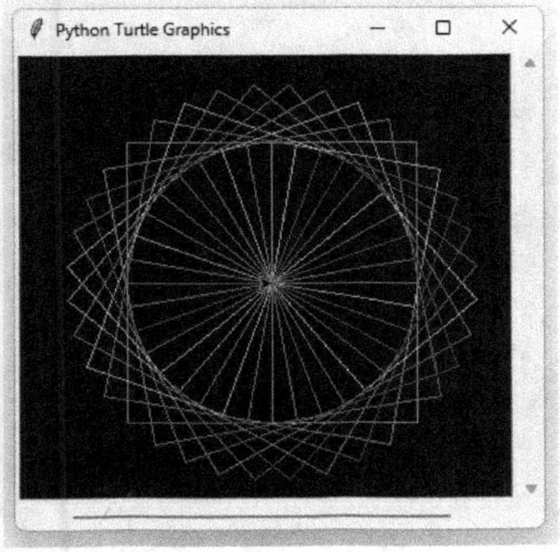

Example 5 – Program to draw square spiral

```python
import turtle

turtle.speed(0)
turtle.bgcolor("#14171A")

colors = ["red","yellow","green","blue","orange","purple"]

for i in range( 100 ):
      turtle.pencolor( colors[ i % len(colors)])
      turtle.forward( i * 5 )
      turtle.right( 91 )

turtle.done()
```

#Output

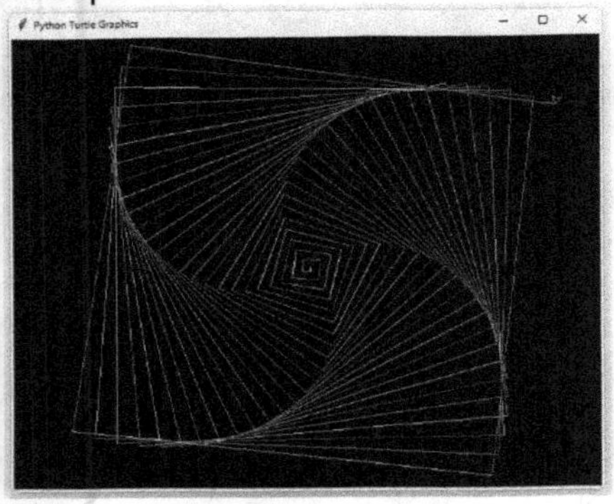

Example 6 – Program to draw colorful hexagonal flower

```
●●● Python
import turtle

turtle.speed(0)
turtle.bgcolor("#14171A")
colors = ["red","yellow","green","blue","orange","purple"]

for i in range( 6 ):
      turtle.pencolor( colors[ i % len(colors)])
      for _ in range( 6 ):
            turtle.forward( 100 )
            turtle.right( 60 )
      turtle.right( 60 )

turtle.done()
```

#Output

Example 7 – A program to draw spiral flower,

```
●●● Python
import turtle
turtle.speed(0)

for i in range( 100 ):
      for _ in range( 3 ):
            turtle.forward( i * 4 )
            turtle.right( 140 )
      turtle.right( 5 )

turtle.done()
```

Key Terms

teleport
Pen Control
penup
pendown
begin_fill
end_fill
done
mainloop

Review Questions

1. Which Turtle method moves the turtle to a specific coordinate without drawing?
   a) goto()
   b) teleport()
   c) penup() + goto()
   d) pendown()
   Answer: c

2. What does turtle.seth(90) do?
   a) Moves forward 90 pixels
   b) Sets the turtle heading to 90 degrees
   c) Rotates the turtle counterclockwise 90 degrees
   d) Rotates the turtle clockwise 90 degrees
   Answer: b

3. Which method is used to start filling a shape with color?
   a) fillcolor()
   b) begin_fill()
   c) end_fill()
   d) color()
   Answer: b

4. What is the difference between clear() and clearscreen()?
   a) clear() clears current object; clearscreen() clears everything
   b) clear() clears everything; clearscreen() clears current object
   c) Both are identical
   d) Both close the window
   Answer: a

5. How do you draw a circle with 6 sides instead of a perfect circle?
   a) circle(radius, steps=6)
   b) circle(radius, extent=6)
   c) begin_fill(6)
   d) dot(6)
   Answer: a

Review Exercises

1. **Basic Shapes**
   Draw a square and a triangle on the same Turtle screen using forward() and right()/left() commands.
2. **Colorful Spiral**
   Create a spiral with 50 iterations, using pencolor() with random colors and forward() incrementing by 5 pixels each time.
3. **Filled Shapes**
   Draw a filled hexagon using begin_fill(), end_fill(), and a custom fill color.
4. **Custom Text**
   Display the text "Python Turtle Rocks!" at three different positions with different fonts, sizes, and alignment using write().
5. **Flower Pattern**
   Create a function flower(petals, size) to draw a flower with a variable number of petals using loops and circle() or forward() + left().

PIL (Pillow)

Pillow, also known as **PIL (Python Imaging Library),** is a core Python module for loading, manipulating, enhancing, and processing images in various formats. It provides a wide range of image-processing capabilities that allow developers to modify images programmatically. Pillow enables tasks such as image resizing, cropping, rotating, filtering, and format conversion, making it an essential tool for applications that involve image processing.

Features and Functionalities

Loading, Showing, and Printing Images

Pillow allows users to load images from different file formats and display them directly. Additionally, it provides the capability to print image details such as size, mode, and format.

Creating Images from Scratch

Developers can generate images from scratch using Pillow, defining colors, sizes, and shapes as needed. This feature is particularly useful for creating placeholders, patterns, or visual data representations.

Image Rotation

Pillow provides built-in methods to rotate images at various angles. This feature is useful in applications requiring image orientation adjustments, such as correcting tilted photos.

Image Cropping

Images can be cropped to extract specific areas of interest. This feature is commonly used in applications requiring face detection, object recognition, or automated document processing.

Scaling Images

Resizing images while maintaining aspect ratio is an essential function in many applications. Pillow enables users to scale images to fit different screen sizes or optimize them for various platforms.

Image Filtering

Pillow provides filtering capabilities to enhance images, including sharpening, blurring, and edge detection. These features improve image quality and can be used for artistic effects or pre-processing in machine learning applications.

Image File Format Conversion

Pillow supports converting images from one file format to another. This functionality is useful for optimizing images for different use cases, such as converting a high-resolution PNG to a more storage-efficient JPEG.

Color Transformation

The library allows changing an image's color mode, such as converting an image from RGB to grayscale. This is useful for reducing file size, improving contrast, or preparing images for further analysis.

Resizing Images

Pillow provides methods to resize images while preserving quality. This feature is particularly useful for creating thumbnails or optimizing images for web applications.

Retrieving Image Statistics

The library includes a histogram method that allows users to analyze pixel distribution within an image. This feature is commonly used in image recognition, segmentation, and color analysis applications.

Installation and Compatibility

While Pillow is often pre-installed with Python, some environments may require manual installation. It is important to ensure that PIL is not installed alongside Pillow, as they may not coexist properly.

> **Note**
>
> In case of compatibility issues, it is recommended to uninstall PIL before installing Pillow.
>
> pip uninstall PIL
>
> pip install pillow

Pillow remains a powerful and versatile tool for image processing in Python, supporting a wide range of functionalities suitable for beginners and advanced users alike. Whether for simple tasks such as resizing and cropping or complex operations like filtering and transformation, Pillow provides a robust solution for handling images programmatically.

Image File Formats

Pillow (PIL) is a powerful image processing library capable of handling various image file formats across different operating systems. It allows seamless conversion between formats while preserving image quality. An image can be loaded in one format, processed, and saved in another without loss of essential details.

Supported Image Formats and Platforms

Pillow supports a wide range of image file formats commonly used across multiple platforms:

Format	Extension	Description	Platform
JPEG / JFIF	.jpg, .jpeg	Common image format, lossy compression	Windows, macOS, Linux
JPEG 2000	.jp2, .j2k, .jpx	Advanced JPEG format with better compression	Windows, macOS, Linux
PNG	.png	Portable Network Graphics, supports transparency	Windows, macOS, Linux
TIFF	.tif, .tiff	Tagged Image File Format, used in professional photography	Windows, macOS, Linux
ICO	.ico	Windows icon format	Windows
ICNS	.icns	macOS icon format	macOS
GIF	.gif	Graphics Interchange Format, supports animation	Windows, macOS, Linux
PPM/PGM/PBM	.ppm, .pgm, .pbm	Portable Pixmap/Graymap/Bitmap	Unix-based systems
SGI	.sgi, .rgb, .rgba, .bw	Silicon Graphics Image format	Windows, macOS, Linux
MSP	.msp	Microsoft Paint format (old versions)	Windows
PCX	.pcx	Paintbrush image format	Windows
BMP	.bmp	Bitmap image format	Windows, macOS, Linux
DDS	.dds	DirectDraw Surface, used in game textures	Windows, macOS, Linux
DIB	.dib	Device-independent bitmap	Windows
EPS	.eps	Encapsulated PostScript	Windows, macOS, Linux
IM	.im	A format used by LabEye and other applications	Windows, macOS, Linux
WEBP	.webp	Modern web image format with better compression	Windows, macOS, Linux
TGA	.tga	Truevision TGA, used in 3D graphics and gaming	Windows, macOS, Linux
XPM	.xpm	X PixMap, used in X11 applications	Unix-based systems
XBM	.xbm	X Bitmap, used in X11 GUI systems	Unix-based systems
SPIDER	.spi	Multi-image format used in electron microscopy	Windows, macOS, Linux
PFM	.pfm	Portable Float Map, used in high-precision images	Windows, macOS, Linux
FITS	.fli, .flc	Flexible Image Transport System, used in astronomy	Windows, macOS, Linux
CUR	.cur	Windows cursor format	Windows
MIC	.mic	Microsoft Image Composer format	Windows

PSD	.psd	Adobe Photoshop format	Windows, macOS, Linux
WMF, EMF	.wmf, .emf	Windows Metafile / Enhanced Metafile, used for vector graphics	Windows

Table 11.1

Insight

With Pillow's image file conversion capabilities, you can easily convert an image from one format to another, including converting images to PDF.

The PIL Modules

Pillow (PIL) consists of several modules, each designed to provide specialized classes and methods for handling different aspects of image processing. These modules focus on various functionalities such as image filtering, color manipulation, special effects, image composition, painting, 2D graphics, and other advanced graphic features. Each class within these modules offers distinct methods that enable efficient image and graphic processing.

Some essential Pillow modules

Image Module (PIL.Image)

- Provides the core functionality for opening, creating, and saving images.
- Supports multiple image formats.

ImageChops Module (PIL.ImageChops)

- Supports image arithmetic and logical operations.
- Used for blending, compositing, and enhancing images.

ImageEnhance Module (PIL.ImageEnhance)

- Provides methods to adjust brightness, contrast, sharpness, and color balance.

ImageFilter Module (PIL.ImageFilter)

- Offers predefined filters such as BLUR, CONTOUR, DETAIL, EDGE_ENHANCE, SHARPEN, etc.

ImageDraw Module (PIL.ImageDraw)

- Allows drawing shapes, lines, and text onto images.

ImageFont Module (PIL.ImageFont)

- Handles different font styles for rendering text on images.

ImageGrab Module (PIL.ImageGrab)

- Captures screenshots (Windows and macOS only).

Note

Pillow includes many modules, some of which extend beyond the scope of this book. The modules listed above are essential for graphic design.

Insight

There are four simple ways to utilize the modules or classes provided by PIL:

1. Importing a single module by its name from PIL.
   ```
   >>> from PIL import Image
   ```
2. Importing multiple modules from PIL at once.
   ```
   >>> from PIL import Image, ImageDraw, ImageFilter
   ```
3. Importing all classes using the * wildcard.
   ```
   >>> from PIL import *
   ```
4. Importing PIL and creating instances of classes when needed.
   ```
   >>> import PIL
   >>> img = PIL.Image.open("mypicture.jpg")
   ```

The Image Module

The **Image** module in Pillow provides a class with various methods, each offering unique functionalities for handling images. This module allows you to open, load, display, rotate, create, crop, and retrieve image information seamlessly.

Methods

open	show	blend	core
close	save	alpha_composite	deprecate
new	merge	annotation	effect_noise
frombyte	split	atexit	enum

frombuffer	math	builtins	eval
module	abc	cast	fromarray
fromqimage	fromqpixmap	getmodebans	getmodebase
getmodetype	init	io	is_path
item	linear_gradient	logger	logging
preint	os	radia_gradient	re
isImageType	register_extensions	register_save	register_open
tempfile	register_mime	register_save_all	register_extensions

Table 11.2

show( )

Displays the image using the system's default image viewer. It creates a temporary file to preview the image.

new(mode, size, color)

The *new()* method creates a new image from scratch by specifying its mode, size, and color.
mode →(string): Defines the type of color bands (e.g., "RGB", "RGBA", "L", or "CMYK").
size → (float,float): A 2-tuple (width, height) representing the image dimensions.
color → *(Optional)*: Defines the image color as:

- A single integer (e.g., 156).
- An RGB or RGBA tuple (red, green, blue, alpha).
- A string representing a color name (e.g., "red").
- A hex color name (e.g., "# F5F8FA").

Python

```
from PIL import  Image
img = Image.new(mode="RGBA", size=(600,800),color="#1DA1F2")
img.show()
```

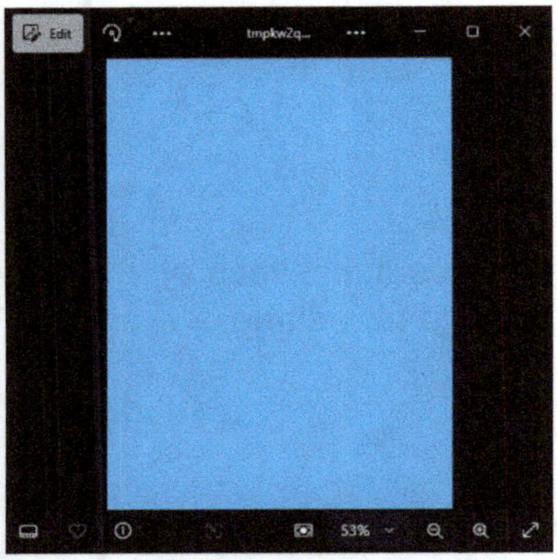

open(path, mode, format)

This method loads an image from a specified path.

path → (string): The file location (as a string or bytes).

mode → (string) [Optional]: Specifies read 'r' (default) or write 'w'.

format → (Optional): Defines the format if not inferred from the file.

Methods and Attributes of an Open Image

height	custom_mimetype	format	getexif
app	decoderconfig	fp	getextrema
applist	decodermaxblock	frombytes	getim
histogram	get_format_mimetype	entropy	getpalette
bits	effect_spread	filename	getpixel
close	get_child_images	getbands	getprojection
convert	has_transparency_data	getchannel	getxmp
copy	apply_transparency	getcolors	load_djpeg
crop	alpha_composite	getdata	load_prepare
draft	format_description	filter	quantization
icclist	putpalette	load_read	quantize
info	putpixel	point	readonly
layer	palette	putalpha	reduce
mode	paste	putdata	remap_palette
rotate			

Table 11.3

Insight

To retrieve the methods and attributes of an image opened with Image.open(), use the dir() function on the image object.

```
>>> img = Image.open("path/to/image.jpg")
>>> dir(img)
```

Note

The **close()** method closes the image and frees up system resources, such as memory and file handles, that were allocated when the image was opened for editing.

Example - Opening an image

```python
from PIL import  Image

img =  Image.open("flower_girl.jpg")
img.show()
```

Saving Images and File Conversion

save(fp, format, save_all, append_images, loop, duration, quality, disposal, transparency, interlace)

The *save()* method in Pillow plays a crucial role in saving and converting images. It provides multiple functionalities depending on the file format used. For instance, saving an image as a GIF requires parameters that might not be applicable when saving as a JPEG.

Key Functions of save()

- Saving an edited or manipulated image as a new file.
- Converting an image from one format to another.
- Stacking multiple images into a single file.
- Creating animated images such as GIFs.

Parameters

fp →(str) [required]: The filename or file path to save the image. The file extension must be included (e.g., "myimage.jpg").

format →(str) [Optional]: Specifies the file format (e.g., "JPEG", "PNG", "GIF"). If omitted, the format is inferred from fp.

save_all →(bool) [Optional]: If True, saves all frames of a multi-frame image (e.g., GIF). Default is False, which saves only the first frame.

append_images →(list of Image objects) [Optional]: A list of additional images to be appended, useful for stacking images or creating animations.

loop →(int) [Optional, GIF-specific]: Specifies how many times an animated image should loop. 0 means infinite looping.

duration →(int) [Optional, GIF-specific]: Sets the display duration (in milliseconds) for each frame in an animated image.

quality →(int) [Optional, JPEG-specific]: Determines the quality of the saved image (1 to 95). Higher values yield better quality. Default is 75.

disposal →(int)[Optional, GIF-specific]: Determines how the previous frame is handled in animations. Default is 0.

transparency →(int or None)[Optional, GIF/PNG-specific]: Defines a transparency color index.

interlace →(bool)[Optional, PNG-specific]: If True, enables interlacing for progressive loading.

Example – Saving an image,

Python
```python
from PIL import  Image

img =  Image.open("flower_girl.jpg")
img.save("new_image.jpg")
```

Insight

File Conversion

You can convert an image to a different format by changing the file extension in the filename.

```
>>> from PIL import  Image
>>> img =  Image.open("image.jpg")
>>> img.save( "new_image.png" )          # conversion from JPG to PNG
```

Creating GIFs or Animated Images

Example,

Python
```
from PIL import  Image

img1 = Image.open("image1.jpg").resize(size=(600, 800))
img2 = Image.open("image2.jpg").resize(size=(600, 800))
img3 = Image.open("image3.jpg").resize(size=(600, 800))

imgs = [ img2, img3]

img1.save(fp="animate.gif", save_all= True, append_images= imgs,
        duration= 500, loop=0)
```

Creating PDFs

Example – Creating PDF from images

Python
```
from PIL import  Image

pic1 = Image.open("picture1.jpg").resize(size=(600, 800))
pic2 = Image.open("picture2.jpg").resize(size=(600, 800))
pic3 = Image.open("picture3.jpg").resize(size=(600, 800))

imgs = [ pic2, pic3]

pic1.save(fp="sample.pdf",format="PDF",save_all= True,append_images= imgs)
```

Insight

A multi-frame image is a single file that contains multiple images, allowing for animation or layered content. Formats that support multi-frame images include **GIF** and **TIFF**, which can store multiple frames within one file.

Color Conversion and Filters

Pillow provides various methods for converting colors, applying filters, and manipulating image color channels. These functions help in changing image modes, adjusting transparency, and processing pixel values.

convert(mode, colors)

The ***convert()*** method is used to change an image from one color mode to another.
mode →(string)[optional] : Specifies the target color mode. Common modes include:

- RGB – Red, Green, Blue
- CMYK – Cyan, Magenta, Yellow, Black
- L – Luminance (grayscale)
- RGBA – RGB with an Alpha (transparency) channel
- LAB, HSV, P, 1, I, F – Other modes for various image types

colors →(optional): An integer (0–256) specifying the number of colors when using the Palette.ADAPTIVE mode.

Example,

```
Python
from PIL import  Image
img =  Image.open("flower_girl.jpg")

gray_image = img.convert( mode = "L" )
img.show()                # Showing the original image
gray_image.show()         # Showing a gray image
```

> **Note**
>
> In grayscale conversion, the formula used is:
> L=(R×299/1000)+(G×587/1000)+(B×114/1000)L = (R \times 299/1000) + (G \times 587/1000) + (B \times 114/1000)L=(R×299/1000)+(G×587/1000)+(B×114/1000)
> Where: R = Red, G = Green, B = Blue

putalpha(alpha)

This method adjusts the transparency (alpha) of an image.

alpha → (int): An integer that defines the transparency level. Lower values increase transparency. A value of **0** makes the image almost completely invisible.

Example,

```python
from PIL import  Image
img =  Image.open("flower_girl.jpg")
copied = img.copy( )        # creates a copy of the image
img.putalpha( alpha = 100 )
copied.putalpha( alpha = 20 )
img.show()             # showing the first image with alpha - 100
copied.show()          # showing the copied image with alpha - 20
```

point(lut)

It applies a function to modify pixel values across all bands in the image.

lut →(function): A required function that takes a single argument and returns a new pixel value.

Example – Program to convert dark areas into white and white area, dark,

```python
from PIL import  Image
img =  Image.open("africa_woman.jpg")

#Function to inverts each pixel's value
inverted = img.point( lut = lambda x: 255 - x )

img.show( )          # showing the original image
inverted.show( )     # showing an inverted image
```

split( ) and merge(mode, bands)

The *split()* divides an image into individual color bands. This is useful for processing specific channels separately. For example, Splitting an RGB image results in three separate images for Red, Green, and Blue.

The *merge()* combines individual image bands into a single image.
mode→ : The target mode for merging, such as "RGB" or "CMYK".
bands →: A sequence of images, each representing a single color channel.

```python
from PIL import  Image
img =  Image.open("africa_woman.jpg")

# Splitting image into 3 color bands ( red, green, blue)
r, g, b =  img.split( )
r.show()
g.show()
b.show()
```

```
# Merging the color bands
merged_img =  Image.merge(mode= "RGB",bands = [ r, g, b] )
merged_img.show()
```

Red Color Band

Green Color Band

Blue Color Band

Merged Color Bands ([r, g, b])

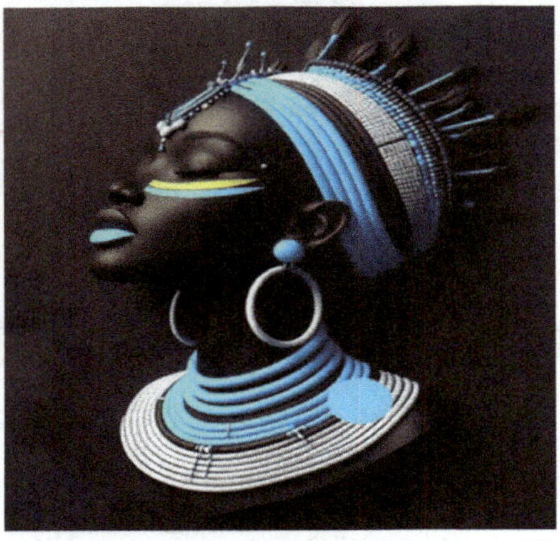

Merged Color Bands([b, g, r])

Merged Color Bands([g, b, r])

Geometric Transformations

Image Transformation refers to modifying an image's structure, size, orientation, or content without altering its core data. Pillow provides various transformation methods such as resizing, rotating, cropping, and pasting images. These transformations allow precise control over how images appear and are processed.

resize(size, box, resample**)**

The *resize()* method is used to scale an image up or down, modifying its width and height.
size → (width, height): A required 2-tuple defining the new dimensions.
box → (left, top, right, bottom): An optional 4-tuple specifying the region to be scaled.
resample →: Defines the resampling filter (e.g., Image.Resampling.NEAREST, Image.Resampling.BILINEAR, Image.Resampling.BICUBIC).

Example,

```
Python
from PIL import  Image
img =  Image.open("bird.jpg")
resized = img.resize(size= (600, 800 ) )
resized_with_box = img.resize(size=(600,800),box=(0,0,400,600))

resized.show()
resized_with_box.show()
```

reduce(factor, box)

The *reduce()* method scales down an image by a given factor while preserving quality.
factor →(int or 2-tuple) : Required parameter defining the reduction ratio.

box → (left, top, right, bottom): Optional 4-tuple specifying a region to be reduced.

Example,

```python
from PIL import  Image
img =  Image.open("bird.jpg")
reduced = img.reduce( factor= 5 )
img.show( )
reduced.show( )
```

Insight

The **thumbnail(** size, resample**)** method, similar to **reduce()** resizes an image to fit within a bounding box while maintaining its aspect ratio.

- *size*: *(width, height)* – A 2-tuple defining the maximum size.
- *resample*: Defines the resampling filter (same as resize).

rotate(angle, center, fillcolor, resample, expand, translate)

The ***rotate()*** method rotates an image by a given angle around a specified center point.
angle → (float): Rotation angle in degrees.
center → (x, y): Optional 2-tuple defining the pivot point.
fillcolor → (int or tuple): Optional color for the empty areas.
expand → (bool): If True, resizes the output to fit the entire rotated image.
translate → (x, y): Optional 2-tuple shifting the image.
resample →: Defines the resampling filter (same as resize). The available filters include,

- Resampling.NEAREST
- Resampling.BOX
- Resampling.BILINEAR
- Resampling.HAMMING
- Resampling.BICUBIC
- Resampling.LANCZOS

Example,

```
Python
from PIL import  Image
img =  Image.open("bird.jpg")
rotation_180 = img.rotate( angle=180)
rotation_90 = img.rotate(angle=90, expand=True,
                       resample=Image.Resampling.BICUBIC)
rotation_45 = img.rotate( angle= 45, expand= True, fillcolor="red")
rotation_135 = img.rotate(angle=135,expand=True,center=(300,300))

rotation_180.show()
rotation_90.show()
rotation_45.show()
rotation_135.show()
```

180° rotation

90° rotation

45° rotation

135° rotation

Note

Image.Resampling.BOX is not supported for rotation.

transpose(method)

The *transpose()* method provides predefined rotation and flipping options: The available defined rotation methods are,

Method	Description
Image.Transpose.ROTATE_90	Rotates 90° counterclockwise.
Image.Transpose.ROTATE_180	Rotates 180°.
Image.Transpose.ROTATE_270	Rotates 270°.
Image.Transpose.FLIP_LEFT_RIGHT	Flips the image horizontally.
Image.Transpose.FLIP_TOP_BOTTOM	Flips the image vertically.
Image.Transpose.TRANSVERSE	Rotating 90° counterclockwise, then flipping horizontally
Image.Transpose.TRANSPOSE	Rotating 90° clockwise, then flipping vertically.
Image.Transpose.ROTATE_90	Rotates 90° counterclockwise.
Image.Transpose.ROTATE_180	Rotates 180°.
Image.Transpose.ROTATE_270	Rotates 270°.

Table 11.4

Example,

Python
```
from PIL import  Image

img =  Image.open("bird.jpg")
transpose = img.transpose( Image.Transpose.TRANSPOSE)
transverse = img.transpose( Image.Transpose.TRANSVERSE)
transpose_90 = img.transpose( Image.Transpose.ROTATE_90)
transpose_180 = img.transpose( Image.Transpose.ROTATE_180)

transpose.show()
transverse.show()
transpose_90.show()
transpose_180.show()
```

TRANSPOSE

TRANSVERSE

ROTATE_90

ROTATE_180

crop(box) and paste(image, box, mask)

The ***crop()*** extracts a rectangular region from an image.
box →(left, top, right, bottom): A 4-tuple defining the region to extract.

The ***paste()*** pastes or places an image onto another image at a specified position.
image→: The source image to paste.
box → (left, top): Optional coordinates for positioning.
mask →(Image or None): An optional mask for transparency.

Example,

```
Python
from PIL import  Image

puppy1 = Image.open("puppy1.jpg")
puppy2 = Image.open("puppy2.jpg")
puppy1.show()
puppy2.show()

# extracting a region from puppy1
cropped = puppy1.crop(box= (200, 200, 600,1000) )
puppy2.paste(im = cropped, box = (10, 500) )
puppy2.show()
```

Puppy1

Puppy2

Puppy1 pasted into Puppy2

Image Attributes

Pillow provides several attributes for retrieving essential information about an image. These attributes help in understanding the image's format, size, color composition, and more.

filename and format

The *filename* returns the full name of the image file, including its extension. The *format* returns the image file format, such as "JPEG", "PNG", or "GIF". This corresponds to the file extension of the image.

```
●●● Python
from PIL import  Image
img = Image.open("flower.jpg")
print(f"Filename -> {img.filename}")
print(f"Format -> {img.format}")
```

```
#Output
Filename -> flower.jpg
Format -> JPEG
```

width, height and size

The *width* returns the width of the image in pixel.
The *height* method returns the height of the image in pixel.
The *size* returns the width and height of the image as a tuple (width, height).

```
●●● Python
from PIL import  Image
img = Image.open("flower.jpg")

print(f"Height of the image -> {img.height}")
print(f"Width of the image -> {img.width}")
print(f"Size of the image -> {img.size}")
```

```
#Output
Height of the image -> 1294
Width of the image -> 1024
Size of the image -> (1024, 1294)
```

getpixel(xy) and histogram(maxcolors)

The *getpixel()* returns the pixel value at a specific (x, y) coordinate. The returned value format depends on the image mode.

The *histogram*() method returns a histogram of the image, representing pixel intensity distribution. This is useful for analyzing image contrast and color composition.

```python
from PIL import  Image
img = Image.open("flower.jpg")

print(f"Pixels -> {img.getpixel(xy=(10, 20))}")
print(f"Histogram -> {img.histogram()}")
```

```
#Output
Pixels -> (0, 80, 177)
Histogram -> [477439, 544487, ….]
```

mode, getbands() and getcolors()

The *mode* returns the color mode of the image, defining the number and type of color bands. Common modes include:

- **RGB** – Red, Green, Blue
- **CMYK** – Cyan, Magenta, Yellow, Black
- **L** – Luminance (grayscale)
- **RGBA** – RGB with an Alpha (transparency) channel
- **LAB**, **HSV**, **P**, **1**, **I**, **F** – Other modes for various image types

The *getbands()* returns a tuple listing the names of each color band in the image. For an **RGB** image, it returns ('R', 'G', 'B').

The *getcolors()* returns a list of colors used in the image, limited to the specified maxcolors (default: 256). Returns None if the color count exceeds the limit.

```python
from PIL import  Image

img = Image.open("flower.jpg")
print(f"Mode -> {img.mode}")
print(f"Bands -> {img.getbands()}")
print(f"Colors -> {img.getcolors()}")
```

```
#Output
Mode -> RGB
Bands -> ('R', 'G', 'B')
Colors -> None
```

The ImageDraw Module

The **ImageDraw** module in the Python Imaging Library (PIL) provides methods for drawing 2D graphics, including shapes, geometric figures, and text, onto images. It is used alongside the Image module to create and manipulate images.

Methods

Any	Draw	ModuleType	annotations
AnyStr	Image	Outline	cast
Callable	ImageColor	Sequence	deprecate
Coords	ImageDraw	Union	floodfill
getdraw	math	struct	

Table 11.5

Insight

Use dir(ImageDraw) to list all the methods and attributes available in the ImageDraw module.

```
>>> from PIL import ImageDraw, Image
>>> dir(ImageDraw)
[.........]
>>>
>>> img = Image.open("picture.ico")
>>> draw = ImageDraw.Draw(im = img)
>>> dir(draw)
[.........]
>>>
```

Draw(im, mode)

The **Draw()** class is crucial for adding graphics to images. It provides numerous functions for drawing geometric shapes and applying text.
im →(Image)[required]: A required parameter that specifies the image to be drawn on.
mode → (string)[optional]: Specifies the color mode, such as "RGB", "L", or "CMYK".

Methods and Attributes of Draw

arc	ellipse	im	multiline_textbbox	rectangle
bitmap	fill	ink	palette	regular_polygon
chord	font	line	pieslice	rounded_rectangle
circle	fontmode	mode	point	shape
draw	getfont	multiline_text	polygon	text
textbbox	textlength			

Table 11.6

text(xy, text, fill, font, fill, spacing, align, direction, stroke_width, stroke_fill, embedded_color)

The **text()** method is used to add text to an image.
xy → (tuple (x, y)): Specifies the coordinates where the text should appear.
text → (string): The actual text to be displayed.
font → (ImageFont) [optional]: Defines the font style. Example:
ImageFont.truetype("path/to/font.ttf", size).

fill → (int/str/tuple) [optional]: Defines the text color.
spacing →(float) [optional]: Sets the space between lines in multiline text.
align → (string) = ("left", "right", "center"): Controls text alignment.
direction → (string) = ("ltr", "rtl", "ttb"): Specifies text direction.
stroke_width →(float) [optional]: Sets the stroke thickness.
stroke_fill →(color) [optional]: Defines the stroke color.
embedded_color →(bool)[optional]: Determines whether to use font-embedded color glyphs.

Example 1

```
Python
from PIL import Image, ImageDraw, ImageFont

img  = Image.new(mode="RGB", size=(600,800), color="#324D34")
draw = ImageDraw.Draw(im=img)
```

```
#Setting Font
font = ImageFont.load_default(size=50)
mytext = "Awesome Python!\nGraphics"
draw.text(text=mytext, xy=(100, 350), font=font, align= "center" )
img.show()
```

Note

The ImageFont module in PIL is used for customizing fonts.
The ImageFont.load_default(size) method adjusts the default font size. To use a custom font, **ImageFont.truetype(**font, size, index**)** is used, where font specifies the font file, size defines the font size, and index indicates the font face to load.

```
>>> from PIL import ImageFont
>>> font = ImageFont.truetype( font= "san_serif.ttf", size = 20)
```

You can explore and download fonts from Google Fonts.

Example 2,

Python
```
from PIL import Image, ImageDraw, ImageFont

smile  = Image.open("smile.jpg")
draw = ImageDraw.Draw(im=smile)
font = ImageFont.truetype(font="font.ttf", size=50)
text = "smile with love"
draw.text(
     text=text,
     xy=(50, smile.height-200),
```

```
    font=font,
    align="center",
    fill="#D86350"
)

eagle  = Image.open("eagle.jpeg")
draw = ImageDraw.Draw(im=eagle)
font = ImageFont.truetype(font="arvo.ttf", size=60)
text = "The power of courage!"

draw.text(
    text=text,
    xy=(20, 500),
    font=font,
    align= "center",
    stroke_fill="#ff6700",
    stroke_width=50
)

smile.show()
eagle.show()
```

Insight

Multiline Text

The **multiline_text()** method has the same parameters as text(), but it is specifically designed to render text containing newline characters (\n).

Drawing Shapes

line(xy, fill, width, joint)

The **line()** method draws a line by connecting coordinate points.
xy →(list of (x, y) tuples): Points defining the line path.
width →(float) [optional]: Line thickness.
fill →(color)[optional]: Line color.

Python
```
from PIL import Image, ImageDraw

line  = Image.new(mode="RGB", size=(800, 600), color="#3a6ea5")
draw = ImageDraw.Draw(im=line)
draw.line(xy= [(100,300), (400, 200), (450, 400), (750, 300)],
         width= 5, fill="#ebebeb")

line.show()
```

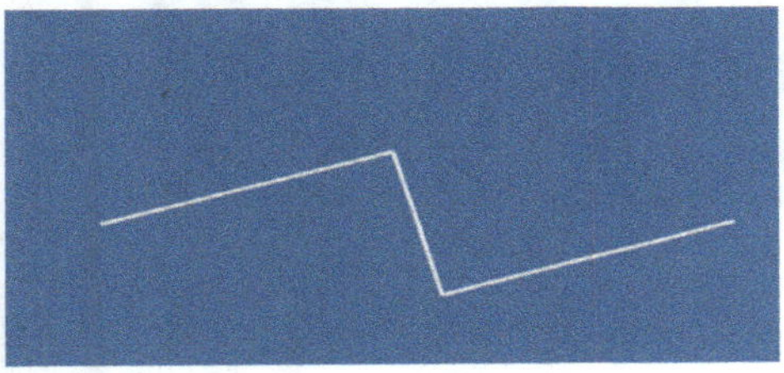

rectangle(xy, fill, outline, width)

The **rectangle()** method is used to draw a rectangular shape on an image.
xy →(tuple or list of tuples (x, y, width, height)): Defines the rectangle coordinates.
fill →(color)[optional]: Background color.
outline →(color) [optional]: Border color.
width →(float)[optional]: Border thickness.

Insight

The **rectangle()** method can also be used to draw squares. This can be achieved by ensuring that the coordinates define equal side lengths.

```python
from PIL import Image, ImageDraw

rectangle  = Image.new(mode="RGB", size=(500,500), color="#3a6ea5")
draw_rec = ImageDraw.Draw(im=rectangle)
draw_rec.rectangle(xy= (100,100, 400, 300), width= 2, fill="#ebebeb")

square  = Image.new(mode="RGB", size=(500,500), color="#3a6ea5")
draw_sq = ImageDraw.Draw(im=square)
draw_sq.rectangle(xy= (100,100, 400,400), width= 5, outline="#ebebeb")

rectangle.show()
square.show()
```

Rectangle

Square

rounded_rectangle(xy, fill, outline, width)

The **rounded_rectangle()** method is used to draw a rectangle with rounded corners.
radius →(float): Defines corner rounding.
xy →(tuple or list of tuples (x, y, width, height)): Defines the rectangle coordinates.
fill →(color)[optional]: Background color.
outline →(color)[optional]: Border color.
width →(float)[optional]: Border thickness.

```python
from PIL import Image, ImageDraw

round_rec  = Image.new(mode="RGB", size=(500,500), color="#324D34")
draw = ImageDraw.Draw(im=round_rec)
draw.rounded_rectangle(
      radius= 25,
      xy= (100,150, 400, 300),
      width=2,
```

```
      fill="#ebebeb"
)

round_rec_pic  = Image.open("girl.jpeg")
draw2 = ImageDraw.Draw(im=round_rec_pic)
xy = (100,100, round_rec_pic.width-100, round_rec_pic.height-100)
draw2.rounded_rectangle(radius=20, xy=xy, width=5, outline="#c57284")

round_rec.show()
round_rec_pic.show()
```

circle(xy, radius, outline, width, fill)

The **circle()** method is used to draw a circle with a defined radius and center point.

xy →(x, y) [required]: Defines the center coordinates of the circle.

radius →(float) [required]: Specifies the radius of the circle.

width → (float)[required]: Determines the thickness of the circle's outline.

outline → (int or "string" or "#hex" or (red, green, blue))[optional]: Specifies the boundary color of the circle.

fill → (int or "string", "#hex" or (red, green, blue))[optional]: Defines the background color of the circle. It is transparent by default.

```
Python
from PIL import Image, ImageDraw

circle  = Image.new(mode="RGB", size=(500,500), color="#151419")
draw = ImageDraw.Draw(im=circle)
draw.circle(radius= 100, xy = (250,250,), width= 5, fill="#EB5E28")
```

```
circle_pic  = Image.open("potrait.jpg")
draw2 = ImageDraw.Draw(im = circle_pic)
draw2.circle( radius=200,xy=(370,300),width=10, outline="#EB5E28")

circle.show()
circle_pic.show()
```

ellipse(xy, width, outline, fill)

The **ellipse()** is used to draw circles by specifying a bounding box.
xy → (x, y, width, height) [required]: Defines the center coordinates of the circle.
width → (float)[optional]: Determines the thickness of the circle's outline.
outline → (int, "string", "#hex" or (red, green, blue)) [optional]: Specifies the boundary color of the circle.
fill → (int, "string", "#hex" or (red, green, blue)) [optional]: Defines the background color of the ellipse. It is transparent by default.

```
●●● Python
from PIL import Image, ImageDraw

img  = Image.new(mode="RGB", size=(500,500), color="#3A6EA5")
draw = ImageDraw.Draw(im=img)
draw.ellipse(
        xy= (100, 100, 400, 400), width= 20,
        outline="#0D2137", fill="#ebebeb"
)

draw.ellipse(xy= (150, 150, 350, 350), width= 10, fill="red")
img.show()
```

arc(xy, start, end, width, fill)

The **arc()** method draws an incomplete circle or a portion of a circle outline..
xy → (x, y, width, height) [required]: Defines the center coordinates of the circle.
start , end → (float) [required]: Define the start and end angles of the arc.
width → (float) [optional]: Determines the thickness of the circle's outline.
fill → (int, "string", "#hex" or (red, green, blue)) [optional]: Defines the background color of the arc. It is transparent by default.

Python
```
from PIL import Image, ImageDraw

arc  = Image.new(mode="RGB", size=(500,500), color="#3A6EA5")
draw = ImageDraw.Draw(im=arc)
draw.arc(xy= (50, 50, 350, 350), start=10, end=150, width= 10,
         fill="#EBEBEB")

arc.show()
```

chord(xy, start, end, width, fill, outline)

The chord() method draws an arc whose ends are connected by a line.

xy → (x, y) [required]: Defines the center coordinates of the circle.

start , end → (float) [required]: Define the start and end angles of the arc.

width → (float) [optional]: Determines the thickness of the arc's outline.

fill → (int, "string", "#hex" or (red, green, blue)) [optional]: Defines the background color of the chord. It is transparent by default.

```python
from PIL import Image, ImageDraw

chord  = Image.new(mode="RGB", size=(500,500), color="#3A6EA5")
draw = ImageDraw.Draw(im=chord)
xy = (50, 50, 400, 400)
draw.chord(
      xy= xy, start= 10, end=200,
      width= 15, fill="#ff6700", outline="#0D2137"
)

chord.show()
```

polygon(xy, width, fill, outline)

The ***polygon()*** method is used to draw a polygon by connecting multiple coordinate points.

xy → ([(x1, y1), (x2, y2), (x3, y3), ...]) [required]: – A list of coordinate points that define the vertices of the polygon.

width → (float) [optional]: Determines the thickness of the polygon's outline.

fill → (int, "colorname", "#hex" or (red, green, blue)) [optional]: Defines the background color of the polygon. It is transparent by default.

Example,

```
●●● Python
from PIL import Image, ImageDraw

poly  = Image.new(mode="RGB", size=(500,500), color="#3A6EA5")
draw = ImageDraw.Draw(im=poly)
xy = [(150, 450),(350, 450),(450, 250),(250, 50),(50, 250),]
draw.polygon(xy= xy, width= 10, outline="#ebebeb")

poly.show()
```

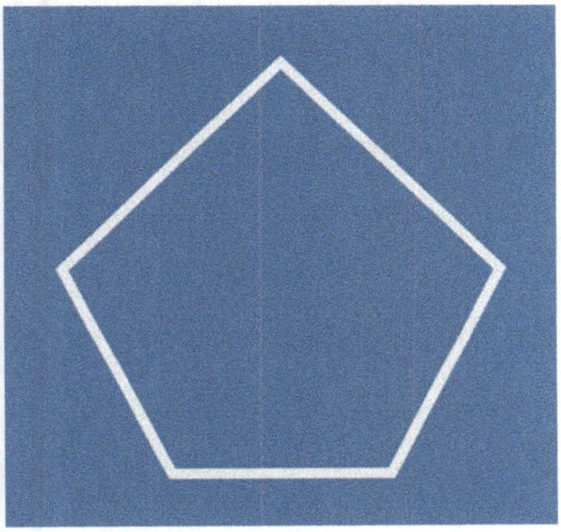

The ImageEnhance Module

The **ImageEnhance** module provides various classes for enhancing images by adjusting their **color**, **contrast**, **brightness**, and **sharpness**. These classes take an image as a parameter and modify its appearance using an enhancement factor, typically ranging from **0.0** to **1.0**, where **1.0** represents the original image.

Methods

Brightness	Contrast	ImageFilter	Sharpness
Color	Image	ImageStat	annotations

Table 11.7

Insight

To explore the available methods and attributes of the ImageEnhance module, use the **dir()** function.

```
>>> from PIL import  ImageEnhance
>>> dir(ImageEnhance)
```

The ImageEnhance module provides **three key objects** for each enhancement class:

image

Represents the input image and provides methods for manipulation and data retrieval.

degenerate

This generates the **least enhanced version** of the image, often used as a reference for scaling enhancements.

enhance(factor)

Applies the enhancement effect to the image based on the specified factor, where 1.0 represents the original image.

Brightness(image)

The **Brightness()** class controls the light intensity of an image:

- A factor of **0.0** results in a completely dark image.
- A factor of **1.0** preserves the original brightness.
- A factor above **1.0** increases the brightness.

Python

```python
from PIL import Image, ImageEnhance

img  = Image.open("girl.jpeg")
enhanced1 = ImageEnhance.Brightness(image=img).enhance(factor=0.3)
enhanced2 = ImageEnhance.Brightness(image=img).enhance(factor=2)
enhanced3 = ImageEnhance.Brightness(image=img).enhance(factor=5)

img.show()
enhanced1.show()
enhanced2.show()
enhanced3.show()
```

Original Image

Brigthness factor: 0.3

Brigthness factor: 2

Brigthness factor : 5

Contrast(image)

The **Contrast()** class adjusts the difference between the darkest and lightest parts of an image:

- A factor of **0.0** results in a completely gray image.
- A factor of **1.0** maintains the original contrast.
- A factor above **1.0** increases contrast.

```python
from PIL import Image, ImageEnhance

img  = Image.open("cute_girl.jpeg")
img.show() #Showing original Image

ImageEnhance.Contrast(image=img).enhance(factor=0.6).show()
ImageEnhance.Contrast(image=img).enhance(factor=2).show()
ImageEnhance.Contrast(image=img).enhance(factor=4).show()
```

Original image

Contrast factor :0.6

Contrast factor :2

Contrast factor :4

Color(image)

The **Color()** class manages the **saturation** or **intensity** of colors in an image:

- A factor of **0.0** converts the image to black and white.
- A factor of **1.0** keeps the original colors.
- A factor above **1.0** increases color vibrancy.

Python
```
from PIL import Image, ImageEnhance

img  = Image.open("parrot.jpeg")
enhanced1 = ImageEnhance.Color(image=img).enhance(factor=0.0)
enhanced2 = ImageEnhance.Color(image=img).enhance(factor=0.4)
enhanced3 = ImageEnhance.Color(image=img).enhance(factor=3)

img.show()
enhanced1.show()
enhanced2.show()
enhanced3.show()
```

Original image

Color factor : 0.0

Color factor : 0.4

Color factor : 3.0

Sharpness(image)

The **Sharpness()** class controls the **clarity of edges and fine details** in an image:

- A factor of **0.0** results in a completely blurred image.
- A factor of **1.0** maintains the original sharpness.
- A factor above **1.0** enhances the sharpness.

```python
from PIL import Image, ImageEnhance

img  = Image.open("snow_trip.jpeg")

img.show() #Showing the original image
ImageEnhance.Sharpness(image=img).enhance(factor= -10.0 ).show()
ImageEnhance.Sharpness(image=img).enhance(factor= 0.0).show()
ImageEnhance.Sharpness(image=img).enhance(factor=15.0).show()
```

Original image

Sharpness factor:-10.0

Sharpness factor:0.0

Sharpness factor:15.0

The ImageFilter Module

Image filtering enhances an image's appearance by modifying pixel values using predefined functions. The ImageFilter module in PIL provides various classes for applying different filtering effects.

Predefined Filters in Pillow

Pillow includes several built-in filters:

Filter	Effect
SMOOTH	Applies a subtle smoothing effect
SMOOTH_MORE	Enhances the smoothing effect
BLUR	Softens the image
SHARPEN	Enhances image sharpness
FIND_EDGES	Highlights edges in the image

CONTOUR	Creates a contour-like effect
DETAIL	Enhances fine details
EDGE_ENHANCE	Enhances image edges
EDGE_ENHANCE_MORE	Stronger edge enhancement
EMBOSS	Creates an embossed effect

Table 11.8

Insight

To explore the available methods and attributes of the ImageFilter module, use the **dir()** function.

```
>>> from PIL import  ImageFilter
>>> dir(ImageFilter)
[........]
```

Example,

```
Python
from PIL import Image, ImageFilter
img  = Image.open("orange_love.png")

img.show() #Showing the original image
img.filter( ImageFilter.BLUR ).show()
img.filter( ImageFilter.CONTOUR ).show()
img.filter( ImageFilter.SMOOTH_MORE ).show()
img.filter( ImageFilter.EMBOSS ).show()
img.filter( ImageFilter.FIND_EDGES ).show()
img.filter( ImageFilter.DETAIL ).show()
img.filter( ImageFilter.SHARPEN ).show()
```

Original image

BLUR

CONTOUR

SMOOTH_MORE

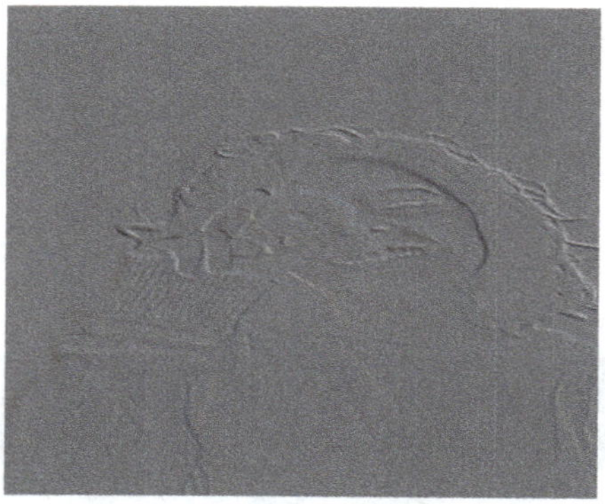

EMBOSS

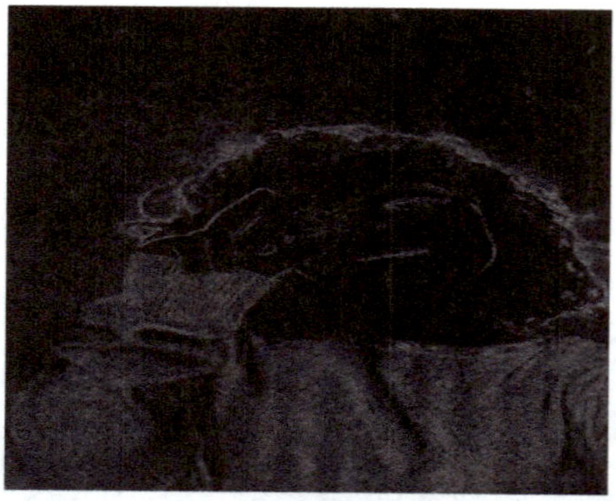

FIND_EDGES

DETAIL

SHARPEN

ImageFilter Classes

RankFilter(size, rank)

Sorts all pixels in a window of the specified size and returns the rankth value.
size → (int)[required]: The kernel size in pixels.
rank → (int)[required]: The pixel value to pick.

- 0 → Minimum filter
- size*size/2 → Median filter
- size*size - 1 → Maximum filter

Example,

```python
from PIL import Image, ImageFilter

img  = Image.open("orange_lover.png")
img.filter( ImageFilter.RankFilter( size = 7, rank= 2) ).show()
```

MinFilter(size)

Selects the lowest pixel value in a given window size.

size → (int)[required]: Kernel size in pixels.

MaxFilter(size)

Selects the highest pixel value in a given window size.

size → (int)[required]: Kernel size in pixels.

MedianFilter(size)

Selects the median pixel value in a given window size.

size → (int)[required]: Kernel size in pixels.

ModeFilter(size)

Selects the most frequent pixel value in a given window size. Pixels that appear only once or twice are ignored.

size → (int)[required]: Kernel size in pixels.

MultibandFilter

Used for filtering multi-band images.

BoxBlur(radius)

Blurs the image by averaging pixel values in a square box extending radius pixels in each direction.

radius → (float or list of floats)[required]: Defines the blur area.

- radius = 0 → No blur applied

Example,

```python
from PIL import Image, ImageFilter

img  = Image.open("orange_love.png")
img.filter( ImageFilter.BoxBlur( radius = 10)).show()
```

GaussianBlur(radius)

Blurs the image using a Gaussian kernel approximation with extended box filters.

radius → (float or list of floats)[required]: Defines the standard deviation of the Gaussian kernel.

The ImageChops Module

The **ImageChops** module in Pillow provides a collection of channel operations ("chops") for performing arithmetic image manipulations. These operations are useful for image comparison, blending, masking, and logical operations.

Methods

add	composite	duplicate	logical_and	add
add_modulo	constant	hard_light	logical_or	add_modulo
annotations	darker	invert	logical_xor	annotations
blend	difference	lighter	multiply	blend
offset	overlay	screen	soft_light	offset
subtract	subtract_modulo			subtract

Table 11.9

Insight

Use the dir() function to explore the available methods and attributes of the ImageChops module.
>>> from PIL import ImageChops
>>> dir(ImageChops)
[........]

add(image1, image2, scale, offset)

This method **adds** one image to another with an optional **scale** and **offset**.
image1→ (PIL.Image) : First image.
image2 → (PIL.Image): Second image.
scale → (float)[optional- default=1.0]: The resulting image is divided by this scale factor.
offset → (int)[optional- default=0]: A value added to the result to adjust brightness.

Python
```
from PIL import Image, ImageChops

img1 = Image.open("freshview.jpeg")
img2 = Image.open("warmview.jpeg")
img1.show()
img2.show()
ImageChops.add(image1=img1,image2=img2,scale=3,offset=10).show()
```

freshview.jpeg

warmview.jpeg

combined images

add_modulo(image1, image2, scale, offset)

This method **adds** two images without applying a scale factor, meaning pixel values wrap around (modulo 256).
image1→ (PIL.Image) : First image.
image2→ (PIL.Image) : Second image.
📌 **Use Case**: Prevents image values from clipping when they exceed the maximum pixel value.

subtract(image1, image2, scale, offset)

Subtracts image2 from image1 and divides by a **scale** factor, with an optional **offset**.
image1 → (PIL.Image): First image.
image2 → (PIL.Image): Second image.
scale → (float)[optional- default=1.0]: Controls the degree of subtraction.
offset → (int)[optional- default=0]: Adjusts the resulting image brightness.
📌 **Use Case**: Used to detect changes between images.

Example,

```python
from PIL import Image, ImageChops

img1 = Image.open("freshview.jpeg")
img2 = Image.open("warmview.jpeg")
img = ImageChops.subtract(image1=img1,image2=img2, scale=3, offset=10)

img.save("new_image.jpg")
```

subtract_modulo(image1, image2)

Subtracts image2 from image1 without clipping pixel values (wraps around if values go negative).

image1→ (PIL.Image): First image.

image2→ (PIL.Image): Second image.

📌 **Use Case**: Works well for periodic images where wrapping pixel values is desired.

difference(image1, image2)

Computes the **absolute difference** between two images, pixel by pixel.

📌 **Use Case**: Commonly used in image comparison and detecting changes between two images.

Example,

```
Python
from PIL import Image, ImageChops

img1 = Image.open("girl_with_orange.jpeg")
img2 = Image.open("girl_with_glass.jpeg")
img1.show()
img2.show()
ImageChops.difference(image1=img1, image2=img2).show()
```

girl_with_orange.jpeg

girl_with_glass.jpeg

difference

lighter(image1, image2)

Creates an image where each pixel is the **lighter** value of the two images.

📌 **Use Case**: Useful for highlighting bright areas.

Example,

●●● Python
```
from PIL import Image, ImageChops

img1 = Image.open("girl_with_orange.jpeg")
img2 = Image.open("girl_with_glass.jpeg")
ImageChops.lighter(image1=img1, image2=img2).show()
```

hard_light(image1, image2)

This method applies the **Hard Light** blending mode, which enhances contrast by either multiplying or screening the pixel values of two images based on the brightness of the top image.

📌 **Use Case**: Used for adding dramatic lighting effects by intensifying highlights and shadows

Example,

●●● Python
```
from PIL import Image, ImageChops

img1 = Image.open("girl_with_orange.jpeg")
img2 = Image.open("girl_with_glass.jpeg")
ImageChops.hard_light(image1=img1, image2=img2).show()
```

invert(image)

This method **inverts** an image, meaning dark areas become bright and vice versa.

📌 **Use Case**: Used for negative effects.

```
Python
from PIL import Image, ImageChops

img = Image.open("dark_girl.jpeg")
img.show() #Showing the original image
ImageChops.invert(image = img).show()
```

multiply(image1, image2)

Multiplies pixel values of two images, making dark areas **darker** and bright areas **brighter**.

image1→ (PIL.Image): First image.

image2→ (PIL.Image): Second image.

📌 **Use Case**: Often used for shadow effects.

screen(image1, image2)

This method **blends two inverted images** and superimposes them.

image1→ (PIL.Image) – First image.

image2→ (PIL.Image) – Second image.

📌 **Use Case**: Used in graphics editing for soft light effects.

overlay(image1, image2)

Applies the **Overlay blending mode**, enhancing contrast by mixing highlights and shadows.

image1→ (PIL.Image): First image.

image2→ (PIL.Image): Second image.

📌 **Use Case**: Used in photo filters and color correction.

blend(image1, image2, alpha)

Blends two images with a constant **transparency weight** (alpha).

image1→ (PIL.Image): First image.

image2→ (PIL.Image): Second image.

alpha→ (float)[required]: A value between 0.0 (fully transparent) and 1.0 (fully visible).

📌 **Use Case**: Used in fading effects.

constant(image1, image2, value)

This method fills a channel with a given **gray level**.

image1→ (PIL.Image): First image.

image2→ (PIL.Image): Second image.

value → (int)[required]: Level of gray (0-255).

📌 **Use Case**: Used for background manipulation.

The ImageGrab Module

The **ImageGrab** module in Pillow is primarily used for capturing screenshots of the entire computer screen or retrieving content from the clipboard. It provides two key functions: one for taking screenshots and another for extracting clipboard content.

Taking Screenshots

grab(bbox, include_layered_window, all_screens, xdisplay)

The **grab()** function captures a screenshot of the screen. If no bounding box (bbox) is specified, it captures the entire screen.

bbox → (tuple)[optional]: Defines the region of the screen to capture in the format (x, y, width, height).

x, y → Coordinates of the top-left corner.

width, height → Dimensions of the region to capture.

include_layered_windows → (bool)[optional]: If True, captures layered windows (Windows-only).

all_screens → (bool)[optional]: If True, captures all screens in a multi-monitor setup (Windows-only).

xdisplay → (string): Specifies the display to capture (Linux-only).

For example,

Python
```python
from PIL import ImageGrab

img  = ImageGrab.grab()

img.show()                      #Showing the screenshot
img.save("screenshot.png") #Saving the screenshot
```

Capturing Clipboard Content

grabclipboard()

The **grabclipboard()** function retrieves the current clipboard content if available.

Return Values:

- If an image is stored in the clipboard, it returns a PIL.Image object.
- If file paths are stored, it returns a list of filenames.
- Returns None if the clipboard is empty or contains unsupported data.

For example,

Python

```python
from PIL import ImageGrab

content  = ImageGrab.grabclipboard()
print(content)
```

KeyTerms

resize
rotate
transpose
truetype
Brightness
Contrast
Sharpness
BLUR
EMBOSS
DETAIL
Add
Subtract
difference
grab
thumbnail

Review Questions

1. Which method in Pillow rotates an image around a specific point?
A) rotate()
B) resize()
C) transpose()
D) crop()
Answer: a

2. What does ImageEnhance.Sharpness factor of 0.0 do?
A) Maintains original sharpness
B) Completely blurred
C) Increases sharpness
D) Converts to grayscale
Answer: b

3. Which method draws multiline text on an image?
A) text()
B) multiline_text()
C) textbbox()
D) draw()
Answer: b

4. Which filter highlights edges in an image?
A) BLUR
B) CONTOUR
C) FIND_EDGES
D) SMOOTH
Answer: c

5. Which ImageChops method computes absolute pixel differences?
A) add()
B) difference()
C) multiply()
D) invert()
Answer: b

6. Which ImageDraw method draws a rectangle with rounded corners?
A) rectangle()
B) rounded_rectangle()
C) ellipse()
D) polygon()
Answer: b

7. What does ImageGrab.grab() return?
A) Clipboard text
B) PIL.Image object
C) File path
D) Pixel array
Answer: b

8. Which enhancement factor in ImageEnhance.Color converts an image to grayscale?
A) 0.0
B) 0.5
C) 1.0
D) 2.0
Answer: a

9. Which transpose method flips an image horizontally?
A) FLIP_LEFT_RIGHT
B) FLIP_TOP_BOTTOM
C) ROTATE_90
D) TRANSVERSE
Answer: a

10. Which ImageFilter selects the most frequent pixel value in a window?

A) MedianFilter
B) ModeFilter
C) MinFilter
D) MaxFilter
Answer: b

Review Exercises

1. Load an image, resize it to 800×600, rotate 45°, and save the result.

2. Use ImageDraw to draw a filled red circle with radius 50px at the center of a 500×500 image.

3. Enhance the brightness and contrast of an image using ImageEnhance and compare before and after.

4. Apply ImageFilter.SMOOTH_MORE and ImageFilter.EMBOSS to the same image and describe the differences visually.

   Capture a screenshot using ImageGrab.grab() and save it as "screenshot.png"; then retrieve any image from the clipboard using grabclipboar()

Index

Author's Remarks

On behalf of the entire Ouereila team, I would like to express my sincere gratitude to everyone who contributed, directly or indirectly, to the completion of **Python For Everyone**. Most importantly, I would like to thank you, our cherished reader, for investing your time, resources, and trust in this book. Your support means a great deal to us, and we are truly grateful.

It is our hope that this book has given you a strong foundation in Python and helped you progress from fundamental programming concepts to more advanced techniques and practical applications. If you have completed this book from beginning to end, you have taken an important step in your journey as a Python programmer. However, reading alone is never enough. True mastery comes through consistent practice, experimentation, problem-solving, and continuous learning.

We encourage you to go beyond the examples presented in this book. Modify the programs, experiment with the code, develop your own projects, explore Python libraries, and find creative ways to apply what you have learned. Every program you write, every error you encounter, and every problem you solve contributes to your growth as a programmer.

Python continues to evolve, and its ecosystem continues to expand across areas such as automation, data processing, artificial intelligence, web development, software development, and many other fields. We encourage you to remain curious, keep learning, follow new developments, and continue exploring what Python can accomplish.

Ouereila is a growing publishing and software development organization committed to producing practical, accessible, and high-quality learning resources. Our progress is made possible not only through dedication and hard work but also through the continued support, encouragement, and constructive feedback of readers like you.

We warmly welcome your comments, suggestions, corrections, and recommendations. If you discover an error, have an idea for improving a future edition, or simply wish to share your experience with this book, please do not hesitate to contact us. Your feedback helps us improve our publications and create better learning resources for the programming community.

You can reach us through:

Email: oureila@gmail.com
Feedback Form: https://forms.gle/oCEzyKpXgf1zbiV46

Once again, thank you for choosing **Python For Everyone**. We sincerely hope this book becomes a valuable companion throughout your Python programming journey and inspires you to keep learning, building, and creating.

Keep learning. Keep coding. Keep building.

May God richly bless you and grant you success in all your endeavors.

Warm regards,
Williams Asiedu
Ouereila

About the Author

Williams Asiedu is a computer engineer, author and philanthropist with a deep passion for technology and social impact. He earned his Ph.D. from the Illinois Institute of Technology in Chicago, USA and currently works as a Data Analyst, applying advanced computational and analytical techniques to solve real-world problems.
Beyond his professional career in technology, Williams is a dedicated writer who has authored several books, including programming guides and works of fiction. His writing reflects both technical expertise and a commitment to making knowledge accessible to learners at all levels. Through clear explanations and practical examples, he aims to empower readers to develop skills that can transform their careers and communities.

Williams is also actively engaged in philanthropic efforts. Through his publications and personal initiatives, he supports individuals and communities in the fight against poverty, discrimination and abuse—particularly in parts of Africa. He strongly believes that social responsibility is a collective obligation and that meaningful change happens when individuals contribute in their own unique ways.
Mr. Asiedu maintains that knowledge, opportunity and compassion are powerful tools for transformation. He encourages readers not only to pursue professional excellence but also to use their skills and resources to uplift others.

Through both technology and service, Williams Asiedu remains committed to building solutions that improve lives and inspire hope.

Acknowledgement

This book would not have been possible without the support, encouragement and contributions of several remarkable individuals.
First, I extend my heartfelt gratitude to my dear friend, Anokyewaa Theresa, whose encouragement and thoughtful support throughout this journey meant more than words can express. Your belief in this project gave me strength during both the exciting and challenging moments of writing.

To my family, especially my beautiful sisters, Alice and Vero, thank you for your constant love, patience and motivation. Your support has always been a source of inspiration and I am truly grateful to have you in my life.
I would also like to sincerely thank every member of the Ouereila Team for their dedication, careful review, constructive feedback and incredible support. Your commitment to excellence helped refine this work and bring it to its final form.

To everyone who contributed in any way—through encouragement, technical insight, proofreading, or simple words of motivation—please accept my deepest appreciation.
This book is not just the result of one person's effort; it is the outcome of collective support and shared belief. Thank you all.

www.ingramcontent.com/pod-product-compliance
Lightning Source LLC
LaVergne TN
LVHW060435061126
851857LV00016B/1635
* 9 7 9 8 2 4 0 8 0 2 4 3 0 *